CAMBRIDGE STUDIES
IN ENGLISH LEGAL HISTORY

Edited by
D. E. C. YALE
Fellow of Christ's College
and Reader in English Legal History at the University of Cambridge

THE LEGAL FRAMEWORK OF ENGLISH FEUDALISM

THE MAITLAND LECTURES
GIVEN IN 1972

troud Francis Charles

S. F. C. MILSOM

CAMBRIDGE UNIVERSITY PRESS

CAMBRIDGE

LONDON · NEW YORK · MELBOURNE

Published by the Syndics of the Cambridge University Press
The Pitt Building, Trumpington Street, Cambridge CB2 1RP
Bentley House, 200 Euston Road, London NW1 2DB
32 East 57th Street, New York, NY 10022, USA
296 Beaconsfield Parade, Middle Park, Melbourne 3206, Australia

First published 1976

Printed in Great Britain
at the
University Printing House, Cambridge
(Euan Phillips, University Printer)

Library of Congress Cataloguing in Publication Data
Milsom, Stroud Francis Charles.
The legal framework of English feudalism.
(Cambridge studies in English legal history)
Includes index.
1. Land tenure – Great Britain – Law – Addresses, essays, lectures.
2. Feudal law – Great Britain – Addresses, essays, lectures. I. Title.
KD835.A75M54   346′.41′0432   75–2351
ISBN 0 521 20947 1

CONTENTS

[v]

PREFACE

With some expansion in detail, this book consists of lectures given in Cambridge in 1972 at the invitation of the Managers of the Maitland Memorial Fund; and it is now published with the aid of a generous grant from the Fund. To the Managers, to Mr David Yale, and to those historians and lawyers who so bravely listened, I am deeply grateful. There were power cuts at the time, and the lecturer peered from a wavering patch of candle-light much as his lectures tried to make out what sort of world lies in the darkness behind our earliest legal records. These are lights that cannot come on again; and we may never be sure of the answers to many individual questions. I shall be content if it is agreed that the questions arise, and therefore that the world cannot have been quite as we have supposed.

S.F.C.M.

ABBREVIATIONS AND MODES OF CITATION

A. Printed Plea Rolls

References are to entry numbers in publications which number entries, and to page numbers in those which do not. In the following list a note at the end of each description shows to which class the publication belongs. When a page reference seems insufficient for ready identification the name of a principal party, is added in parentheses.

When several references to a case have been found, they are listed in an order which is only approximately chronological: strict chronology would cause repetition by separating entries printed in the same volume. Italic type for page or entry numbers in such cases distinguishes the less important and not the more important references: the entries for which the case is particularly cited are thus in roman type like all other page and entry numbers. A series of references separated only by semicolons comprises the entries found of a single case or a series of cases concerning the same dispute: when more than one case is cited, each is prefixed by (*a*), (*b*), etc.

Quotations reproduce the text as printed, and therefore follow differing editorial conventions.

Beds.	*Rolls of the Justices in Eyre at Bedford, 1202*; ed. G. H. Fowler; Bedfordshire Historical Record Society, vol. I (1913), pp. 133–247. Entry numbers.
BNB	*Bracton's Note Book*; ed. F. W. Maitland; 3 vols. (1887). Entry numbers.
CRR	*Curia Regis Rolls* (1922–). Page numbers in vols. I–X, entry numbers thereafter.
Gloucs.	*Rolls of the Justices in Eyre for Gloucestershire, Warwickshire and [Shropshire], 1221–1222*; ed.

D. M. Stenton; Selden Society, vol. 59 (1940). Entry numbers.

Lincs. The Earliest Lincolnshire Assize Rolls, 1202–1209; ed. D. M. Stenton; Lincoln Record Society, vol. 22 (1926). Entry numbers.

Lincs.-Worcs. Rolls of the Justices in Eyre for Lincolnshire, 1218–1219 and Worcestershire, 1221; ed. D. M. Stenton; Selden Society, vol. 53 (1934). Entry numbers.

Northants. The Earliest Northamptonshire Assize Rolls, 1202–1203; ed. D. M. Stenton; Northamptonshire Record Society, vol. v (1930). Entry numbers.

PKJ Pleas before the King or his Justices, 1198–1212; ed. D. M. Stenton; vols. I–IV; Selden Society, vols. 67 (1948), 68 (1949), 83 (1966), 84 (1967). Entry numbers.

PRS, xiv Three Rolls of the King's Court in the Reign of King Richard the First, 1194–1195; ed. F. W. Maitland; Pipe Roll Society, vol. xiv (1891). Page numbers.

PRS(NS), xxxi Memoranda Roll for the Tenth Year of King John [etc.]: 'Curia Regis Roll 5 (1196)' and 'Curia Regis Roll 8B (1198)'; ed. R. Allen Brown; Pipe Roll Society, New Series, vol. xxxi (1955), pp. 69–118. Page numbers.

RCR Rotuli Curiae Regis; ed. F. Palgrave; vols. I–II (1835). Page numbers.

Staffs. 'Staffordshire Suits extracted from the Plea Rolls, temp. Richard I and King John'; ed. G. Wrottesley; William Salt Archaeological Society, vol. III (1882), pp. 25–163. Page numbers.

Yorks. Rolls of the Justices in Eyre for Yorkshire, 1218–1219; ed. D. M. Stenton; Selden Society, vol. 56 (1937). Entry numbers.

B. Other Materials

Bracton   Henry de Bracton, *De Legibus et Consuetudinibus*
                   Angliae; ed. G. E. Woodbine; 4 vols. (1915–42).
                   Reissued with translation and notes by S. E.
                   Thorne (1968–).

Brevia Placitata *Brevia Placitata*; ed. G. J. Turner and T. F. T.
                   Plucknett; Selden Society, vol. 66 (1947).

Glanvill   *The treatise on the laws and customs of the realm of*
                   England commonly called Glanvill; ed. G. D. G.
                   Hall (1965). To avoid circumlocution, 'Glanvill'
                   is used as the name of the author of *Glanvill*.

Registers   *Early Registers of Writs*; ed. E. de Haas and
                   G. D. G. Hall; Selden Society, vol. 87 (1970).

DISCIPLINARY JURISDICTION

History is difficult because people never state their assumptions or describe the framework in which their lives are led. To the extent that you do not unthinkingly supply these from your own experience, you can only guess at them from what your actors said and did. There will be no more evidence for the most important lines in your picture than that they fit with the demonstrable detail. They are either obvious or wrong. Maitland's indestructible memorial is that the great outlines he drew of the history of the common law, for which so much material survives, have so long seemed obvious. New or unnoticed detail at last begins to obtrude: but you cannot usefully erase an outline, only propose what seems a better fit.

This book will be about a small part of his picture, but one in which our understanding of the law is peculiarly entwined with our understanding of contemporary life. It will try to reconstruct what may be called the feudal component in the framework of English society in the years around 1200, the earliest time at which we know enough of what people said and did to make out what did not need saying and what it was not thinkable to do.

The things said and done are nearly all taken from *Glanvill* and from the plea rolls surviving from the reigns of Richard and John; and the lawyer trespassing in historians' country knows that he compounds his offence by concentrating on the legal sources. But somebody must make a start. It is in these sources, if anywhere, that the formal structure of society at this time must be reflected; yet they have never been seriously examined with that in mind. And they are so intractable that a lifetime may be too little even for the single-minded lawyer.

Can this intractability be analysed? Why is it that we do not immediately see the daily life of a society which left such copious records of its litigation? Partly it is because we confront those records with anachronistic questions, and turn away when they do not immediately answer. To us a law-suit should first ascertain the facts and then apply the law. Relevant facts are therefore stated; and although we cannot know whether any particular party is telling the truth, we can be fairly sure that it would be lawful to act as he did if the facts were as he says. This last of course is always so; and to the extent that facts are stated at all in the earliest records the legal and social order is faithfully reflected. But the reflections are fragmentary because early law-suits did not work by ascertaining and examining the facts. The plaintiff alleged the basic ingredients of his case in a set form of words – for example that his ancestor was seised of the land in dispute and that he was heir; the defendant normally made a general denial; and the business of the court was to decide which side should swear to the justice of his cause and how the oath should be tested – for example by battle. The only facts stated are those required of the plaintiff, and most of what actually happened is lost in that general denial.

It follows that direct and explicit answers to our questions will be rare indeed. But we may do better with our own questions if we first try to understand theirs; and their questions were mostly about proof. That this was the end to which the legal process was directed is obvious. That it was also the pivot upon which its logic turned is something that has been hidden behind a contrary assumption. The network of assumptions implicit in the phrase 'the forms of action' sees the first step in a law-suit as logically primary. Its identity lies in the writ or other mode of initiation, and proof is just one of the things that follow from that: there must be battle because it is a writ of right. The mischief is that this necessitates another assumption, that writs embody concepts: it is not the writ but 'the right' that demands the battle. In much this way mysticism eventually came into the law itself. But it was not there to begin with. Writs were practical pieces of machinery, as they are for Glanvill; and there was a direct and, in its own day, a rational relationship between the facts and the mode of proof. What a party sought to allege, sometimes even what writ he started with, were dictated by the proof he would have to offer. That was what law-suits were about.

It is naturally in the context of certain writs concerning land that this point will matter to the present inquiry. But an easier and more dramatic application in a different context illustrates a second theme: we have over-estimated the magnitude of legislative innovation. Henry II and his advisers did great things; but they did not reach out from their own world. The appeal of felony and the indictment are traditionally distinguished in terms of initiation and motive: the victim's desire for vengeance proved insufficient to protect public order and royal rights, and so a new procedure of public accusation was invented. Important work has suggested that after all the Assize of Clarendon did not create the indictment process, and has pointed to what it probably did do, which was to alter the mode of proof.[1] The change was not in giving any effect to the suspicion of the countryside, but in giving it greater effect. Now it would put a man not just to compurgation but to the more drastic 'law' of the ordeal. But still we have not thought through the implications of this. Glanvill does not see two separate entities, distinguished by their mode of initiation: he sees only two modes of proof.[2] Either there is a specific accuser or not. If there is, he can swear as one who saw or otherwise knew, and can prove his oath by the test of battle. If there is no specific accuser, but only the suspicion of the countryside, there can be no affirmative oath and therefore no battle. It must be the accused who swears to his denial, who must wage and make his law. Consider Glanvill's special worry about the taking of treasure trove,[3] an offence which leaves no corpse, no wound, not even anything known to have gone. Unless it was otherwise established at least that some metal had been found, the custom was that public suspicion could not put a man to the ordeal: he thinks the assize may have altered this, and seems to disapprove. That is the kind of question with which law courts dealt, and the kind of change which legislators could make.

Changes in what we should call substantive law could equally result from changes in the proof which courts themselves required; and important developments in warranty, for example, seem to have followed from an increasing insistence upon charters. But our immediate concern is with the records as evidence; and our chance of learning the facts is another of the things governed by considerations of proof. Charters provide a good example, so long as we remember that they were only proof and not the dispositive deeds of a later time. The party who has a charter may formally rely upon the fact which the charter proves, and the law-suit may

[1] Hurnard, 'The Jury of Presentment and the Assize of Clarendon', *English Historical Review*, LVI (1941), 374.

[2] *Glanvill*, XIV, 1ff. [3] *Glanvill*, XIV, 2.

follow a different course in consequence: if he is plaintiff it may even begin with a different writ; if he is defendant there may be a special issue instead of the general denial. And yet what we should regard as the substantive dispute may be the same: it is not that we learn more of the facts than we otherwise would have.

What does it matter if we learn them for reasons turning upon proof rather than upon substance? If we assume that facts are stated whenever they are substantively relevant, we also assume that whenever they are not stated they are either not relevant or not present. The harm is to our understanding of the ordinary, of that great majority of early cases in which the defendant formally puts forward no facts of his own and makes the customary general denial. The scale of misunderstanding that may result is most simply seen in an example again outside the scope of the present study. Throughout the middle ages defendants sued for certain kinds of harm often plead specially that indeed they did it but because of some justification, never that it happened by accident. Modern minds have drawn both the modern inferences: that the early cases all concerned deliberate wrongs, or that liability was strict so that accident was no defence;[1] and the latter implies something important and unlikely about the intellectual climate. The truth seems to be that such a defendant said, as he would in a criminal trial to this day, that he was Not guilty. The accident was not substantively irrelevant, but it did not affect the proof. The defendant had no charter or the like, and if he relied formally on the accident it would still go to the same jury as if he said Not guilty. In such a situation, the rule for centuries is that the special matter may be pleaded only if the general question might somehow mislead the jury. The justification is an example: the defendant may formally rely upon it because he admittedly did and meant to do what the plaintiff says he did.

It has been suggested elsewhere that the possibility of a jury being misled was the sole reason for allowing defendants to advance special facts instead of making the general denial, and therefore that the whole fruitful process began as juries replaced the older and supposedly infallible modes of trial.[2] This may be an over-

[1] See, e.g., Holmes, *The Common Law* (ed. 1938), pp. 4, 101; Plucknett, *Concise History of the Common Law* (5th ed., 1956), p. 465; Holdsworth, *History of English Law*, vol. III (5th ed., 1942), p. 375.

[2] Milsom, 'Law and Fact in Legal Development', *Toronto Law Journal*, XVII (1967), 1.

simplification. A defendant who had some other proof of his fact – for example, a charter or the record of a court – may always have had greater latitude. But juries generated most of the logic that kept defendants from stating and us from learning the facts. It seems, for example, that you could not make anything of the possibility that a jury might be misled if you yourself chose it instead of an alternative. The grand assize was always chosen, being in principle alternative to battle; and this may be why actions in the right so rarely disclose the facts underlying the dispute. The petty assizes, on the other hand, were imposed. The writ itself ordered the general question to be put, and the defendant had considerable freedom to advance his own facts by way of exception. But, and this is a difficulty which affects all forms of special plea at first, the question was whether he could take this course, not whether he must. If the proof involved was burdensome, for example, he might prefer to let the general question go to the jury; and a petty assize would be taken although he did not even come. If his fact was overlooked in consequence or not given proper weight, the loss was his. In any event it is also ours. Even in a case in which we might have expected to see them, the facts are hidden behind the usual general verdict.

The inscrutability of general issue and general verdict, all we know of most concluded cases on the plea rolls, is our central difficulty. Most work seems to have assumed that the dispute was just about the brute event: did it happen and is this the man? That has always been the normal question in criminal cases, but even today is not the only question raised by Not guilty. In civil cases, it was roughly the effect given to the general issue by nineteenth-century rules of court; and projected back into the early rolls it conjures up an agitated and arid world, fundamentally a criminal world. Malefactors hurry about attacking people, ejecting them from their lands, hoping to get away with obvious wrongs. It is a world we can unthinkingly assume, but cannot consciously believe in. The general issue contained all possible questions, and often hides a more or less honest dispute about the details of an event which is not itself disputed. Those details were what juries and assizes commonly discussed; but for centuries we hardly ever hear anything but their final decision, the blank verdict for the one side or the other. Occasionally on the early rolls we may learn something if the jurors disagree among themselves, or if the loser seeks to attaint them as liars.[1] Occasionally they give a reason which evidently goes to the detail in dispute, but may still be cryptic without the context.[2] Very occasionally we find them doing what Glanvill says the grand assize can do, tell the story and leave it to the court to work out which side should win.[3] Reason suggests that this would not be infrequent, but would be treated as a request for direction. The court would declare for which side the verdict should go, and that verdict is what the clerk would enter.

The methods of the clerks form a further screen through which the facts must pass. Of course it was not their business to inform us; but frustration can almost imagine a censorship at work, so consistently do they leave out what we need just because they did not need it themselves. They did not need anything said in court which was not formally relied upon. A century after the period now under consideration, the year-books begin to show us what rich discussions might leave no trace on the rolls. A little earlier, statute had to provide for the possibility that a rejected exception might after all be needed in some review.[4] Earlier still, we forget even that such discussions may be going on; and only a rare rehearsal can show us what actually lay behind a short entry in

---

[1] A disagreement: *CRR*, VII, *340*; *CRR*, I, *37*; *PKJ*, II, *78*; *RCR*, I, *285, 399*; *PKJ*, I, *2056, 2885*; *RCR*, II, *100* (Walesham), *105–6, 148*. Revealing attaints: (a) *CRR*, III, *97–8*; (b) *CRR*, III, *131, 134–5, 138*; (c) *CRR*, III, *128, 332–3*; (d) case in n. 1, p. 15, below. But the entry of an attaint is often as blank as that of an assize: (a) *PKJ*, III, *909*; (b) *Gloucs.*, *642*.

[2] See, e.g., (a) *CRR*, IV, *33, 73, 165, 199–200, 247–8*; *CRR*, V, *4–5*, where the dispute must have turned on a gift to a younger son which the reason does not even mention, and which may be compared with the case below, p. 142, n. 1; (b) the cases below, p. 23, n. 1. But reasons are occasionally informative: (a) *Lincs.*, *1419*; (b) *PKJ*, I, *2774*; *CRR*, I, *205, 244, 473*; *CRR*, II, *27, 199–200*; *PKJ*, III, *584*; *Northants.*, *532*; *CRR*, III, *13, 67, 179, 229, 254–5, 307, 341* (Alneto); (c) *CRR*, II, *260, 296*; *Northants.*, *680*; *CRR*, III, *309–10*; *CRR*, IV, *17, 58–9, 118, 141, 173*.

[3] *Glanvill*, II, 18. Grand assize declaring facts: (a) *CRR*, I, *16*, 75 (Nuers); *PRS*(NS), XXXI, *80?, 102, 107*; *RCR*, I, *288?*; *CRR*, II, *184, 307*; cf. consequential litigation, *RCR*, I, *281, 376–7, 254*; *PKJ*, I, *2151*; *RCR*, II, *147*; (b) *Gloucs.*, 390, leading to concord; (c) cases below, p. 179, n. 6, arising out of gifts to younger sons before death of Henry I. For a grand assize which did not know, see *CRR*, III, *313–14*; *CRR*, IV, *86*. Assizes of novel disseisin declaring facts: (a) *PKJ*, III, *1002*; (b) *CRR*, VI, *81–2*; (c) *CRR*, VII, *81–2*. A story might lead up to a general verdict, *CRR*, VI, *333–4*; and it might or might not be included by the clerk, as twin enrolments show, *CRR*, II, *146, 149* (Ditton). On judicial direction in the thirteenth century see Sutherland, *The Assize of Novel Disseisin*, p. 73. Recognitors were eventually allowed to insist on returning a special verdict, Stat. Westminster II, c. 30.

[4] Stat. Westminster II, c. 31.

common form.[1] But other chances can show us the kind of thing we may be missing. Once it is a work of fiction. A writer describing how various lawcourts work chooses as an illustration something that may be happening out of our sight in countless real cases.[2] Once it is a clerk who has not mastered the drill. Some mishap must have brought him into service when king John was in the west country in 1204. He is less precise than usual, and feels obliged to note more of what was actually said; and his entries seem to show us a more vivid world.[3]

It is also a world in three dimensions; and one of the important things about which these various distortions have deceived us, or helped us to deceive ourselves, is the seignorial dimension. The adjective is here used, for want of a better, to mean the qualities flowing from the relationship of lord and tenant at every level of lordship. Consider actions in the right. We have been content to see disputes between equals about something like ownership, with the lord playing at most a jurisdictional part. But in a substantial proportion of early cases the question is itself seignorial: is one of the parties entitled to hold the land of the other? This is something we have simply failed to take into account: the rolls do nothing to disguise it.[4] In any particular case, however, they do not tell us until near the end, if at all. Of the claim itself, the clerk often gives us nothing beyond a bare recital: the demandant *petit* the land against the tenant *ut jus suum*. Even if he enrols the count, we shall learn only about the ancestor's seisin and the hereditary descent: the logic of the law-suit required no more. Hardly ever will there be any hint that the demandant's claim is to hold of the tenant, if that is the case; and yet, in a sense that we shall see, that was the normal case.[5] If the claim is the converse, that the tenant is not entitled to hold of the demandant, the logic of proof may

---

[1] *CRR*, VII, 190, *288*, *321*, 322–5 (n.b., prior of Rochester's exception as recited in last entry).

[2] *Consuetudines Diuersarum Curiarum*; below, p. 56.

[3] *CRR*, III, 121 ff., esp. 131–8.

[4] Instead of being asked which party has the greater right, a grand assize may be asked (*a*) whether the tenant has greater right to hold of the demandant or the demandant to hold in demesne, or conversely (*b*) whether the tenant has greater right to hold in demesne or the demandant to hold of him. This book refers to the two latter as 'special mises', as opposed to 'general mises'; and in the early rolls they are about as frequent. Claims in the vertical dimension are discussed below, pp. 80–102.

[5] See generally below, chapters 2 and 3, and especially pp. 41–2, 71–4.

give us early warning in some phrase about the tenant's *ingressum*. But, almost as though regretting this, the clerk refuses to tell us whether the phrase was part of the writ or only said in court.[1] It is indeed over writs that his needs differ most disastrously from ours. He hardly ever tells us even whether a case was begun by *precipe* in the king's court or by writ patent in the lord's, let alone who the lord was. Could it have been the tenant to the action himself? Often, as we shall see, it probably was: but only once does the clerk tell us so, and then by mistake. Absent-mindedly he copied the writ (though turning it into indirect speech) on his roll.[2] Perhaps he was in trouble for wasting parchment.

The writ patent to the lord introduces the last and largest difficulty in interpreting our evidence, the easiest to overlook and the hardest to reckon with when seen. We have no records from lords' courts at this time. Something of their life a little earlier has been reconstructed by Sir Frank Stenton.[3] Substantially later a good deal can be seen in records. To the extent that we have consciously attended to the matter at all, we have read back the later picture, so supposing that Stenton's vigorous world disappeared without trace in decades or even years. We have assumed that at the time of Glanvill and the earliest rolls lords' courts were doing the same kind of thing as the king's court but less important, and doing it less effectively. Inferior jurisdictions administering the same law are in decay, their work just being taken over by national courts. The innumerable petty assizes, for example, reflect mere disorder: the thief of land and the prospector for tenements vacant by death are working in a society in which lords and their order might as well not exist. This book will suggest that the law was not like that: nor was the world.

*   *   *

Thomas is one of Ralph's tenants, and he fails to do the services due from his tenement. What happens? This was an everyday question, and its answer must have been familiar to every man alive. As a matter of words, the answer is familiar to us: Ralph

[1] Below, pp. 96–102.
[2] *PRS*(NS), XXXI, 105, 100–1; *CRR*, I, *41*; *CRR*, VII, *346*. Entries apparently concerning the warranty are: *PRS*(NS), XXXI, *105*; *RCR*, I, *342, 348*; *PKJ*, I, *2147, 2579, 2816*; *CRR*, I, *364*.
[3] *The First Century of English Feudalism* (2nd ed.), esp. lecture II.

distrains. But that may not mean in the twelfth century what it had come to mean by the fourteenth. A number of accounts survive from the years around 1200, surprisingly similar in different parts of England; and since they are given in law-suits by persons concerned to show that they have acted rightly, they tell us at least what ought to happen when Thomas fails to do his services.[1] He is summoned to Ralph's court: summoned by equal tenants, once, again, and a third time. If by the fourth court day he has not come, the court orders that he be distrained by chattels taken on the land; and this also is ordered three times. If that fails, the tenement itself is taken into Ralph's hand, and held if necessary until a third set of three court days has passed. After that, the theory seems to be that the court can order the forfeiture of all Thomas's rights in the tenement to Ralph, who can allocate it to another; but in practice Ralph probably continues to hold it only as a means of coercing Thomas.[2]

This looks like the common source of two things which became distinct. The first is mesne process, the steps by which courts in general compel persons to come and answer. Ralph's court would proceed similarly upon a claim by Ralph other than for services, or upon a claim by somebody other than Ralph.[3] If a third party claimed the tenement, for example, there would be the same three summonses, the same three orders for distress by chattels, and the same taking of the tenement into Ralph's hand; but if Thomas still

---

[1] Below, pp. 13–14, and references there given.

[2] *Glanvill*, IX, 1: *de iure de toto feodo quod de illo domino suo tenet exheredabitur* (below, p. 11, n. 1). But the power seems to have fallen into disuse by the time of even the earliest plea rolls. The only clear reference to a loss of all right *per judicium pro defectu servicii* is in an urban context, *CRR*, VI, 290–2. Cf. *Borough Customs*, I, Selden Society, vol. 18, pp. 297 ff. In *CRR*, V, 266–7 one who claims to have taken in hand for failure of service and held for eight years relies upon an eventual waiver by the tenant in his court. Cf. *Gloucs.*, 249. But as late as 1221 loss by judgment is referred to as alternative to waiver in such a case for the purpose of barring a mort d'ancestor by the defaulting tenant's heir, *Lincs.-Worcs.*, 981. Cf. *BNB*, 370; Bracton, f. 262.

[3] Instead of claiming services, the lord may be questioning the tenant's right to the tenement in the manner considered in chapter 2, below. Examples reciting the process are: (*a*) *Northants.*, 782 (below, pp. 53–4); (*b*) *CRR*, III, 161–2 (arrears and *quo waranto*, below, p. 53); (*c*) *RCR*, I, 62–3, *134–5* (guardian of newly succeeded lord taking homage of tenants); (*d*) *Gloucs.*, 406 (similar). Examples of claims to the tenement by a third party in which the process of the lord's court is recited are: (*a*) *Northants.*, 809; (*b*) *Lincs.*, 1384; *CRR*, IV, *233?*; (*c*) *PRS*(NS), XXXI, 87–8; cf. *PKJ*, II, *79*; *CRR*, I, 72, 93; *RCR*, I, *240, 269, 451*; (*d*) *CRR*, I, 59 (court of Arnold de Bosco), *61?*.

did not come to answer the claim and replevy the tenement, it would be adjudged to the claimant.[1] Nor is the routine fundamentally different in the king's court; and when first it ordered a tenant's lands to be taken into the king's hand, perhaps it was not the court or the hand of an abstract ruler, but specifically of a lord king.

But that threefold process in Ralph's court looks like the starting-point of something more central to our present study, namely distress. Later developments have led us to see distress as a distinct entity, an extra-judicial remedy which happened to be used in judicial process. With unwitting prodigality, we have even argued whether in the earliest days some judgment was necessary to make a distress lawful.[2] But there is little trace of this separate entity in the earliest rolls, and no apparent place for it in the scheme of coercion we are now considering.[3] We have been led to antedate it, perhaps seriously, by an ellipsis of language. Glanvill may speak of distraining for rightful aids;[4] but in connection with the failure to do services, as with other feudal wrongs, he inserts the understood words: the lord distrains his man *ueniendi in curiam suam ad respondendum de seruicio.*[5] So completely have we been taken in, that the insertion in a statute eighty years later of similar words about coming to court has caused us to understand a general prohibition of distraint out of fee as being limited to the obligation of suit of court.[6] When Ralph speaks of distraining for services,

---

[1] e.g., (a) *RCR*, I, 174–5; (b) *CRR*, I, 58–9; (c) cases at the end of last note·

[2] *Select Cases of Procedure without Writ under Henry III*, ed. Richardson and Sayles, Selden Society, vol. 60, p. xciii, n. 1.

[3] The only early case noted in which it may be suggested that a taking into hand for failure of service might be proper without as well as with judgment is *RCR*, II, 58–9, 117 (Tichesie). A defendant seems to plead first that he took by judgment, then that he took without judgment. But it is possible that the judgment is assumed in his second statement, and that he is really modifying a plea of disseisin by judgment to one of taking in *namium* (also by judgment). Cf. below, p. 11, n. 1.

[4] *Glanvill*, IX, 8: *ad huiusmodi auxilia reddenda possit aliquis dominus tenentes suos ita distringere.* But this summarises the preceding sentence: *Possunt autem domini tenentes suos ad huiusmodi rationabilia auxilia reddenda eciam suo iure sine precepto domini regis uel capitalis iusticie per iudicium curie sue distringere, per catalla que in ipsis feodis suis inuenerint uel per ipsa feoda si opus fuerit; ita tamen quod ipsi tenentes inde iuste deducantur iuxta considerationem curie sue et consuetudinem rationabilem.*   [5] *Glanvill*, IX, 1.

[6] Stat. Marlborough, c. 2. Cf. the justification offered in Stat. Westminster II, c. 2, for the provision that lord as well as tenant can procure the removal of a replevin action to justices: though nominally defendant, the lord *distringit & sequitur* for his customs and services.

like Glanvill he means only that Thomas is being distrained to answer for their non-performance in his court. The legal system within which the tenant holds his tenement has been set in its customary motion through summons to the taking of chattels, and from that to the taking of the land. But so long as the lord's own is the only relevant legal system, the steps can only be customary: there is nobody to make him answer if he abridges due process, or abandons it and acts on his own will without any judgment. Until a generation before 1200, his own was indeed the only relevant legal system, and there was no outside authority to which the tenant could regularly look for help.

The king to the sheriff: Thomas has complained to us that Ralph wrongfully and without judgment disseised him of his free tenement in such a place since such a date. So if Thomas gives security to pursue his claim, you are to have the tenement reseised of the chattels that were there taken, and to see that the tenement with the chattels is undisturbed until such a date, when you are to have twelve lawful men before our justices to pronounce upon the matter; and you are to attach Ralph to be there to hear what they say, or, if he cannot be found, his bailiff.

That is the essence of the writ of novel disseisin; and it is always assumed to have been invented, perhaps under Roman influence, for the purpose it came to serve – namely, the protection of possessors against wrongdoers. To this purpose, and to the assize for most of its working life, tenure is irrelevant: the plaintiff's lord and his court play no part and indeed might as well not exist. But if we remember their existence, remember the threefold process just described, and look again at the words of the writ as the only truly contemporary evidence of their own intention, a different picture comes to mind. The lord is not an unnoticed spectator, worrying if at all about a royal encroachment upon his jurisdiction. He is the defendant, and he is being made to answer for an abuse of his power. Against him the phrase *injuste et sine judicio* is not platitudinous: he could disseise lawfully by judgment.[1]

---

[1] Sutherland, *The Assize of Novel Disseisin*, at pp. 82 ff., says that the limit of the lord's power was to distrain by the fee, and that he could never lawfully disseise his free tenant or treat the tenement as forfeit. This rule he characterises as 'rather strange', and so it would be as a part of feudal custom; but it seems to be a factual result of external control. *Glanvill*, IX, I, states the possibility of forfeiture three times over: one who acts to the disinheritance of his lord *feodum quod de eo tenet iure amittet et heredes eius*; one who uses violence against his lord *in misericordia domini sui de toto feodo quod de eo tenet remanebit*; and one who withholds service *de iure de toto feodo quod de illo domino suo tenet exheredabitur*

Against him too, the provision about chattels makes particular sense: a wrongdoer who removed them at all would consume or dispose of them; and this part of the writ accordingly became a dead letter, being replaced, without any adjustment in the wording, by the award of damages. But the lord's first distraint was regularly by chattels, and the sheriff could sensibly be told to have them put back.[1] Then there is the mere tenement which does not

(above, p. 9, n. 2). Perhaps of the first, certainly of the last two, he affirms that proceedings will be in the lord's own court; and the point which he emphasises is that no writ is needed (below, pp. 25–6 and 30). A fourth mention appears over purprestures in IX, 13: *tenementum quod de illo domino suo tenuit sine recuperatione amittet*. This also is done in the lord's own court, but by writ (below, pp. 26–7). For reasons considered later (pp. 27 ff.), the jurisdiction itself disappears, except over the withholding of services; and for that lords' courts cease to proceed beyond taking and holding the fee in *namium*. Glanvill's *de iure* suggests that even in his day it would be extreme to enforce a forfeiture; and his mention of heirs may suggest that the extremity would lie in barring their right (as to which see below, pp. 59 ff., 177 ff.). Probably, however, the assize itself was mainly responsible: lords were careful to act so that recognitors would say *non ita disseisivit eum* (below, p. 15). On the conceptual framework proposed in this book (especially below, pp. 40 ff.), there could originally be no separate step of disinheritance: seisin would be the tenant's only right, and disseisin the lord's extreme sanction; but of course a disseisin would not be irrevocable. Two pleas of disseisin by judgment have been found, both failing for lack of warrant: (*a*) *CRR*, III, 62 (Revell), *129, 129–30, 138, 146, 149*; (*b*) *PKJ*, III, 932. Cf. *CRR*, I, *119*; *RCR*, II, *28*, 194 (Gilbert de Norf'), where recognitors so explain a general verdict. There seems no way of telling whether these represent a stage beyond the usual taking in *namium*, or whether the verbal or factual distinction between such taking and disseisin was a product of the assize or existed in the original framework. In *RCR*, II, *58–9*, 117 (Tichesie), the two things are equated on one view (Sutherland, op. cit. p. 83, n. 4), distinguished on another (above, p. 10, n. 3). It seems *a priori* likely that custom alone had produced a final stage of process by which the tenant was put out without benefiting the lord. But any impropriety in earlier stages would make this as much a disseisin as ultimate forfeiture; and it may have been the assize which produced the verbal distinction. For the taking into the king's hand by way of process, see *CRR*, II, 263–4 and Bracton, f. 365b (*captio…simplex*); and for the position of religious houses during the Interdict, see *CRR*, VII, *3*, 6 (St Benet of Hulme), *24*, *40*, referring back to *CRR*, IV, *3*, *49*, *194*, *243*; *PKJ*, III, *1929*; *PKJ*, IV, *2620*; *CRR*, V, *201*, 271. The further verbal sophistication of 'simple seisin' is used occasionally of a taking in *namium*, e.g., *BNB*, 348, more often of a lord's position on the death of a tenant, e.g., (*a*) *CRR*, VII, *168–73*; (*b*) *Lincs.-Worcs.*, 256; and it owes less to novel disseisin than to mort d'ancestor (below, p. 169). The earliest example noted is *CRR*, V, 169 (Mantel), where *simplex* is contrasted with *plenaria seisina*. See also below, p. 169, n. 3.

    [1] Revealing entries are: (*a*) *CRR*, II, 120 (second of two assizes against Roger Clericus, bailiff of earl de Insula); (*b*) *CRR*, II, *190*, 195 (earl Ferrers); (*c*) *Northants.*, 925; (*d*) *RCR*, I, *154*, *169*; *CRR*, I, 151 (Furnivall). The rule that one need not answer for his tenement while disseised could be invoked by a tenant who had got his land back but not his chattels: (*a*) *CRR*, I, 20–1;

need to be specified in acres or virgates as in every other writ concerning land. There is the freedom of the tenement, which has significance of a different order if it is the lord we are concerned with, and not casual wrongdoers and police measures.[1] There are the uniquely seignorial implications of some at least of those varieties of novel disseisin concerned with nuisances.[2] There is the provision about the bailiff: not, as in effect it became, a kindly arrangement whereby an absent defendant could be represented, but a regular order for the attachment of one whose existence is assumed, the lord's local agent.[3] But there is nothing else, nothing outside the words of the writ except the world within which it was formulated. The fit is obvious, or it is wrong.

By the time of the earliest rolls, and indeed by the time of Glanvill, it is clear that novel disseisin is not being used only for the protection of tenants against their lords.[4] What do the rolls show us of that use? Most obviously, they show us the customary scheme of distraint itself. Almost all our accounts of that come from assizes in which the defendant is indeed the lord, and in which he pleads specially.[5] The assize should not proceed, says Ralph, because though he did take the tenement into hand it was by judgment of his court following a failure by Thomas to do his services.[6] But it is not enough for him to say this. He is making his exception because he does not want the propriety of what he did to be left at large to the recognitors; and unless Thomas admits it, he must tender his own proof.[7] He must always produce his court to testify to the steps taken;[8] and, at any rate if the judgment was

(b) *CRR*, VI, *52, 55–6, 133–4, 273, 284*. This protected the tenant who had recovered in novel disseisin but had not been paid his damages: (a) *RCR*, II, *192*; *CRR*, I, 411 (Huuell); (b) *Yorks.*, *353*, 198, *287*, *1115*.   [1] Below, pp. 22 ff.

[2] Milsom, introduction to Pollock and Maitland, *History of English Law* (2nd ed., reissue of 1968), vol. I, pp. xlii f.

[3] Ibid. pp. xli f.; below, p. 21.

[4] In connection with purprestures, Glanvill expressly contemplates the assize being used by lord against tenant (IX, 11) and by neighbour against neighbour (IX, 13).

[5] It is convenient so to speak of exceptions, although strictly there is no pleading in an assize. Good examples of distraint by the fee raised by way of exception are: (a) *RCR*, II, 22–4, *67*; *CRR*, I, *139, 308, 318*; (b) *CRR*, III, 133–4. Sometimes accounts come on to the rolls in other ways, e.g., *BNB*, 2.

[6] The court must have adjudged the taking and not just advised it, *Lincs.-Worcs.*, 946 (also interesting on jury conduct).

[7] Admission by tenant: *CRR*, III, 156 (abbot of Pershore).

[8] Court not produced: (a) *CRR*, III, 161–2; (b) *PKJ*, III, 932. Cf. (a) *Northants.*, 786; (b) *Lincs.-Worcs.*, 946.

by default, he must produce the men who had summoned Thomas to it.[1] If he does not have his court there, or if the men he has are not enough to make a court,[2] he loses without more. Equally, of course, he loses if his court acted wrongly – for example, by proceeding directly from summons to a taking of the land without first distraining by chattels.[3] Even if the court is present and attests all the necessary steps leading to a judgment by default, Thomas can undermine it all by denying that he was in fact summoned, and can prove his denial against the summoners by compurgation.[4] Even if the procedure cannot be faulted in any way, there seem to be circumstances in which a lord should not proceed to disseisin, whatever the cause – for example, if there are infants and their father is away.[5] And even if nothing whatever is wrong, the end may be that Ralph is told to replevy the land to Thomas and deal justly with him in his court.[6]

About all this there is no doubt. In the years around 1200 the assize can sometimes be seen doing the work for which a literal reading of the writ suggests it was designed, not replacing seignorial jurisdiction but providing a sanction against its abuse. But the proportion of cases in which it can clearly be seen doing this is very small. How can this be so if that was indeed the purpose for which it was invented? If we can hardly hope to know what Henry II was aiming at, still less can we learn the thoughts of our

---

[1] Express mention of failure to produce summoners: *CRR*, III, 133 (Mery), *137*. Express mention of summoners produced: (a) *CRR*, III, 133–4; (b) *Northants.*, 782.   [2] *PRS*, XIV, 40 (Clement f. Walter). Cf. *Northants.*, 816.

[3] *CRR*, III, 133 (Mery), *137*. In *BNB*, 2, not an assize, issue is offered on this point. The absence of chattels is commonly asserted; see, e.g., the first two cases cited above, p. 13, n. 5; cf. *PKJ*, III, 897.

[4] *RCR*, II, *58–9*, 117 (Tichesie). This is what probably lies behind an unexplained wager, e.g. *RCR*, I, 227, *302*; *RCR*, II, 41 (John f. John); *CRR*, I, 274, *333*: but not necessarily, as appears from the case cited below, pp. 45–6. The possibility of such a denial was of course not confined to proceedings for services; see, e.g. *RCR*, I, 447–8; cf. ibid. 368.

[5] *CRR*, I, 434 (Ambly); *CRR*, II, *10*. Ambly seems to be the centre of many law-suits of seignorial cast, but the records are all fragmentary: (a) *CRR*, II, 9–10; *PKJ*, III, *424* (below, p. 172, n. 5); (b) *CRR*, I, 434; *PKJ*, III, *250, 620*; (c) *PKJ*, I, 3529; (d) *RCR*, I, 430; *RCR*, II, 197; (e) *CRR*, III, 307, 317; *CRR*, IV, 23; *PKJ*, III, *1517*; (f) *PKJ*, III, 1047, 1238; *CRR*, VI, 182, 236; (g) *RCR*, I, 226, 263, 279?; *RCR*, II, 96.

[6] (a) *PRS*, XIV, 134 (prior of Leighton Buzzard); (b) *RCR*, I, 366 (B'wes). Cf. (a) *CRR*, III, 156 (abbot of Pershore); (b) *PKJ*, III, 897; (c) *BNB*, 1767, and Bracton, f. 205b. Note also the continuing offer to replevy in *CRR*, III, 133–4. But it would be wrong to assume judicial hostility to proper distraint: see (a) *CRR*, II, *226*, 282; *CRR*, III, 69–70 (below, pp. 118–19); (b) *Yorks.*, 46.

litigants. But it is not far-fetched to imagine a pensive Ralph after the experience we have taken him through, and one conclusion he might reach would close the door in our faces: next time a distress is challenged in this way, he will not make his exception to the assize. He will allow it to proceed, and leave to the recognitors the propriety of what he did.

Can he do this? In a handful of cases, some chance enables us to catch him at it. An entry in common form with a blank general verdict is followed by an attaint[1] or by a more casual questioning of the recognitors[2] or by a statement from the defendant,[3] from which the facts appear. But these cases do little more than alleviate the discomfort of saying, once again, that it is obvious, that the question itself is topsy-turvy. The assize was not created with the pleading of exceptions in mind, and it proceeds even if the defendant and his bailiff both fail to come. The matter is catered for in the question to be put to the recognitors: not just whether Ralph disseised Thomas but whether he did so *injuste et sine judicio*. Usually in the earliest rolls, increasingly rarely as time goes on, these words are expressly imported into the record of the verdict: not just he did or did not disseise, but *ita* or *non ita disseisivit eum*.[4] This verdict is given on oath, in the fear not only of ultimate perdition but also of instant attaint, the process by which the loser in an assize could charge the recognitors with perjury. The recognitors of one assize, so charged in respect of a verdict actually enrolled without any *ita*, just *non disseisivit eum*, explain themselves: the tenement was taken in hand for arrears of service, after due process which they recite just as the defendant would have recited it in an exception, *et ideo non videbatur eis quod injuste et sine judicio disseisitus*.[5] The parallel but different case, in which

---

[1] *CRR*, II, *212–13*, *294* (Euermou; the assize); *CRR*, III, *98*, *117–18*, *124–5* (the attaint); a sequel to *CRR*, I, *474*, *476*; *PKJ*, III, *96*.

[2] *CRR*, I, *119*; *RCR*, II, *28*, 194 (Gilbert de Norf'). For a similar special verdict apparently given on the recognitors' own initiative, see *CRR*, VI, *383–4*. Sometimes the assize, taken because of other land or the like, confirms such matter first put forward by way of exception, e.g., (*a*) *BNB*, 270; *CRR*, XIII, 388; (*b*) *BNB*, 1767 (in the last sentence of the first paragraph, *cartam* should presumably read *curiam*).   [3] *Northants.*, 786.

[4] Examples (in this note each entry number refers to a separate case): *Beds.*, 60, 76, 131, 145, 147, 152; *Lincs.*, 25, 27, 44, 62, 67, 70, 125, 150; but contrast *Lincs.*, 108, 111, 112 (a different clerk: see editor's notes preceding 103 and following 118). For a particularly laconic clerk, see *PKJ*, II, *599–617*. Some clerks use the phrase '*sicut breue dicit*', e.g., *Gloucs.*, 70, 72, 73, 79, 80, 85, 101, 102, 103, 106 (the last particularly interesting).   [5] See above, n.1.

the defendant is not the lord but one claiming to have gone in by judgment of the lord's or a local court, is similarly most often visible because the defendant makes an exception and vouches the court;[1] but that too may lie invisibly behind a general verdict, as appears from the occasional explanation: *non ita disseisiuerunt eum quia ipse recuperauit inde seisinam uersus eum per judicium curie* of such a lord.[2]

It is therefore at least possible, and probable if we take at their face value the words of the writ, that the lord whose case was that he had properly taken the tenement into hand would normally allow the assize to proceed. Even if, as the Charter was to insist, assizes were taken at county meetings where his men were likely to be available,[3] the production of court and summoners was a cumbersome as well as a hazardous business; and since it was his own court, the responsibility fell entirely upon him. Perhaps

---

[1] Sometimes this is cast in the usual form of an exception, *assisa inde non debet fieri quia*..., e.g., (a) *CRR*, III, 229 (court of William de Humez), *346*; (b) *Northants.*, 814 (a county court, as in the two following cases); (c) *CRR*, V, *44, 73*, 141 (Lucell'), 150, 160, 176; (d) the curious case at *CRR*, I, 72 (Hensteworth). But more often it is in some such form as: *dicit quod per judicium comitatus recuperavit ipse seisinam...et inde vocat comitatum*; *CRR*, III, 136–7, *146*. Other county examples are: (a) *RCR*, II, 21 (Leviva f. William), 24, 118–19; *PKJ*, I, *2795*; *CRR*, I, 134, *284*; cf. *CRR*, I, *204*; (b) *Northants.*, 887; (c) *CRR*, III, 139–40, 140, 142–3; (d) *PKJ*, II, 434. Examples from seignorial courts are: (a) *RCR*, I, 174–5; (b) *Northants.*, 592; (c) *CRR*, I, 400 (court of bishop of Rochester), 458; (d) *CRR*, II, 168 (court of Odo de Danmartin), *190, 197*; (e) *CRR*, VI, 388 (court of William de Bocland, *set non audet vocare curiam ejus*). For the relationship between the assize and false judgment, see: (a) *CRR*, III, 66 (Buistard); (b) *Staffs.*, 61 (prior of Stafford); (c) *CRR*, V, *44, 73*, 141, 150, 160, 176 (above).

[2] *Northants.*, 821. It is possible that this verdict was not conclusive: the entry adds that the plaintiff *retraxit se*, and there is a marginal note perhaps ordering the court to be produced. In three other cases it appears that the matter was first raised by verdict and that the court concerned was then summoned; (a) *Northants.*, 809; (b) *Lincs.*, 249, in which the court does not corroborate the verdict and the recognitors *conuicti sunt de periurio*; (c) an assize recited in *CRR*, I, 181 (Chishamton). But there is no such summons in: (a) *PRS*, XIV, 69 (Huggeford); (b) *Lincs.*, 326. Conversely there are two cases in which the matter is first raised by the defendant, but disposed of by verdict: (a) *RCR*, I, 424 (Hugging); (b) *CRR*, V, 265–6, in which defendants, *quesiti si vellent vocare curiam inde ad warantum, dicunt quod non; set bene ponunt se super juratam utrum ipsi disseisiuerunt eum necne*. If what had happened in the court was essentially a grant, a general verdict was presumably appropriate: (a) *CRR*, V, 261 (Welle); (b) *PKJ*, II, 634.

[3] *Magna Carta* (1215), c. 18; (1225), c. 12. In mort d'ancestor, but not apparently in novel disseisin, the county sometimes testifies to relevant facts, e.g., (a) *RCR*, I, 190 (Taiden'); (b) *PKJ*, II, 469, 510; (c) *PKJ*, II, 669; (d) *PKJ*, III, 906. It could happen in other proceedings, e.g., *Lincs.*, 263.

only special circumstances would drive him to so onerous a course; and unless chance has played a trick on us, we can even say what one set of such circumstances might be. In no less than three of the few surviving cases in which the exception was made, it turns out that Thomas is denying that his tenement is held of Ralph.[1] Legally that was an important and difficult situation and we shall come back to it; but it cannot have been so common as to be the issue underlying any significant proportion of disputed distraints. The exception has almost certainly been pleaded to force it into the open, and so prevent the question of title from being lost behind a general verdict.

This assessment of our litigants' position makes our own clearer; we know less than we thought. Most assizes end in a general verdict: 'thus' or 'not thus did he disseise him'. And this is not always, probably not often, a statement about a mere happening. The justices are not being told whether the land had been stolen or not, but whether an undisputed event was an exercise or an abuse of rights. Through exceptions and other chinks we can see that the rights in question were often essentially non-seignorial; but even then we should not forget that they existed in a seignorial world. The point is obvious when William brings the assize against Thomas, and Thomas claims to be in under a judgment of Ralph's court.[2] If it is a judgment of the county court that Thomas relies on, we may or may not remember that the matter can have got to the county only because there was in the background a Ralph whose court had failed to deal with it. But if Thomas could rely upon Ralph's authority in some informal statement to the recognitors, who base a general verdict on it, there will be nothing at all to put us on our guard. These are matters to which we shall come back in considering disputes about the right to the tenement.[3] Our present concern is with the power of a lord to make his undoubted tenant carry out his obligations: and we can never hope to know

[1] (a) RCR, I, 62–3, 134–5; (b) RCR, II, 22–4, 67; CRR, I, 139, 308, 318; cf. CRR, II, 44, 71; (c) RCR, I, 48 (Bard'). Cf. (a) the case cited above, p. 15, n. 1, especially at CRR, III, 98, where the membrane is unfortunately damaged; and (b) CRR, III, 133–4, discussed below, pp. 113–14.

[2] See the cases from seignorial courts cited above, p. 16, n. 1. Sometimes the assize is brought not against the new tenant but against the lord himself, e.g., (a) CRR, I, 156 (prior of Monmouth); RCR, II, 264; (b) PKJ, II, 430; (c) CRR, IV, 41 (Longo Campo). In CRR, II, 19 (count of Eu) the tenant is named as in mort d'ancestor.

[3] Below, pp. 55–6.

how often a general verdict represents a decision about the propriety of a distress or the like.

We can, however, be sure that it was no rarity for the assize to be directed against the lord or persons acting for him. Sometimes we learn of the relationship between the parties by the chance discovery of other litigation between them. Those named in an assize with the usual general verdict may turn up elsewhere in a *de homagio capiendo* concerning land in the same place,[1] or in a grand assize on a mise by which one claims to hold of the other.[2] Often, although the relationship cannot be established, it is the readiest explanation of the novel disseisin entry itself. Cases with groups of defendants are frequent, and they suggest community action which is more likely than not to be directed by the usual management. In one case in which the lord makes his exception of taking by judgment, he is only the first of some two dozen defendants; and there is good reason to think that the others are the members of his court.[3] If he had allowed the assize to proceed to a general verdict, the record would have conjured up a riotous invasion by strangers. In another assize against a group, a lord's steward comes and says that they acted on his orders, and that the plaintiff had already brought an assize against the lord himself.[4] It is to his second assertion that we owe our knowledge of the nature of this case: issue is joined on the identity of the events complained of in the two assizes; and had there been no earlier assize we can be pretty sure that whatever the lord's steward had to say would have been said to the recognitors, and lost to us behind another general verdict. Once, on the other hand, it is an

---

[1] (a) *RCR*, I, 422 (the assize; Trim = Grim); *CRR*, I, 86; *RCR*, I, *280, 326–7*; *PKJ*, I, *3067* (*de homagio capiendo*); (b) *RCR*, I, 177 (the assize; Hereford); *PKJ*, II, 874, *1134*; *CRR*, II, 259–60 (*de homagio capiendo*); (c) *CRR*, II, 55 (the assize; Braibof); 60 (*de homagio capiendo*). Cf. (a) *CRR*, VI, 372 (Veteri Ponte); (b) *CRR*, VI, 373 (Bray), in which the assize is ended by agreement, the defendant taking the plaintiff's homage.

[2] *PKJ*, I, 3151 (mistaken editorial comment at p. 73: tenement in Herefordshire, and London hearing possibly because defendant a baron); *RCR*, II, 166, 187 (the assize); *CRR*, II, 75; *CRR*, IV, 186, 293–4 (claim in the right first by assize defendant himself, then by his son). For another assize between the same parties, see below, p. 20, n. 7.

[3] *RCR*, II, 22–4, *67*; *CRR*, I, *139, 308, 318*. Only the lord himself plays any part, and the other defendants are only named in this assize. But in another, brought by another plaintiff concerning land in the same place, formal entries show one appearing as attorney of the lord's court; *CRR*, II, 44, 71.

[4] *CRR*, III, 22 (steward of Gilbert de Aquila), *80, 195*, 227. See also below, p. 20, at nn. 2, 3.

unusually explicit verdict that allows us to see what sort of thing was happening: of seven defendants, the first two named *disseisiverunt eum ita quod ceperunt cum eis* the last three *et plures alios de curia et per visum illorum ceperunt tenementum illud in manum domini sui*; and three weeks later came the remaining two, who were merchants, and bought timber *dum fuit in manu domini*.[1]

It will be noticed that in this last case the lord himself is not a defendant, and that the first two defendants, presumably his bailiffs or the like, are not named as such. Accident sometimes tells us that defendants not so described are in fact seignorial officers,[2] and this may not be uncommon. It is relatively uncommon to find a defendant identified as bailiff of a named lord,[3] much more common to find groups of defendants which include one or more persons named as reeve, serjeant, bedel, and so on.[4] In one such there is a second entry in which the plaintiff appoints an attorney; and then the defendants are not named at all but identified simply as the *homines* of a named lord.[5] Another feature of that case is not unique, and suggests that the reeve or other officer at least played some leading part: he is amerced more than the other defendants.[6] But he is by no means always the first defendant named in the writ; and, assuming that the order was not random, other possible principals suggest themselves, the lord himself, for example, or the person in whose interest his men had been acting.

---

[1] *CRR*, VI, 383–4.

[2] (*a*) *CRR*, VII, 80–1 (the assize), 53 (second assize identifying bailiff); (*b*) *CRR*, VII, 243–4 (the assize), 245–6, *308* (other litigation identifying serjeant).

[3] (*a*) *CRR*, II, 120 (*Rogerus Clericus baillivus comitis de Insula*); (*b*) *CRR*, VI, 387 (*Arnulfus serviens Ade de Port*); (*c*) *CRR*, V, 238 (*abbas de Hageman et Alvredus senescallus ejus*); (*d*) *CRR*, VII, 81, 82, 140–1, 204 (various parts played by Clement de Santerdon, steward of William de Windsor). Sometimes the relationship emerges only in a verdict, e.g., (*a*) *CRR*, V, 70–1 (assize of nuisance against Robert de Crec, Roger de Gedinges, and five others: *ita fregerunt omnes ...preter corpus Roberti, qui ibi non fuit, set Rogerus de Gedinges senescallus ejus et alii*); (*b*) *CRR*, I, 27 (assize against William de Curtenay, Thomas and Emma: *Willelmus predictus non disseisivit eum set Johannes de Holt ballivus ejus, et Thomas et Emma disseisiverunt ita eum inde*).

[4] e.g., (*a*) *Lincs.*, 1140 (17 named defendants *et alii*, of whom first is *Gilebertus seruiens de Baston* and fifth *Johannes prepositus*); (*b*) *CRR*, VI, 385 (14 defendants headed by *Radulfus prepositus de Estokes*).

[5] *CRR*, I, 73, 105 (*Woluinus prepositus de Blacend'*). Cf. *CRR*, IV, *121*, 163 (*quare aramiavit assisam...versus homines precentoris de Welles*), 195–6.

[6] Cf. the nice graduation in *CRR*, V, 262–3; 4 defendants not amerced, 16 amerced ½m., 3 amerced 8s., and Petrus Prepositus amerced 10s.

Against this background one would expect to find questions of vicarious liability arising; and so they did. It is not unknown to find plaintiffs proceeding separately against the lord and against his agents.[1] We have already seen one such case in which the steward objected to an assize against the men on the ground that one had already been brought against the lord.[2] But this plaintiff may have been in a genuine quandary. A few years earlier an assize by another plaintiff against the same lord had ended in a verdict that the disseisin was done not by the defendant himself but by three of his *servientes*; and this time the steward intervened to point out that only the defendant was named in the writ, and that at the time he had not been in England.[3] Since inquiry was ordered into this, its truth would presumably exonerate the defendant.[4] But even a defendant out of England was liable for a taking which he had expressly ordered.[5] And one available in England who had not ordered it might escape amercement and perhaps damages if he was willing to put it right.[6] A defendant himself disseised by the king may have been altogether immune: once a sheriff attests that the defendant's lands are indeed in the king's hand, but in such a way that neither his steward nor his serjeant nor his reeve have been removed. The assize thereupon proceeds and passes against the defendant: he retains enough control to be responsible for what his local administration has done.[7] But questions about vicarious liability are something else normally hidden behind blank general verdicts. Only the coincidence of timorous recognitors with a scrupulous clerk will leave us the occasional finding

---

[1] *RCR*, I, 155 (Robert f. Walter), 398.

[2] *CRR*, III, 22, *80*, *195*, 227 (Gilbert de Aquila; above, p. 18 at n. 4).

[3] *CRR*, I, *325*, *350*, *400*, *455–6*, 460 (Aquila).

[4] Cf. Bracton, f. 172b. In *PKJ*, IV, 4132, the jurors say that the defendant was overseas and the disseisin done on his behalf by his brother and bailiff.

[5] *Gloucs.*, 85. Cf. *Lincs.*, 1321, *1511*: verdict that defendant's wife and *homines* disseised at his order.

[6] (a) *CRR*, III, 135 (William de Lond' and Osbert Clericus); (b) *BNB*, 779. Cf. Bracton, f. 172b. In *Lincs.-Worcs.*, 947, an assize fails against a lord and succeeds against his bailiff and reeve, possibly because the plaintiff did not hold of the lord. But an abbot is absolutely responsible for any disseisin done by his monks; *CRR*, III, 159 (Evesham).

[7] *PKJ*, III, 773, 774 (same parties as case above, p. 18, n. 2). Conversely, the king's committee might disseise: (a) recital in *CRR*, v, 60–1; (b) *CRR*, v, *311*; *CRR*, VI, *14*, *23*, *55*, 117 (cf. *CRR*, VI, 381, showing John f. Hugh as committee of lands of William de Windsor). Sometimes an assize is held up because the lands of a third party, presumably the lord of the fee, are in the king's hands: (a) *CRR*, I, 52 (St Alban's abbey); (b) *CRR*, I, 78 (earl Baldwin).

that the defendant himself did not do it but his men did, to wit, as one entry has it, Osbert the reeve and Albert the bedel. But even our lucky glimpse of those functionaries does not take us to the heart of that particular case: from another entry we learn that the defendant so made liable was not the lord but his steward; and a separate assize against the lord himself failed.[1]

All this seems to make yet more sense of the provision made in the writ for the bailiff to act in the law-suit itself. If the assize went against the lord, the bailiff could not attaint the recognitors;[2] but it seems that he could take any defensive step, and that he could yield to the plaintiff's claim in the sense of binding his lord by an undertaking to deliver up the tenement. Usually, of course, the reason for such a yielding, whether by bailiff or lord himself, is not recorded.[3] Sometimes it is because the exception of taking by judgment cannot be sustained.[4] But sometimes, and here we turn to a fresh aspect of the problem, it is because another exception cannot be sustained: the assize should not proceed, says the defendant, because the plaintiff is his villein.[5] The question so raised was of more moment to the parties than the mere disseisin; and for each of them the consequences of losing might be serious.[6] This is probably why we find plaintiffs abandoning their claims and placing themselves in mercy,[7] and defendants or their bailiffs yielding up the tenements or otherwise settling the case at considerable cost.[8] If it was fought, the definitive procedure was for the defendant to prove his assertion by record,[9] or by the production

---

[1] *RCR*, I, 398 (William f. Walter: the other assize, ibid., 155, shows that he was steward of Robert f. Walter, lord of Benington). Similar verdicts: (a) *RCR*, I, *246, 249*; *RCR*, II, 134–5; *PKJ*, I, *3014*; *CRR*, I, *199*; (b) *Lincs.-Worcs.*, 947; (c) last two cases above, p. 19, n. 3. In *Lincs.-Worcs.*, 256, the actual disseisor seems to have been serjeant of the vill but not of the lord. In *CRR*, v, 227 (Norensis), the verdict seems to emphasise that the lord did play a direct part.

[2] *Lincs.*, 173.

[3] e.g., *Lincs.*, 51.

[4] *Northants.*, 816.

[5] Examples in usual form of exception, *assisa non*: (a) *CRR*, I, 187 (Holebeche), 262, 278; (b) *Gloucs.*, 1044; (c) *BNB*, 281; *CRR*, XIII, 508. Not in that form: (a) *RCR*, I, 84 (Thomas f. Thomas); (b) *Lincs.-Worcs.*, 1057.

[6] See, e.g., award of damages in *CRR*, III, 140 (Neville), and amount paid for licence in *Lincs.*, 423, 279.

[7] (a) *CRR*, I, 142 (Pictaviensis); (b) *Lincs.*, 1311; (c) *CRR*, v, *193*, 212 (Gerard persona de Beniton); (d) *Gloucs.*, 540; (e) *Gloucs.*, 1044.

[8] (a) *Lincs.*, 423, 279; cf. *CRR*, III, 47; (b) *Northants.*, 663; (c) *CRR*, II, 93 (Cameis), *94*, 132.

[9] (a) *PRS*, XIV, 73 (Bigog); (b) *RCR*, I, 366 (Burnham).

of the plaintiff's kin;[1] and the case would then proceed as on a *de nativo habendo*. It may even turn out that some entries showing lords claiming villeins grew out of assizes.[2] But it was possible for even this issue to be left to the recognitors; and one entry, which does not record defendant or bailiff as saying anything or even being present, seems to show the recognitors explaining a verdict against the plaintiff by saying that he is a villein and holds in villeinage.[3] If this was the fact, and if the defendant did not even come, it is hard to imagine what else they could do.

It follows that even so large a matter as the personal unfreedom of the plaintiff may possibly lie behind a blank general verdict, that again the true issue is not whether an event happened but whether it was lawful, whether a lord was acting within his powers. But this particular issue was one which could at least be raised by exception, and therefore within our sight. Now suppose that a free man holds in villeinage: as a matter of law, at least the king's law, the lord may equally disseise him at will;[4] and yet in the earliest rolls this is not raised expressly by exception.[5] Why should it be when this question, like the *injuste et sine judicio*, is squarely put to the recognitors by the *liberum tenementum* of the writ? For the purpose of winning the assize, it is enough for the lord that the tenement is unfree; and even if the plaintiff was also personally a villein the lord may have preferred to raise no exception and leave it at large to the recognitors. The freedom of the tenement may often have been the real issue they had to decide;[6] but only a chance will let us see it. Sometimes the

---

[1] (a) *CRR*, I, 187 (Holebeche), 262, 278; (b) *Lincs.*, 423 (p. 21, n. 8); (c) *CRR*, V, *193*, 212 (Gerard persona de Beniton); (d) *Gloucs.*, 540; (e) *Gloucs.*, 1044; (f) *Lincs.-Worcs.*, 78.

[2] *CRR*, IV, *121*, 163, 195–6.

[3] *CRR*, VI, 383 (Sumetarius). In *BNB*, 63; *CRR*, VIII, 75, the recognitors seem to have given a general verdict, and now explain it on certification. If the assize proceeds after a defendant has raised the question but without tendering suit, it may apparently still be in issue; *RCR*, I, 84 (Thomas f. Thomas). Cf. *CRR*, III, 140 (Neville). The position is, or becomes, clearer in mort d'ancestor; (a) *Lincs.-Worcs.*, 137; (b) *CRR*, XI, *817*; *BNB*, 225.

[4] See terms of verdict in *CRR*, II, 122–3. And for an express statement made in the course of another kind of action, see *CRR*, VII, *46*, 108 (Norbroc), *133*.

[5] See terms of verdict in *Lincs.-Worcs.*, 174; cf. ibid. 176. In later rolls like these, generally in special circumstances, the matter is sometimes raised expressly: but no independent proof is possible and it still goes to the recognitors; (a) *Lincs.-Worcs.*, 101; (b) ibid. 318; (c) *CRR*, VI, 355 (Kime).

[6] Compare the termor: it is not that he cannot bring the assize, but that he will not win it. Cf. *CRR*, I, 400 (Lega).

recognitors say the plaintiff had no free tenement.[1] A little more frequently, and much more significantly, they say they do not know whether the tenement is free: *nesciunt utrum sit liberum tenementum an non*,[2] to which once they add an express finding that the plaintiff himself *non est villanus*.[3] In the earliest such case the plaintiff is told to ask for other recognitors if he wants to pursue the matter;[4] but what comes to happen shows how as between the parties the question must have gone unasked: the recognitors detail the services and conditions attaching to the tenement, often including the payability of merchet, and leave it to the court to decide whether it is free or not.[5] Sometimes after such a recital the plaintiff withdraws without waiting for judgment.[6] But we shall never know how often such a sequence lies behind the scores of unexplained withdrawals, or the hundreds of verdicts saying *non ita disseisivit eum*.

Even in the cases in which we can see the point coming up, it is of course still possible that the defendant is a mere wrong-doing stranger. But consider the implications of an entry in which nine defendants, headed by 'Richard the serjeant of' a named lord, face novel disseisin brought by eleven plaintiffs. Nine of the plaintiffs come and admit that they are customers, but it is attested that the other two are free men and hold freely. One of these two is not there, so the assize proceeds for just the one survivor and finds that *ita disseisiverunt eum*.[7] It is not impossible that the defendants are marauders who have, as it were, struck lucky with most of their victims; but it is not likely. The lord's local administration has distrained upon all eleven, forgetting that against two they were not entitled to proceed so summarily. Perhaps there had

---

[1] (a) *CRR*, I, *346*, *401*, 446 (Swaffham); (b) ibid. 446 (Edward f. Edward); (c) *Lincs.*, 345; (d) *Gloucs.*, 1113. Cf. *CRR*, II, 99 (Ferendon) where the recognitors confirm an admission by the plaintiffs.

[2] *PRS*, XIV, 70 (le Cras).

[3] *CRR*, II, 122–3. The tenement was held in right of the plaintiff's wife.

[4] *PRS*, XIV, 70 (le Cras).

[5] (a) *Northants.*, 789, 793, *795*; *CRR*, III, *16*; (b) *CRR*, VI, 335 (Valoines); (c) *CRR*, VII, 240–1. Sometimes it is clear that the tenement was once villeinage, and the doubt concerns a possible enfranchisement: (a) *CRR*, VII, 60–1; (b) ibid. 150–1, 225, *307*. For a recital of services in mort d'ancestor, see *CRR*, I, 120–1, *192*, 216; *RCR*, II, *192*.

[6] (a) *CRR*, III, 143 (Alan f. Rolland); (b) *CRR*, VI, 373 (William de Bocland named as lord, not as defendant). Cf. *CRR*, II, 99 (Ferendon).

[7] *Staffs.*, *102*, 110 (lord is John de Kilpeck).

been some forgotten act of enfranchisement: such acts are sometimes directly reflected in the earliest rolls.[1] But, on any view of
their original nature, it was only the assizes of novel disseisin and
mort d'ancestor that had introduced a test of the freedom of
tenements external to the lord's own court, and early doubts must
have been common. The recognitors who could only recite the
facts about services and the like had surely never before needed to
attach a label, 'free' or 'unfree'. The overwhelming majority of
all early assizes seem to be brought in respect of peasant holdings;
and it is not impossible that more of them turned on the *liberum
tenementum* than the *injuste et sine judicio*.

But, although it is implicit in all that has so far been said, there
is still a point to be emphasised about the sense of *disseisivit* itself.
On the traditional view of the assize, the connotations were always
those of theft: a taking necessarily wrongful and probably intended
to be permanent. This is certainly the later sense, when the assize
and other controls have had their unintended effects. Lords rarely
or never proceed even to a taking of the tenement in *namium*
(which, perhaps as another effect of the assize, is not regarded as
a disseisin if done according to the customs); and a final con-
fiscation becomes unthinkable. Then indeed a disseisor must be
a wrongdoer, and it is mere coincidence if he happens to be the
victim's lord doing wrong. But to begin with the word itself
seems to be seignorial. 'Seisin' as a noun is a late derivative of the
verb. A tenant was seised by a lord, not as a modern delivery of
property but as one side of the feudal arrangement. The other side
lay in the tenant's obligations; and if he failed in these the lord
might disseise him.[2] In the rolls our evidence of taking by way of
sanction, even taking in *namium*, comes almost wholly from the
manorial level. It is rare, though not unknown, to read of the
holder of a knight's fee being disseised by a great lord for some
failure.[3] But from other sources we know that the greatest lord of
all freely used this means of discipline; and since there was no
superior jurisdiction to be invoked, the king's disseisins were often

---

[1] (a) *RCR*, I, 227?, 289, 301, 416; *RCR*, II, 89–90; (b) *RCR*, II, 100–1; *PKJ*,
I, 2669; (c) *CRR*, VI, 109, 163, 195–6, 248–9; (d) *CRR*, VII, 219 (Magnus);
(e) enfranchisement cases above, p. 23, n. 5.

[2] On the meanings of 'seisin' and 'disseisin' see also above, p. 11, n. 1, and
below, pp. 39–41.

[3] *RCR*, II, 207; *CRR*, I, 136, 177–8, 343, 458; *CRR*, II, 61, 277; *CRR*, III,
75.

avowedly *per voluntatem*.[1] Perhaps it is no coincidence that at the lowest level, that of the unfree tenure where again no superior jurisdiction would interfere, similar language takes hold: if the lord can demand renders at will he can also take away the tenement at will. For free tenants, even the humblest, what the assize first required was that this means of discipline must be used not *per voluntatem*[2] but by due process. And when the Charter requires that the king should disseise only by judgment,[3] it seeks to make him treat his own men as his law already makes them treat theirs. In this respect, as in some others, the myth should be allowed to stand, but on its head.

*   *   *

The concept of discipline may be used to set the power of Ralph over Thomas in a wider context. For Glanvill the proceedings for default of service are only an example, though an important one, of a lord exercising what may be called his disciplinary as opposed to his proprietary jurisdiction; and what matters is that the disciplinary jurisdiction is exercisable on the lord's own authority and without writ. The dogma that a tenant cannot be made to answer for his tenement without writ applies to proprietary disputes.[4] A third party's claim to Thomas's tenement will be made in Ralph's court, but a writ is needed. Ralph's own claim that Thomas was never rightfully his tenant, and that he is himself

---

[1] Jolliffe, *Angevin Kingship* (2nd ed.), esp. chapter III; Painter, *The Reign of King John*, esp. chapter VI. Supporters of John's rebellion disseised by king Richard: (*a*) *RCR*, II, 159–60; *PKJ*, I, *3123, 3399, 3424*; *CRR*, II, *68*; *Northants.*, 557, *564, 584*; (*b*) *RCR*, II, *247*; *CRR*, I, *196*, 207–8, 245, *265–6*, 338 (discussed below, p. 49, at n. 2); (*c*) *Beds.*, 70. Other royal disseisins: (*a*) *CRR*, V, 135 (Heriz, unexplained disseisin by Henry II); (*b*) *CRR*, I, *456*, 464–5; *CRR*, II, *118* (*per voluntatem* of Henry II); (*c*) *CRR*, V, 147–8 (*sua voluntate et sine judicio* by Henry II); (*d*) *CRR*, VI, *133*, 176–7, 287, 296, 393; *CRR*, VII, *239* (*per voluntatem* of Henry II); (*e*) *CRR*, VIII, 27, *156*, 357–8; *BNB*, 114 (*per voluntatem* of Henry II *pro quadam discordia* with 3rd party). Cf. *CRR*, III, 124 (count of Meulan lost lands *ob suam culpam*; for consequential orders, see Painter, op. cit. p. 99). In *PKJ*, III, *1817*; *CRR*, IV, *84, 100*, 111 (Hersin), an interesting case on escheat, the tenant is said to have been seised *per voluntatem* of king John. In *CRR*, IV, *163*, 233 (Solers), the demandant's father was *exheredatus per voluntatem Henrici regis patris*.

[2] Disseisins *per voluntatem* recited: (*a*) *CRR*, I, 285 (Turpin; by one who knew that the tenant had incurred king Richard's *malevolentia*); (*b*) *CRR*, V, 305–6 (by earl of Salisbury as custodian of the honour of Eye: issue whether present tenant had *ingressum per* the earl).

[3] *Magna Carta* (1215), c. 39; (1225), c. 29.   [4] Below, pp. 57 ff.

entitled in demesne, equally needs a writ; and we shall see that the writ does not even bring the case to Ralph's court.[1] But if Thomas is Ralph's undoubted tenant, and is in breach of his tenurial duties, Ralph needs no authorisation to deal with the matter in his own court; and his court may even adjudge that Thomas be disinherited.

About this Glanvill is explicit, and he mentions a number of cases. There are failures to do services and customs[2] and to pay relief and rightful aids.[3] Homage itself is not included: in principle it is not a duty of the tenant but a condition precedent to his tenure. The common claim is against the lord, requiring him to take homage and so accept the tenant as entitled; and claims by a lord for homage are rare and special.[4] There are, however, various wrongs which may arise out of homage or at least out of the relationship: acts of personal disloyalty;[5] acts which may tend to the disinheritance of the lord;[6] felony (if it is anything different);[7] the heiress in ward who is incontinent;[8] even, though Glanvill is plainly uneasy about this, the tenant having only daughters who marries them without the lord's consent,[9] a case to which we shall return.

In these cases Glanvill repeatedly says that the lord may act *sine breui* or *sine precepto* of the king or the chief justiciar or the justices; and the point is emphasised by the last of the feudal wrongs he discusses. This is the purpresture, an encroachment upon the lord's demesne. For this the offending tenant not only, and obviously, loses the land he has wrongfully occupied: he is also liable to be disinherited of his undoubted tenement.[10] But the

---

[1] Below, pp. 94 ff.   [2] *Glanvill*, IX, 1.   [3] *Glanvill*, IX, 8.

[4] For *de homagio capiendo*, see below, p. 172. But a few claims to homage are found. Some probably arise from grants of service, e.g., (a) *RCR*, II, 159–60; *PKJ*, I, 3123, 3399, 3424; *CRR*, II, 68; *Northants.*, 557, 564, 584; (b) *RCR*, I, 331; *RCR*, II, 70, 73–4, 240, 252; *PKJ*, I, 2925; *CRR*, I, 368; *Lincs.*, 1137, 1174–5, 1210; *CRR*, II, 36; as well as resisting the grantee in this case, the terre-tenants proceed against the grantor, *CRR*, I, 364–5; *CRR*, II, 250–1; (c) *CRR*, VII, 228–9. In others, the real claim is probably for relief, normally made by distraint or the action of customs and services, below p. 162, e.g., (a) *RCR*, I, 32–3, 71, 272 (confusion; cf. ibid. 276, 282); (b) *CRR*, I, 111 (de Bosco); (c) *CRR*, VI, 354–5; *PKJ*, IV, 4487, 4528, 4693; (d) case in n. 3, p. 24, above. In some there is no telling the real dispute, e.g., (a) *RCR*, I, 68 (Rose, granddaughter of Richard de Lucy and wife of John de Dover); (b) *PKJ*, III, 1154; *CRR*, III, 224 (Dummer).   [5] *Glanvill*, IX, 1.   [6] *Glanvill*, IX, 1.

[7] *Glanvill*, VII, 17.   [8] *Glanvill*, VII, 12, 17.

[9] *Glanvill*, VII, 12; below, pp. 104, 157   [10] *Glanvill*, IX, 13.

procedure open to the lord is interesting in two ways. Just to recover what has been taken, if the taking was recent enough, Glanvill assumes novel disseisin to be the simplest remedy for lord against tenant as for neighbour against encroaching neighbour;[1] and this passage shows how quickly the assize must have been extended from what seems to be its original purpose of protecting tenants against lords. For the case of lord against tenant, however, if the assize is not available, Glanvill gives a writ, and an odd one. Writs to the sheriff start proceedings in the county or the king's court; and proceedings in a lord's court are started by writs patent to the lord. This writ is unique in requiring the sheriff to make Thomas answer in Ralph's court.[2] It had to be Ralph's court because of the disciplinary element and the possibility of forfeiture; and a writ telling Ralph to do justice to himself might not sound sensible. But why have a writ at all? Why is this case different from the other disciplinary cases? The answer must lie not in Thomas's undoubted tenement, which may be forfeited, but in the land upon which he has encroached. His right to that is being challenged, and as to that Ralph cannot make him answer in court without writ. Suppose that he holds no other tenement of Ralph, so that, whereas Thomas is claiming to be Ralph's tenant, Ralph regards him as a mere interloper: if it is not within the assize, Glanvill prescribes the ordinary writ patent directed to Ralph's lord.[3] We may find the case of some help in working out the principle underlying the proprietary jurisdiction;[4] but its immediate use is to point the contrast with the disciplinary jurisdiction of Ralph's own court.

What happened to this jurisdiction? For Glanvill it is a clear reality, though perhaps it needs emphasis just because it is already being squeezed out by novel disseisin on one side and by misunderstanding about the need for writs on the other. There is almost no visible trace in the surviving rolls. But we must

---

[1] *Glanvill*, IX, 11, 13.

[2] *Glanvill*, IX, 12. Mr Hall's index of writs, ibid., pp. 199 ff., shows that Glanvill gives no other writ addressed to the sheriff and originating action in the lord's court. There is no trace in the rolls. It may, for reasons to be considered in chapter 3, have given way to the writ patent; see *CRR*, I, 398 (Bissup; note the claim of court); *PKJ*, I, *3428*. The possibility of forfeiture disappeared with it.

[3] *Glanvill*, IX, 13. For a possible example of such a claim, see *RCR*, I, *271*; *PKJ*, I, *2337*, *2845*; *RCR*, II, 230 (Abruncis); *CRR*, I, 448; *CRR*, II, *16*.

[4] Below, p. 94.

remember that it may lie behind those blank verdicts on assizes, or behind other formulae equally opaque. Suppose that Thomas's heir brings a writ of right against, say, Ralph's heir, who puts himself upon the grand assize: the question for the knights would be whether Ralph's heir has the greater right to hold in demesne or Thomas's heir to hold of him. There are many such entries; and the claim must be that a tenement has wrongfully come back into the lord's hands. But there are also many ways in which that might happen, and we hardly ever know which of them was really in issue.

Apart from the claim to services, to which we shall return, it is clear that the disciplinary jurisdiction did disappear; and if we cannot be sure when, we can at least say something about why. On the one hand there can be little doubt that the personal element in homage was waning rapidly. The word 'felony' is still in the earliest rolls used more widely than in its criminal sense, but outside that sense it seems always to denote some denial of the lord's proprietary rights.[1] Breaches of personal duty sometimes appear, but as the subject of trespassory complaints in the king's court. One lord, for example, complains that his man has gone surety for the prosecution of a third party's claim against the lord: significantly, the man says he acted on the orders of a second lord, whose man he also is; even more significantly, this dispute is ancillary to a proprietary dispute between the two lords.[2]

But it is not only that the personal aspects of the relationship are receding, so that the ambit of escheat shrinks with the ambit of felony. Even in the area that remains, the judgment of a lord's court without writ becomes either unnecessary or insufficient; and, except to the extent that it may lie unseen behind the general

---

[1] (a)...*nequiter defendunt quod non tenuerunt terram illam de eo et predictum servicium nequiter ei negant;* opponents *defendunt feloniam; RCR*, II, 22–4, *67; CRR*, I, *139, 308, 318;* (b) *nequiter* denying quantum of service agreed when homage done; *CRR*, I, *326,* 469 (Hausard'); (c)...*contra ius et rationem et in feloniam et causa eum exheredandi fecit homagium* to another *de feodo suo quod de eo tenere debet;* opponent *defendit feloniam; Lincs.,* 1348. (This dispute was protracted. A claim first appearing in *RCR*, I, *79; PRS*(NS), XXXI, 81, was settled by fine; *Feet of Fines, 1196–7, PRS*, XX, 85. The entry cited is an action in 1198 to enforce that fine, and it ended in another fine, which is itself the subject of proceedings in *PKJ*, I, *2917, 3171; RCR*, II, *173; CRR*, I, *173,* 207, and again in *Lincs.,* 1350 – the reason for the survival of the record here quoted. The original proceedings are mentioned in *CRR*, VI, 138–9); (d) *nequiter et in felonia defendit ei servitium suum et ad exheredationem suam fecit alii homagium de feodo suo; CRR*, XII, *36, 751,* 1453, 2293, 2480; *BNB*, 1687.

[2] *CRR*, II, 124 (Richard f. Bive); cf. ibid. 124 (Bret), *154, 196.*

verdicts of assizes, we rarely find it alleged. Consider a case of 1202: a lord, warranting his present tenant, says that a former tenant *convictus fuit de felonia ita quod ipse et heredes sui abjudicati fuerunt inperpetuum*.[1] This may have been a feudal felony and a judgment in the disciplinary jurisdiction of the lord's court. If, as seems more likely, it was a criminal felony, then either this is a unique reference to an independent judgment in the lord's court, or the criminal judgment itself was supposed to carry the forfeiture. We cannot tell. But nor would it matter. So long as Ralph takes the tenement directly Thomas is hanged, or directly it is freed from the king's hand, there will be nobody who can say he is disseised; and the judgment of Ralph's court will be unnecessary in the sense of making no difference. If on the other hand somebody else has got in, a judgment of Ralph's court may be insufficient. Consider an assize of novel disseisin in 1199. The defendant makes the exception of taking by judgment of his court; and the court warrants that it was the lord's escheat for failure of the former tenant's heirs, and that they adjudged that the fee should be taken into his hand. Had the tenement been empty, this would have been proper, though since nobody could have brought the assize the judgment would have been otiose. But it was not empty: the plaintiff, whoever he was, had been put out; and his reply to the exception is that he was not summoned and, more significantly, that there was no writ. The lord and all the members of his court are thereupon amerced.[2] So far as this plaintiff was concerned, and the same would have been true if the escheat had been for felony, the claim was a proprietary one. The disciplinary jurisdiction covers a wrong by and a judgment against the lord's accepted tenant and nobody else. If somebody else is in, the lord's claim against him requires a writ. What is more, the writ will not bring it to his own court, though, as we shall see, that result seems to be accidental: the only writ available is the writ patent to his lord.

We now return to the withholding of services or relief and the like, the only item in Glanvill's disciplinary jurisdiction to survive as a reality, because it is the only remaining cause of forfeiture which can be committed by a living tenant who is still in the

---

[1] *CRR*, II, 110 (Parco).

[2] *RCR*, I, 447–8; cf. ibid. 368. For lords taking, apparently without judgment, see, e.g., (a) *Beds.*, 63; (b) *CRR*, VII, 136–7; (c) *Lincs.-Worcs.*, 357. See also below, p. 159.

tenement and can himself be made to answer. But this too, though for different reasons, becomes affected by proprietary logic. Three cases are possible. In the first, Thomas admits that his regular dues are of the amount alleged by Ralph, but denies that he is in arrear or just cannot or will not pay. In the second, Thomas claims to hold his tenement for less services than those demanded by Ralph. And in the third, Thomas refuses any services because he denies holding the tenement of Ralph.

Of the last we need say no more at the moment than that it would be a prime case of feudal felony for which, if the disclaimer was made in Ralph's court, one would expect immediate disinheritance to follow; though of course this might be challenged elsewhere by Thomas himself or by the other lord of whom he claimed to hold.[1] Our immediate concern is with the other two: Glanvill does not distinguish between them. Both are within the disciplinary jurisdiction of Ralph's court, exercisable without writ; and, in particular, issue may there be joined on the amount of the services due from the tenement. This may go to battle, the witness being one of Thomas's peers who saw the services done, or to the grand assize.[2] Elsewhere Glanvill gives the writ of peace appropriate if Thomas claims the grand assize. This underlines the point: unlike the adjacent writ of peace for use when a third party is claiming the tenement from Thomas, it does not specify that Ralph's court is hearing the case by writ.[3] Indeed, if Glanvill does distinguish the mere failure to pay from the denial of the amount due, it is the latter which is the heinous offence, and which is immediately followed by his statement that the convicted tenant should be disinherited. Like the disclaimer, it is a denial of Ralph's rights.

But of course, if Ralph's claim to the greater services is wrong, that is equally a denial of Thomas's rights. A tenement worth holding for the service of one knight may be valueless if two knights must be found; and it is not unknown for such a dispute in the rolls to end in the surrender of the tenement.[4] This is the aspect of the matter that comes uppermost; and the result is to take the case out of Ralph's disciplinary jurisdiction. The reasoning appears

---

[1] Below, p. 44.

[2] *Glanvill*, IX, I.

[3] *Glanvill*, II, 9 (services); cf. II, 8 (land: *per breue meum*).

[4] *CRR*, II, 273–4; *PKJ*, III, *1182*; *CRR*, III, 206–7. For surrender of urban tenement after fire, see *Gloucs.*, 249.

from Bracton's account of distress by chattels.[1] Whatever the realities are in his day, he assumes almost consistently that his lord has a court and is working through it:[2] the limits of distress are therefore the limits of what the lord's court can do without writ, of what this chapter has called the disciplinary jurisdiction. And distress is in principle improper if the tenant does not admit the amount of the services with which the lord says the tenement is burdened. If that is the situation, there must be a writ,[3] and two correlative writs are available:[4] Ralph may have a writ of customs and services which starts proceedings in the county; or Thomas may halt the process of Ralph's court with a prohibitory *ne vexes*, which in effect equally obliges Ralph to claim in the county. Bracton's logic leads to a difficulty. Suppose Ralph has long been getting the equivalent of two knights: can Thomas by merely asserting that one is due, stop Ralph's distress and make him claim by writ? Certainly Thomas can stop it with a *ne vexes*. But he cannot otherwise make the present distress unlawful; and in the ensuing replevin proceedings the services that Ralph has in fact been getting will be taken as the standard. The hierarchy of possessory and proprietary rights is being established.

All this would have seemed strange to Glanvill, and strangest of all the proposition that so intimately feudal a question as the rightful amount of the services could not be settled in a feudal court. That result appears to be accidental. The proprietary logic has made writs necessary, and by chance there were already writs to hand. Glanvill has both the customs and services and the *ne vexes*. But probably he did not see them as a pair, or as playing the parts assigned by Bracton.

His *ne vexes* is not described at all. The writ is one of a series recited without discussion to illustrate the kinds of matter which may be referred to the sheriff.[5] But it is not addressed to the sheriff: it is a writ patent addressed to the lord, and it orders the sheriff to act only if the lord fails to do so. Glanvill has two other writs in this form. The writ of right of dower comes in his discussion of dower.[6] But it is only a variant of the great writ of right patent,

---

[1] Bracton, ff. 155b ff., *De vetito namii.*
[2] Especially at f. 157b: the lord, having said that he took *secundum considerationem curiae suae* for services, *inde poterit curiam suam vocare ad warantum si voluerit.*
[3] Bracton, ff. 156–156b.   [4] Bracton, f. 158.
[5] *Glanvill*, XII, 10.   [6] *Glanvill*, VI, 5.

which comes immediately before his *ne vexes*, and leads into his survey of the sheriff's jurisdiction.[1] Claims started by these two writs came to be regularly removed by the sheriff, and the following chapter will consider reasons why lords to whom they were addressed might feel obliged to disobey.[2] These reasons would not apply to *ne vexes*, but we cannot tell how far obedience was expected or even what would constitute obedience. Would the sheriff remove the plea unless the lord abandoned his claim to more service than that acknowledged by the tenant, or could the lord's court continue provided it allowed the tenant's assertion to be put in issue? Neither Glanvill nor the early rolls answer this,[3] and the question may be unreal: a tenant would get the writ only after his lord's court had refused to let him raise the question. What matters is that for Glanvill they could let him raise it if they chose, could let the question go to battle or grand assize, and could and perhaps should disinherit the tenant if he lost; and they needed no writ.[4] There was no jurisdictional incapacity. The tenant needed the writ, and perhaps the consequent removal, because the lord's court was treating his question as closed. In this we shall see an analogy with the great writ of right itself.[5] There may prove to be another. Glanvill's *ne vexes*, like counts in the right, refers to the state of things in the time of Henry I, and may first have been aimed at usurpations during the anarchy rather than at a commonly recurring dispute.[6] Within the closed world of a lord's court, genuine disputes about quantum of service would not easily arise.

---

[1] *Glanvill*, XII, 1–9.

[2] Below, pp. 58 ff.

[3] By the time a case has reached the royal court and its rolls, *ne vexes* is hard even to recognise. An early recital shows that in that particular instance *per illud breve venit loquela in Comitatu*; *Staffs.*, 108–9, *123*. But what other writ could have figured in a lord's claim for services *per breve recti in curia sua*; *CRR*, I, 11 (Gerpunvill)?

[4] *Glanvill*, IX, 1. Even in the king's court in the time of the early rolls, disputes about quantum of service lead to revealing offers of proof: (*a*) *per...parem... qui interfuit ut dicit ubi ei fecit humagium nomine* so much service; *CRR*, I, *326*, 469 (Hausard'); (*b*) *per unum parium*; *CRR*, II, 242–3; *CRR*, III, 36, *183*, 253; *CRR*, IV, 20; (*c*) *per* one *qui illud servitium recepit ut ballivus...qui hoc offert etc. ut de receptione sua*; *CRR*, II, *27*?, 32–3; *PKJ*, III, *1179*. Cf. a disclaiming party said to have done service to the lord's serjeant, which the lord offers to prove by the serjeant who received it or by a witness to the receipt; *CRR*, XII, *36*, *751*, 1453, *2293*, *2480*; *BNB*, 1687 (less explicit).

[5] Below, p. 58.

[6] *Glanvill*, XII, 10. For the frequency with which counts in the right begin at the death of Henry I, see below, p. 178.

Glanvill does explain the use of his writ of customs and services, and it is not about quantum at all. After discussing aids, in which there was some discretion about amount, he says that they are enforced like reliefs and customs and services by the lord's own court, as of right and without any writ. But, he goes on, *si dominus potens non fuerit tenentem suum pro seruiciis suis uel consuetudinibus iusticiare...tale breue inde habebit*; and this introduces his *justicies* writ telling the sheriff to enforce the customs and services due.[1] It is a mode of enforcement auxiliary to the lord's own jurisdiction, and there is no question of the dispute being seen to touch the right and so falling within the requirement of a writ.

Why should a lord not be *potens* to *justiciare* his tenant? Glanvill may have been thinking of conditions more specific than factual weakness. The tenant might have some immunity, and this is a point to which we shall return in connection with grants to religious houses.[2] But grants could produce a more widespread form of impotence. Subinfeudations for service seem to have been made even when the aims of the parties would be better met by a substitution. We shall see that this may itself have followed from royal interference in the seignorial structure; but it certainly weakened it by introducing artificial lords, lords without courts.[3] If distress is the process of a court, you need a court to distrain; and how many tenants make a court? The later riddle may echo a real problem: in early assizes two men seem not enough to warrant a seignorial taking by judgment.[4] Nor is it only the disciplinary jurisdiction that is affected. The writ of right patent goes to the person of whom the demandant claims to hold; and Glanvill may have the same artificiality in mind when he warns that it must not be directed to any one else, 'not even to the chief lord'.[5]

The writ of right going to a peasant grantor was incongruous, but little more of a nuisance than the same writ going to a real lord whose court would not act on it.[6] But substantial inconvenience would result if every grantor for a rent, having no court to *justiciare* his grantee, applied for a *justicies* order to the sheriff to do it for

---

[1] *Glanvill*, ix, 8–9. Cf. ix, 1 : *Sin autem non possit quis tenentes suos iusticiare...*
[2] Below, pp. 118–19.   [3] Below, p. 111.
[4] Above, p. 14, n. 2.
[5] *Glanvill*, xii, 8.
[6] Below, pp. 58–9.

him. This must have contributed to the changes which gave him
the power of distress by chattels, and so disguised as an independent
remedy the last vestige of Glanvill's great disciplinary jurisdiction.
Routine enforcement became extra-judicial because the judicial
load would have been too great for the sheriff and the county
machinery to bear. As it was, they had to carry the load of settling
disputes when the liability was denied; and the work-a-day
replevin, under which the county did what had been the regular
business of lords' courts, seems to have been developed from heavy
armament used against lords who refused to allow that business
to be done.[1] The lord who refused gage and pledge had been
fighting against the order of things in not allowing his dispute with
his tenant to be put to his own court; and the allegation seems to
bring it to the county when there is nowhere else for it to go. Nor
was this aspect of the jurisdictional transfer without its incon-
gruities. They followed because public justice lacked the ultimate
sanction of the lord's own court. In that court, the tenant who
denied holding of his lord would get short shrift. In a replevin in
the county, he found that he could do it with impunity and profit.
Statute had to allow the lord to procure a removal to the king's
court, where at least the disclaimer would be of record;[2] and even
then the lord had to enforce his forfeiture by the king's writ of
right. Again, in the lord's own court there had been no difficulty
about the tenant who in effect abandoned his tenement so that there
were no chattels to take. That court could proceed to take the
land; and statute had in the end to counterfeit this power, providing a new writ by which the land itself could be recovered by
judgment of the king's court.[3]

By the end of the thirteenth century, tenure has been drained of
all the life implied in *justiciare*, an organic life in which tenement
and dues are interdependent and kept in balance by the lord's
court.[4] Now they are independent properties fixed in an external

---

[1] Pollock and Maitland, *History of English Law* (2nd ed.), II, pp. 577 f.

[2] Stat. Westminster II, c. 2; Plucknett, *Legislation of Edward I*, pp. 61 f.

[3] *Cessavit*: Stat. Gloucester, c. 4; Stat. Westminster II, c. 21.

[4] Early usage even speaks of services as due not to the lord but to his court,
as it were a continuing corporation: (*a*) *PRS*, XIV, *136*?; *PRS*(NS), XXXI, 72–3,
77; (*b*) *PRS*(NS), XXXI, 108 (Henry f. Ailmer); (*c*) first document printed in
notes to *PKJ*, I, 3487; (*d*) *CRR*, V, *125*, 191 (Bocland), *290*; (*e*) *CRR*, V, 202–4.
Cf. *CRR*, VII, *25*, 41 (Punchardon), *48* on the significance of the capital messuage.
For services done *ad comitatum*, see *RCR*, I, *239*, *323*; *PKJ*, I, *2012*, *2956*; *RCR*,
II, *111*; *CRR*, I, *180*, 406 (Hauville).

system of law. And the lord's jurisdiction is an antiquarian reminiscence, perhaps seen by lawyers at the end of the thirteenth century as it is by historians today: an obsolete item among the lord's proprietary rights, once valuable for the money it brought in. What had really been lost was an altogether different distribution of power and an altogether different framework of ideas.

2

PROPRIETARY IDEAS

Glanvill's disciplinary jurisdiction was considered first partly to give substance to propositions hard to reckon with when stated in the abstract. For us, property rights have some absolute existence; and the jurisdiction protecting them is a secondary matter having no effect upon the substantive rules. The legal system may allocate a dispute concerning my house to this court or to that; but the same rules will be applied and the same results reached. On this basis we have assumed that the growth of royal jurisdiction over land was a process of transfer, analogous to the transfer of personal actions from local to royal courts. Whether the desire was that of royal officials or of litigants, what happened was that claims formerly made in lords' courts came to be made in the king's; and though they might there receive more sophisticated treatment, especially in the matter of proof, the same justice would be done and the same result reached. The new jurisdiction was set up alongside the old, its superiority important only for the political reason that lords could not stop it. The operating relationship was one of rivalry between parallel institutions making little direct contact with each other.

But if the original role of novel disseisin was that depicted in the preceding chapter, the original relationship was entirely direct: it was one of control. The assize was a response not to a failing seignorial order for which some alternative must be provided, but to an order which had been sovereign within its own sphere and was subject to sovereign abuse. Lords and their courts had inherent powers, but there had been no sanction if these were exercised without satisfying the customary requirements. A sanction was provided by the assize. This book will suggest that mort d'ancestor and the great writ of right itself were equally conceived as mechanisms by which the customs were enforced upon lords and their courts, and that the transfer of jurisdiction which in fact followed was neither intended nor foreseen.

Seignorial jurisdiction was not, however stealthily, to be replaced by royal: it was to be made to work according to its own rules. Even on that basis, we must not imagine a confrontation, with abuse having become general: the customs were no doubt commonly followed, or at least the common intention was to follow them. The remedies began as safeguards of the unquestioned order of things, with novel disseisin, for example, providing a kind of judicial review. They were to destroy the seignorial order. But that was a juristic accident, altogether beyond foresight; and it has eluded hindsight because our hindsight has been preoccupied with the most tangible of the consequences – namely, the transfer of jurisdiction which in fact came about.

It is the most intangible of the consequences that is of most interest to the historian of legal thought – namely, a transformation of elementary legal ideas. In assuming a transfer of jurisdiction, we have also assumed that the disputes themselves and the terms in which they were conducted were removed unchanged. Bracton and the copious records of royal courts in the thirteenth century have familiarised us with seisin and right as abstract concepts, untidy versions of possession and ownership; and so we have imagined seignorial courts in the twelfth century as dealing in rights *in rem*, rights good against the world. But rights cannot be good against a seignorial world, only a Roman or a modern world; and it is this assumption that has misled us most, and perhaps created most of our difficulties.

In any world, possessive adjectives are used indiscriminately. Today's creditor speaks of 'my money in the bank', today's lodger of 'my home', though neither owns anything. Today's owner and tenant of a rented house each speak of it as 'mine'; and both will go on doing so if the tenancy becomes controlled by statute, so that in reality the house is more the tenant's and less the landlord's. That control was imposed from the outside, not intended to change legal principle and not seen to do so. The writers of land law books did not alter their chapters on leases: they added separate accounts of what seemed only a regulation of rents. A new property interest in the tenant grew from control over the landlord's return. In a developed system when law is written down, the new concept resulting from such control is perhaps necessarily stated in the terms of one body of rules working upon another. An example for lawyers (historians may prefer to take it on trust) is the equity of redemption. But in a customary system the change leaves no such obvious trace.

The unfree and the free tenant of the twelfth century each spoke of the land as his; and at the peasant level there may have been little difference between them in reality. How else can we understand those assizes in which the plaintiff has evidently been put out, but recognitors cannot give their usual blank verdict because, they say, they do not know whether the tenement is free? They have to rehearse the services by which it is held, and leave the result to be deduced by the court.[1] For the plaintiff and his neighbours it must be a new question. It has been raised because he is claiming the protection of a new control; and the assize controls only free tenures. Nor was that an arbitrary refusal to protect property rights at the lowest level of society. It is tenures that are being protected: not property rights, but arrangements by which land is held for a return. At the level of the labour force it was not thinkable to control the arrangement. Security of tenure in land would be correlative to security of tenure in job; and both would be correlative to duties fixed in nature and amount. This became a test of freedom, but it started as the limit of control. Even with tenures unquestionably free, it was external control that finally fixed the lord's return. This seems to be happening in Glanvill's account of aids, which like services are enforced in the lord's own court.[2] His tentative rules about what can be demanded, and not just requested, must derive from customs differing from lordship to lordship and evidently embodying a discretion. Only external enforcement can turn them into uniform rules of law.

Such control, brought to bear upon every point of the relationship, deprived seignorial courts of any power of final decision and therefore of their own law. Held to the common standards, they become agents applying the king's law; and then they drop out altogether. Free tenure becomes unrecognisably different from unfree, and from its own former self in the seignorial world. The obvious difference in jurisdiction masks the conceptual difference produced by separating that power of final decision from the tenurial relationship. The tenant's right to his tenement and the lord's right to his dues become independent properties, each passing from hand to hand without reference to the other. The relationship, if such it can be called, is created by coincidence: for

[1] Above, p. 23.   [2] *Glanvill*, IX, 8.

the time being these two are in privity of estate because this man has the tenement and that man the seignory. Only some ancient mysticism prevents us from calling the tenant owner of his land, and attributing to the lord a sort of servitude over it, a *jus in re aliena*. But in the seignorial world the relationship had been primary, with the rights of the parties interdependent, and the balance between them held by the lord's court. If we are to think of either as owning anything, it must be of the lord as owning the whole of his fee. But this is not some real result of conditions outside: outside he too is somebody's tenant. It is something postulated inside the fee, the internal plenitude of control which the historian like the tenant himself must accept. The *dominium* of this kind of *dominus* was always a relative thing.

As between the parties, proprietary language is out of place. There is a relationship of reciprocal obligations; and its properties were fixed at a time when it is the lord rather than the tenant who should be imagined as the buyer in some initial transaction. He is the buyer in the same sense that he is the owner: he is the one with the wealth, the only form of capital wealth there can be. Later he will turn its produce into a money income, and pay in money for what he needs. Now he buys services and pays directly in land. But of course the land is not transferred out-and-out: the basic purchase is of a life's service for a life tenure. He buys a man. The logic of the matter was to be transformed by heritability, which will not be considered fully until the last chapter of this book. But the elementary particle was the life arrangement between lord and tenant made within a lordship seen in isolation. The lord takes the homage or fealty of his man, and seises him of the tenement. If later the man fails in his service, not just the render but also the devotion required by his homage, the lord will disseise him. But by custom, and later by force of the king's assize, he may do this only after due process; and that is what the disciplinary jurisdiction of his court is about. Otherwise he owes the tenant enjoyment of his tenement as long as he lives; and when he dies the lord and his court will make a new arrangement with a new man.

The appropriate language is that of obligation, and the terms used all involve two persons. A tenement is not a lawyer's long word for a parcel of land, but what a tenant holds of a lord for service. A tenant is not just one physically in possession but one who has been seised by a lord. The lord seises the tenant of his tenement, and to seise is as much a transitive verb as to disseise: the subject of both was a lord and the object was a tenant. It was probably outside interference that brought about the linguistic shift, and the process may have begun before the assize. Suppose a royal command in a common passive form: cause such a tenant to be seised, or to be re-seised, of such land.[1] It may be addressed to the lord of that land; or it may be to a sheriff or other royal officer, but in respect of land directly held of the king. Even if the addressee is a royal officer, and the land held of some other lord, the command may imply an element of constraint upon that lord. But the passive is ambiguous, and slowly the lord drops out. To be seised denotes a condition rather than an event, a relationship between person and land which can be discussed without necessary reference to the lord. This generates a new noun; and 'seisin' will describe the condition which is protected when novel disseisin is used against anybody, lord or other. The original active use of the verb disappears. Lords and others may disseise, but nobody seises a tenant. Indeed, the transitive comes to have the land for its object: a lord will seize the tenement into his own hand. To describe the original transaction, a separate verb has to be combined with the noun. The lord puts his tenant in seisin or makes seisin to him. The original connotations will now have to be made explicit in a case in which they matter – for example, where one put himself in seisin, and because seisin had not been made to him by the lord's bailiff it could be held no seisin for the purpose of the assize.[2] Even in such a case the point comes to be that a conveyance has not been completed rather than that a relationship has not been created; and we shall associate the yet later language of livery of seisin with a delivery between equals, not with the livery that a feudal guardian makes when his tenant comes of age.

As between lord and tenant and within the lordship, there is hardly room for any deeper proprietary concept. Seisin itself connotes not just factual possession but that seignorial acceptance which is all the title there can be. We do not ask whether the tenured professor or judge owns his position. His right to hold it is a matter between him and the controlling authority: there is no

---

[1] *Royal Writs in England from the Conquest to Glanvill*, ed. van Caenegem, Selden Society, vol. 77, pp. 261 ff., 439 ff.

[2] *Yorks.*, 342: a death-bed gift in consideration of past service; cf. below, pp. 121–2.

question of his claiming it from somebody else, and nobody else can claim it from him. He is in and cannot be put out except for cause after due process, and that is all there is to it. A piece of land of course can be wrongfully occupied in a more concrete sense than can a professorial chair or judicial bench. But juristically the position of the tenant was at first the same. Perhaps he should not have been put in in the first place: but he is in and cannot be put out except for cause, and again that is all there is to it.

In such a world the lord's court would police against wrongful invasions and encroachments, and would sometimes have to decide whether, for example, these acres belonged to this tenement or to that. But the question of title to a tenement would not arise during the tenure of a tenant fulfilling his obligations. It was only about the beginning and ending of the relationship that decisions had to be made: who should be seised in the first place; and has the man seised so acted as to justify his being disseised? The latter question is the subject-matter of the disciplinary jurisdiction, about which no more need be said. It is from the former that the proprietary jurisdiction and deeper proprietary ideas seem to grow.

Suppose a sovereign lordship to have its customs of inheritance. On the death of a tenant, his heir has a right to be seised. In the concluding chapter we shall see how that right was to be transformed by external control, and turned like seisin into something abstract and absolute. But it begins as a right existing within the lord's court and availing against the lord, just a claim to be put in. Normally the heir will be put in: that is what we mean by customs of inheritance. But suppose he is passed over, deliberately or by mistake. Of course it should not have happened; but it has. From the preclusive effect on third parties of judicial decisions in the earliest rolls, and from the later records of courts governing unfree tenures, we may guess that at most custom would sometimes allow the right heir to claim within a limited time. But even if it does, this cannot alter the nature of his right. It is not a direct property interest in the land, availing against the world including the new tenant: it is still a right against the lord to be seised, to be made tenant of that tenement. Whether or not he has put somebody else in, it is only the lord who can do anything about it. And when the king interferes, his writ is indeed an order to the lord to do right to the demandant.

Inheritance has been anticipated to this extent to emphasise that the right itself started as a term of obligation rather than property. At first it means no more than the right against a lord to be seised. The customs of inheritance are the commonest source of that right. But consider dower. The widow has a right which equally manifests itself in a writ *de recto*. It is a right against the husband's heir to be seised, to hold a tenement of him. Whether or not the heir or the husband has put somebody else in, it is only the heir who can do anything about it. With curtesy there is no question of right because the widower is in: he was seised by the woman's lord when he married her. The problem for the lord in that case is in getting him out again, if the woman dies without having had a child of the marriage: then it is the heir who will have a right, a right against the lord to be seised.

The last term in the seignorial vocabulary is 'warranty', the only one sounding to modern ears like a matter of obligation. But the root idea was probably that of warrant with its connotations of authority and protection. We shall see that a lord might ask *quo waranto* one claimed to be his tenant;[1] but within the single sovereign lordship it would normally be tautologous to say that one seised was in by the lord's warrant or had his warranty. The seisin itself would bind the lord to keep him until he died or failed in his duty. The idea of an obligation to warrant may first be associated with heritability. If a grant can only be for life, a grantor can reach into the future only with promises; and if by charter he undertakes that he and his heirs will warrant the grantee and his heirs, he may mean no more than that the authority is to be renewed on each change of parties. Warranty as an obligation owed to a tenant who has already been seised, and relating specifically to claims by third parties, must grow with the possibility of claims by third parties. The lordship is no longer sovereign. Although this tenant has been properly seised, there may now be somebody who can enforce a better right to be seised. That right of a claimant who is out induces the equal and opposite warranty of the tenant who is in. His service was bought by the lord, and he is still entitled to his pay. He cannot have the original tenement, because the lord is compelled to cede that to the claimant with a better right. Conflicting arrangements have placed the lord under obligation to both parties, and all he can do for his immediate tenant is to compensate him with another tenement.

[1] Below, pp. 45 ff.

In the earliest rolls this logic is seen most clearly in the simplest case in which conflicting arrangements could as a matter of everyday fact be easily made. The husband who endows his wife of certain land at the time of the marriage can later grant the same land to a tenant for services and both transactions are valid. When the husband dies, his heir is bound to warrant the tenant, who is in by virtue of the grant. But the heir is also bound to do something for the widow, who has a right to be seised and to hold the tenement of him for life. We have seen that this will first manifest itself in her bringing a writ *de recto* to the heir. But if, for reasons to which this chapter will wind its way, the widow's claim is then removed into a royal court, the heir must be joined as a party and the language of warranty becomes appropriate. If the heir warrants her claim to dower, he accepts an obligation to her of the same nature as his obligation to the tenant. The ultimate liability falls upon him; and if he is solvent, in the sense of having enough land by inheritance from the dead husband, he must find an extra tenement for the lifetime of the widow. At first there may be some discretion over who gets what. But the widow has the earlier and prior claim: she must be satisfied whether or not the heir can provide another tenement. She therefore comes to get the original tenement anyway, and the later grantee gets *escambium*, if any is forthcoming, until the original tenement is freed by the widow's death.[1]

The essential difference between this seignorial title, which is one side of a relationship between persons, and a modern or Roman

---

[1] Heir warranting both sides: e.g., *PKJ*, IV, 4432. If the husband made many grants, it may be doubtful whether the heir has enough to honour all claims; *CRR*, VI, *226*, 231 (Wallingeton), *263*, *266*, *267–8*, *315–16*, 364–5; *PKJ*, IV, *4470*, *4483*, *4728*; *CRR*, VII, 33, 95–6, 155. He may even argue (see below, p. 127) that too little will be left for himself; *RCR*, I, 406–9, especially the claim against Pelham at 408; *RCR*, II, 6. On who gets what, see *Glanvill*, VI, 13. Bracton, f. 299b ff., says that the widow gets the tenement and the grantee *escambium* if it was *dos nominata*, the converse if the endowment was general. The widow gets the *escambium* expressly for this reason in *CRR*, VI, 149 (Kersimere against Muleton: the claim against Nereford is interesting in another context, below, p. 127). The same result is reached in *PKJ*, IV, *2633*; *CRR*, V, *26*, 84–5; and though the reason is not stated the endowment was perhaps general. *Dos nominata* is normally signalled by a claim for so much land, as opposed to a proportion of so much land. In the early rolls it is common for the grantee to get the *escambium* not only when the claim is for a whole tenement, e.g., (a) *PKJ*, II, 815; (b) *PKJ*, II, 977, but also when it is for a third part, e.g., (a) *Lincs.*, 1503–4; (b) *Lincs.-Worcs.*, *496*, *498*, *591*, *629*, 891. The matter may of course be settled by agreement, e.g., (a) *CRR*, III, 69 (Passelewe), 95; (b) *CRR*, V, *64*, *133*, 170–1, *223*, *243*.

ownership can most easily be seen from the case of a disclaimer. The improbability of the initial situation should itself warn us against thinking of abstract rights. William is in possession of a tenement, but he does no service to Ralph and has not acknowledged him as lord; and all Ralph wants is that he should do so. There is no action for this purpose. Lordship is not a right that can be claimed: it can only be exercised. What Ralph must do, therefore, is to demand his services and dues, whether by process of his own court or by royal writ. But either course assumes the relationship, and William can bring either to an end in his own favour by denying it. Lordship cannot exist unless it is acknowledged. Whatever had been the true position before, Ralph is not now entitled to William's service, or William to Ralph's warranty. If the tenement was indeed part of Ralph's fee, to be proved by the receipt of services in the past, there is no longer anything to keep him out. He will claim it in demesne, as from a stranger who had merely encroached, by writ patent directed to his lord.

Now suppose, more realistically, that William denies holding of Ralph because he regards himself as holding of Humphrey. Even if Ralph knows this at the outset, he cannot in general claim the lordship as a piece of property from Humphrey. Nor can William leave them to fight it out, an unconcerned owner who will render dues to the winner. He must back the winner now, and his stake is the tenement. Ralph will demand services from William as before, and William must choose whether to acknowledge him and forfeit any right he has under Humphrey, or to vouch Humphrey. If he vouches and if Humphrey warrants him, he can indeed watch the fight; and if Humphrey wins it he will continue to hold as Humphrey's tenant. But he cannot end as Ralph's tenant. If Ralph wins, William loses the tenement for ever, no matter how long he and his ancestors have held it; but Humphrey, having warranted him, will owe him another tenement.[1]

*　　*　　*

[1] Telling cases on the subject matter of the last two paragraphs are: (*a*) a dispute between earl Ferrers, often represented by William de Ridware, his steward (*PRS*, XIV, 22; *PRS*(NS), XXXI, 62), and the Templars and Hospitallers; *PRS*(NS), XXXI, *114*; *CRR*, I, 45, 66 (*Comes querat breve versus eum qui terram illam tenet...*), 90; *157, 299, 460; RCR*, I, *327; PKJ*, I, *2242, 2476, 3213; RCR*, II, 127, 234; (*b*) the pair in *PKJ*, III, *1632; CRR*, V, *42, 51*, 53, *77–8*, 78–9. Disclaimers do not often directly appear. The original logic saw everything

If the warranty of a tenant and the right of a demandant are both matters of relationship, of obligation binding the lord, there is another respect in which we have misled ourselves by thinking of a transfer of jurisdiction. It is not just that we have thought of disputes about abstract rights being removed unchanged: we have also thought of them as being removed from one disinterested tribunal to another. But the lord and his court were not disinterested. Like today's management confronted with rival claimants to a reserved seat, there is more to it than adjudication between persons asserting title against each other: both may have rights against the management. There may also be more to it than a passive readiness to adjudicate upon disputes brought to them by the parties. In their own interest as well as in that of an actual or possible claimant, the management may ask persons already seated to show their tickets. Some entries on the earliest rolls show us initiative on this pattern being taken in the seignorial context; and they give us our most direct glimpse of a vanishing world.

After the dissolution of her marriage with the earl of Clare, the countess Amice had one Richard summoned to her court of Sudbury to answer *quo waranto* he held his tenement. We cannot tell whether she was checking all the tenants as she took fealty on assuming control of her lands, or whether she had picked upon Richard because she knew what he would answer. He had to name the earl as his warrant; and, being unable to produce him, he was put out by judgment of the countess's court. We learn about all this from the entries in 1200 of an assize of novel disseisin which Richard brought against the countess, her steward, and seven of her other men. The countess relied upon the judgment, which her court duly attested; but Richard defeated her by waging and making his law. Law is usually waged in such a case by a plaintiff denying that he had been summoned to the lord's court. But Richard had come and answered all right: what he denied was an

happening within the lord's court. It was the change by which his distress became an independent remedy, with any judicial proceedings following in the county, that produced the anomaly of disclaimers made with impunity; above, p. 34 at n. 2. The need for a 'writ of right upon a disclaimer' is itself an anomaly, and even in the thirteenth century there is little to show what writ was appropriate; below, p. 94, n. 3. Within the king's court a consequence of the logic is that the tenant who vouches or otherwise relies upon one lord cannot later name another; (*a*) CRR, I, 23 (Ruffus); CRR, VII, 330 (if indeed a twin entry, a remarkable example of detail being omitted); (*b*) CRR, III, 277–8. For the converse of disclaimer, a lord refusing to acknowledge the seignory, see below, p. 173.

assertion by the countess that he had answered voluntarily, *quod sponte sua non intravit in placitum nec warantum vocavit*.[1]

This issue depends upon a premise which was too well known to need stating – namely, the need for a writ in a case concerning freehold. The rule was not that there must always be a writ, but that the tenant could not be made to answer without one. The elementary value of the case, therefore, is in pointing the distinction between the disciplinary and the proprietary jurisdictions of a lord's court. The countess could have put her undoubted tenant out for a breach of duty after proceedings without writ. What she could not properly do, unless he answered voluntarily, was to challenge Richard's title to be there at all. For that she needed a writ; and what writ might be proper in this seignorial configuration is a question for the following chapter.[2] But two points must be made at once. First, no writ would ever bring this kind of question to her own court. A writ of right would take it to her lord's court or the king's, a writ of entry always to the king's court; and later in the thirteenth century there would be a writ of entry for such a case, the *cui ante divortium*. And this congener of *cui in vita* introduces the second immediate point: as a matter of substance, the countess was in the right. Richard's ticket came from a former management: it might give him some right against the earl; but, unless she had done something to bind herself, he was not entitled as against the countess. There was no warranty to keep her out, and we need to think more closely about her predicament.

What actually defeated her was the assize itself. Before that external control was introduced, it is likely that lords in the countess's position would act as she did, and certain that tenants treated like Richard could have no redress; Richard after all had no substantive right. What is more, the rule that the assize here enforced, that requiring a writ, could not have existed before the assize did; or rather it could have existed only as a self-denying custom followed by seignorial courts, a proposition to which we shall come back.[3] In the truly seignorial world therefore, which may not have been so far in the past for the countess Amice, no mechanical difficulty would have confronted her. But, at the price

---

[1] *PKJ*, I, 3199; *RCR*, II, 180; *CRR*, I, 186, 225, 249. For the guardian of a newly succeeded lord coming to take homage of the tenants, see *RCR*, I, 62–3; *134–5*.

[2] Below, p. 94.   [3] Below, pp. 57 ff.

of a brief renewal of our linguistic probing, we can perceive the makings of a conceptual difficulty.

Richard had been put in by warrant of the earl, seised in the original sense of that word with its connotation of seignorial assent. But the assent had been the earl's; and in that sense Richard was not seised against the countess, who was neither willing nor bound to warrant him. In the later sense reflected by the noun, however, he was indeed in seisin; and that is why he would be protected against her by the assize, with the anomalous result that although she need not accept him as her tenant she cannot get him out by process of her own court. Are we then to conclude that the later sense of 'seisin' is merely an untidy possession, with the seignorial element entirely subtracted? Probably not. If Richard had been a mere invader, the countess could have put him out without any judgment. He was seised, even against her, because he had been put in with proper authority. Upon a change of parties there may or may not be a duty to warrant; but the tenant is seised if the tenure was ever warranted. It was the nature of Richard's *ingressum* that gave him seisin and therefore the protection of the assize; and it is no coincidence that the writ to which this will drive the countess is a *breve de ingressu.* '*Ingressum*' will turn out to be another item in the seignorial vocabulary.

The practical result was that lords had to stop making such claims by *quo waranto* inquiry in their own courts; and some brought them similarly formulated to the king's court.[1] Sometimes '*ingressum*' is used too. A year before Richard's assize against the countess Amice we find another lady, who seems also to have recently assumed control of her inheritance, having a tenant summoned to answer *quo waranto ingressus sit*; but the summons was to the king's court, not her own.[2]

Most such *quo waranto* inquiries on the early rolls, however, are naturally those made by the king himself. As lord, he was immune from novel disseisin, had no other court to go to, and anyway could issue writs returnable in his own court.[3] The usual challenge

---

[1] (a) *PKJ*, III, 2007 (only essoin shows claim is formally made by lord); *CRR*, IV, 101–2, 198?; (b) *PKJ*, IV, 4477; *CRR*, VI, 342, 351–2.

[2] *RCR*, I, 439 (Petra Ponte); *RCR*, II, 96; *PKJ*, I, 2231; 2740. This lady also faces a *de homagio capiendo* by another tenant and takes the homage of a third, all in respect of tenements in the same place; *RCR*, I, 187, 199.

[3] For a writ and the process, see *BNB*, 258, 268; *CRR*, XIII, 300, 377, 523, 709, 1584, 1782, 2185, 2461. Notice that it led to an issue whether or not the

is to one holding part of a fee which as a unit has come into the king's hand. In 1202 a Lincolnshire jury report the escheat of an eighth of a knight's fee on the death of Roger the Fat, but add that he had kept only one wasted tenement and granted the rest away to six separate tenants: these are all made to answer *quo waranto teneant*, and have to produce their charters, or, in one case, to rely upon ancient tenure of Roger's fee.[1] An entry of the previous year turns upon an escheat which is not directly mentioned. The first husband of a much-married lady held a knight's fee of the honour of Penwortham; and the king alleges that when he died, evidently without heir, it went to his widow in dower and has been treated as her inheritance. A son by her third husband is to answer *quo jure et quo waranto teneat se* in the land since only so *habuit ingressum*.[2] In 1211 the king has taken possession of the Peterborough estates on the death of an abbot; and one who claims as grantee of a wardship arising on the death of an abbey tenant is similarly to answer *quo waranto ingressum habuit*.[3] In 1200 tenants-in-chief have surrendered a knight's fee because they cannot *justiciare* their tenants into doing the service: in their name, but of course in the king's interest, the actual tenants are summoned to say *per quem warantum* they hold; and further commotion represents a scramble for warranty.[4] Such entries disappear from the plea rolls as the king's seignorial business is transferred to separate administrators; and *quo waranto* comes more and more to herald what we shall regard as a governmental inquiry – for example the challenge of franchises[5] or of some action in contempt of a court

tenant's ancestor had *ingressum* on a temporary basis (*de ballio*; below, p. 135) from Henry II. But the initial order might be more specific: in *CRR*, v, 60–1, it apparently told the tenant to produce his charter.

[1] *Lincs.*, 759 (presentment of wapentake); 483, 486 (charters produced by one of Roger's grantees named in presentment); *191*, 479, 480, 485 (same by one not named); 482 (one named says *de veteri tenemento et de antiqua tenura*); 1047 (sheriff accountable for the waste tenement).

[2] *PKJ*, I, *3381, 3423*; *CRR*, I, 433–4. There is no telling whether the *ingressum* was specified in the writ.

[3] *CRR*, VI, 151 (Gibwin), *186*; more of the background of this case emerges in *CRR*, VII, 144–5. Cf. *CRR*, v, 74 (abbot of Crowland), *158*.

[4] *PKJ*, I, 3163, *3238, 3344; RCR*, II, 170, 280; *CRR*, I, 216–17, 258, *364*, 377, 422–3; *CRR*, II, *269–70*; and there are later ramifications. For sub-tenants summoned *ostensuri quo waranto tenent se* in land from which they are preventing the lord paramount from getting his services, see *BNB*, 273; *CRR*, XIII, 423, *728*.

[5] Sutherland, *Quo Warranto Proceedings in the Reign of Edward I*.

order.[1] Now it is a king speaking: but the phrase had first been proper to a lord.

A new dimension is introduced by other early *quo waranto* entries. The lord making such inquiries, like the management asking to see your ticket, may not think just that he himself is being bilked: he may have been approached by another claimant. On the plea rolls, of course, the lord we most often see moved to act in this way is again the king himself; and the usual claim seems to be that land which had been temporarily in his hand was released to the wrong person. For a failure of loyalty king Richard disseised a Brett of his land at Chigwell; and later he released it to a Mauduit who claimed that Brett had held only as gagee from a previous Mauduit. Brett's heir has now made fine with king John to have his ancestor's seisin restored to him; and in 1200 Mauduit is summoned to answer *quo jure et quo waranto tenet villam predictam et quem ingressum in illa habet.*[2] Again on the death of a bishop king Richard took possession of all the Durham lands, which at that time included in wardship the fee of a Hansard who had died leaving an infant son and daughter. The land in question was released to the daughter's husband on the footing that Hansard had given it to her *ad se maritandum*. A later chapter will discuss this kind of gift: it was an anticipatory *maritagium*, and difficulties often arose because the father remained in possession.[3] The son claims that it is simply part of his inheritance; and the daughter's husband, who vouches her, is in 1212 summoned to answer *quo waranto ingressum habuit*. The end of this case may help explain why the seignorial initiative implied by that language ceases to be exercised, even by the king. Persuaded by a proffer from the son, king John ordered an inquest; and after some hesitation this declared that the bishop and therefore king Richard had received the land in wardship in the son's rather than the daughter's name. But the daughter refuses to accept this: she has heard tell of the

---

[1] (a) CRR, II, 265 (Ticheseia), *287*; cf. CRR, III, 10; (b) CRR, III, 94–5, 106–7, 156, 164; (c) PKJ, III, *122*; CRR, II, *55*, 58 (Gilbert de Norf'); CRR, III, 106, 118; (d) Lincs., 492, 1141, 1261, 1441, *1536–7*, 1539 (*quare sine waranto ingressa est...*); CRR, II, 175, *202–3*, 272–3; CRR, III, 317.

[2] RCR, II, *247*; CRR, I, *196*, 207–8, 245, 265–6, 338. Two other law-suits are associated with this: (a) PKJ, I, *2099*, *2472*, *3170*; RCR, II, *173*; (b) CRR, VII, 205–6. For a later and famous example of the king, in form, bringing *quo waranto* against one tenant on behalf of another claimant, see BNB, 750, 857; CRR, XV, 131: notice the alleged delivery by king John *de ballio*.

[3] Below, pp. 134–5, 145–6.

inquest, she says, but never put herself on it; and she demands the grand assize. A second inquiry is unacceptable to the king, and it looks as though he persuades the heir after all to forgo his claim.[1]

The daughter's objection in that case is not that there was no writ. There may have been one, actually in the *quo waranto* form. From the rolls we can hardly ever be sure whether there was any writ or what writ. But by coincidence one of the earliest actual writs to survive, from 1195–7, demands *quo waranto* a lady has intruded into the lands of an infant heir: and though the seignorial setting does not emerge, later entries suggest that they were sister and brother and the case may have been parallel.[2] If the later entries are about the same matter, it proceeded as an ordinary claim by the brother. What seems to have become objectionable is the active seignorial role implicit in the *quo waranto* language. A lord, even the king, should leave the claimant to make his own demand. He should not now, though as a matter of words the *precipe* is little better, of his own motion put the tenant to setting up his title. Consider an entry of 1205: tenants are summoned to answer *quo waranto tenent se* in land which Henry II gave to the lepers of Lincoln. But this is heavily cancelled; and later in the same term an entry in common form, such as would follow from a writ of right, shows the lepers of Lincoln claiming against the same tenants.[3] But the first approach was not yet out of the question, because the converse happens in the same year. One purporting to be prior of Montjoux claims land also said to have been given to his house by Henry II, and the tenant objects that the demandant is not prior but just one of the brothers. He probably regretted it: since this was a gift in alms by the king's father, says the roll, *debet dominus rex illam warantizare et illum in placitum trahere, ut sciatur per quem ipse ingressum habet in terra illa.*[4] In this case at least the active mood into which the king had been provoked was going to make a difference to the outcome. Usually,

[1] *CRR*, VI, *165*, 169–70, 188, *193*, *215*, 220, 224, 226, 241–2. See also Holt, *The Northerners*, p. 46, n.1, p. 57, n.17. Other litigation arose from this minority: (a) *CRR*, II, *37*, 221; (b) *CRR*, III, 70. For other examples of intervention by the king, see (a) *RCR*, I, 421 (Blund'); *RCR*, II, *15*, *106–7*, *147*, 186; *CRR*, I, 122, *172;* (b) *RCR*, II, 185 (Noell); *CRR*, I, 399, *409*, *461*; *PKJ*, I, intro. pp. 89–90; (c) the two claims in *CRR*, VI, 201, 226–7, 233–4, *260*, 287–8, one of which is once entered in *petit versus* rather than in *quo waranto* form.

[2] *PKJ*, I, 3474; *RCR*, II, 57; *CRR*, I, 166–7.

[3] *CRR*, III, 298, 342.   [4] *CRR*, IV, 22.

perhaps, the difference was mainly in attitude. The logic of the thing was the same whichever way it was put. But it was not the logic we have supposed, the horizontal logic of a dispute about abstract rights between the parties. The only right which either could have arose from a relationship with the lord.

If a lesser lord were to sue in the king's court on behalf of one he thought entitled to hold of him, he would simply be question-ing the actual tenant's entitlement as against himself; and his altruistic motive might not even appear. But sometimes it does. As late as 1214 a bishop has one summoned to answer *quid juris clamat*, and explains why: *desicut alii jus in terra illa clama-verunt habere et clamant, quibus idem episcopus..., ut capitalis dominus, rectum tenere debet.*[1] Again in 1194 a demandant casually discloses that his claim is made as warrantor of a religious house.[2] It may once have been common for a grantor in alms to act for his grantee, as a decade later king John was prepared to do for his father's beneficiaries at Montjoux though not for those at Lincoln. Grants in marriage had also been particularly dependent; and such a grant lay behind our most instructive example of a lord suing in the king's court on behalf of his putative tenant. William Butler gave *maritagium* on the first marriage of his sister Aubrey. She had a son by that marriage, then had children by a second marriage, then died. The heir of the first marriage sought to recover the *maritagium* from the second husband in mort d'ancestor, and failed: the second husband was entitled to curtesy. The heir now enlists Butler, who in 1199 makes a seignorial challenge. The second husband is summoned to the king's court to answer *ex cujus dono habuit Albredam...in uxorem cum maritagio ipsius Albrede.* He replies that Butler himself as *dominus predicti feodi et frater ejusdem Albrede dedit ei illam in uxorem cum maritagio suo.* This is answered with an equally seignorial denial upon which, but for a compromise, issue would have been joined: *in feodum suum intraverat sine ejus assensu.*[3]

[1] *CRR*, VII, *161*, 197–8. For a yet later example, though the lord claims to hold on behalf of the heir, see *BNB*, 219; *CRR*, XI, *1490, 2227, 2675*.

[2] *PRS*, XIV, *10*; *RCR*, I, 20 (Extraneus); cf. proceedings between this demand-ant and the religious house, *PRS*, XIV, *14*; *RCR*, I, 23–4. Other cases showing the particular dependence of religious houses on their warrantors: (a) *CRR*, I, 19 (Dacus); (b) the remarkable and obscure case in *PKJ*, I, 3475, and references in the editor's notes thereto.

[3] *RCR*, I, *226, 379?*, 432 (the mort d'ancestor); *PKJ*, I, *2083, 2096*; *RCR*, II, 124–5 (the action in Butler's name). This action must in substance have been

This is a good case to have in mind when we think what was really involved in the transfer of jurisdiction from seignorial to royal courts. In the truly seignorial world, the proprietary consequence of an unauthorised marriage was a question which in principle could not arise. The marriage would not have happened, or at least the husband would not have been accepted as the lord's tenant; and that would have been that. In the king's court, curtesy becomes an abstract property right which is understood to flow from the marriage, not from the lord's acceptance; and the need for consent to the marriage becomes an independent rule which has to be applied *ex post facto*.[1] In 1199 it was evidently thought that the lord, though not the heir himself, could still use the king's court to undo the proprietary consequence of what he had failed to prevent. But this was unworkable, and the lord's control of marriage came to be protected only by the *ex post facto* sanction of damages. In cases like this one, indeed, it disappeared altogether.

There remains the logical possibility of one more kind of *quo waranto* inquiry. Butler's action seems artificial in the king's court. Could not a lord use his own court to question the right of the party in at the instance of the one he thought entitled? When he was not the king himself, we should see this in the rolls of the king's court only in the way we saw the countess Amice questioning a tenant on her own behalf:[2] the party in must be put out and bring novel disseisin, and the lord must make his exception of proceeding by judgment.[3] Two such cases have been found, both

brought by the heir, who acted as Butler's attorney. But in a not dissimilar case, though formulated with an *ingressum*, the lord himself acted and got judgment *salvo jure heredum*; *RCR*, I, 359 (Peverel), *427–8*; *CRR*, I, *136*; *RCR*, II, *65*, 196. It is perhaps worth noting that attorneys with an interest in the litigation are not uncommon. One who vouches to warranty may be attorney for his vouchee: (*a*) *CRR*, II, 18 (Salceto), 156, 206; *PKJ*, III, *1264*; *CRR*, III, 190, *260*, *301*; *CRR*, IV, *17*; (*b*) *CRR*, I, *339*, 403 (Penherst); *PKJ*, III, *127*; *CRR*, II, 65; (*c*) *CRR*, IV, 40 (Bruiera), 42–3 (full references below, p. 99, n. 4). (*d*) *PKJ*, III, 2384 (full references below, p. 142, n. 1). Or the vouchee may act for his vouchor; *CRR*, II, 34 (Berners), *172*, *309*; *Northants.*, 462; *CRR*, III, *28*; *PKJ*, III, *1110*. In *RCR*, I, *225*, 430 (Grafton); *PKJ*, I, *2413*; *CRR*, I, 151, 185; *RCR*, II, *73*, 261, 262, the Bereford who acted for Grafton is stated elsewhere to be his heir; *CRR*, III, 144. In *Lincs.*, 428, a widow appoints the warrant of her dower.

[1] Compare the silent change made when the canons of inheritance came to be applied *ex post facto*; below, p. 182.

[2] Above, p. 45.

[3] Once it is proceedings for deceit that seem to show such a sequence: acting on behalf of Edward, Simon disseised Odo, who recovered in novel disseisin. Edward then recovered from Odo on a writ of right in Simon's court. Odo is

using the *quo waranto* language. The facts behind an entry of 1204 go back to another gift in marriage, this time a humble one. The donor, himself perhaps a peasant, gave a peasant tenement in *maritagium* with his daughter. Probably after the donor's death she died childless, so that the husband was not entitled to curtesy; but he stayed on. The lord of the place summoned the husband to his court to answer both for arrears of service and *quo warento tenuit se in terra predicta, in qua nichil juris habuit nisi per uxorem suam, cujus maritagium fuit et que obiit sine herede.* These words come from the lord's exception to an assize brought by the husband, and may have been only explanation to the king's court; but if they represent matter to be put to the husband in the lord's own court, we are looking at the seignorial equivalent of a writ of entry. The exception goes on to recite summonses, the absence of chattels by which to distrain, the taking into hand of the tenement, and the refusal of offers to replevy it to the husband. For all this the lord vouches his court; and he loses because he does not have it there to warrant him.[1] Nothing expressly tells us in whose interest he is making the *quo waranto* inquiry; but unless coincidence has tricked us with names, an unexplained co-defendant is the original donor's son and heir. Another thing about which nothing is said is the absence of a writ; and it is not impossible that the son actually had a writ patent. But the joinder of a claim for arrears makes this unlikely, and also explains why the absence of a writ would not matter. The husband never answered, and the arrears alone would justify a taking for default.

The background to the second such case is less straightforward. On the lord's side there is an unimportant complication: the fee had been given by father to son, and then returned from son to father to look after. This sequence was not uncommon, as will appear later.[2] In the present case it means that some of the seignorial action was taken by the one and some by the other; and for simplicity we shall speak just of the lord. On the tenant's side there is a more damaging obscurity, partly because a woman's two sons had the same name. The elder died in her lifetime, himslef leaving an infant son over whom the lord assumes wardship and on whose behalf he acts. The disputed tenement was taken on the

---

now alleged to have got the land back again by pretending he had never had execution of the assize; *CRR*, II, 67 (reading Odo for Edward in the 6th line).

[1] *CRR*, III, 161–2.   [2] Below, pp. 134–5.

         M L F

woman's death by her younger son, presumably by a second marriage, on the footing that it was *maritagium* to which he was heir.
The lord supposed that the woman got the tenement from the
elder son by way of dower, that the infant was entitled as heir of
the elder son, and that the younger son was an intruder. On this
basis, and *per querelam* of the infant, he had the younger son
summoned to his court to answer *quo waranto tenuit se* in the land:
but the summonses were ineffective, distraints yielded nothing,
and so by judgment of his court he seized the land itself. All this
is set out in his exception to an assize brought by the younger son
in 1203, and is duly attested by the summoners and warranted by
his court. The younger son denies being summoned, and goes on
to seek an inquest on his assertion that the woman had held in
maritagium rather than dower. But at that point, as soon as it
appears that he is claiming some title, the justices break in and
round on the lord with his own language. They demand *quo
waranto traxit eum in placitum de terra illa et inde curiam suam
tenuit;* and the clerk spoils his own syntax to put the sense beyond
doubt: after '*terra illa*' he inserts by interlineation *et si per breue
tractus fuit in placitum.* Since the younger son had never come, the
lord could not say he had answered willingly, as did the countess
Amice. On the other hand, unlike the countess, he could have been
acting on a writ in the younger son's name. But he was not: *dicit
quod licuit ei hoc facere ut credit sine breui.* His belief was wrong.
The younger son recovered his seisin, and the lord and all the
members of his court were amerced.[1]

*   *   *

How unreasonable was the lord's belief in this last case, and the
action taken by the countess Amice? This lord had even accepted
the infant's homage. It is a lord's duty to see that the right heir
gets in. Glanvill tells us that if there is any doubt who is entitled,
he should keep the tenement in his own hand until he can decide
it.[2] And that decision, it may be noted, is one that he makes
without writ. Is all this frustrated because quick footwork has

---

[1] *Northants.*, 782. For a case in which a lord's court held an inquest on the
right despite the tenant's objection that there was no writ, see *RCR*, I, 61–2.
For a lord himself taking an escheat by judgment but without writ, see *RCR*, I,
447–8; cf. ibid. 368.   [2] *Glanvill*, VII, 17; IX, 6.

enabled an interloper to get in first? And if it is, what is the lord to do? The countess Amice, claiming on her own behalf, could at least get some writ, though not one which would bring the matter to her own court. This lord can only wait for the heir to sue. A tenement belonging to his fee is occupied by one whom this lord must not acknowledge as tenant, in the countess's case by one whom she need not acknowledge. Yet neither can get him out, or even demand services without acknowledging him and so giving him a claim to this tenement or *escambium*.[1] The requirement of a writ seems to make nonsense of lordship against this kind of wrongdoer; and yet it does not touch the disciplinary jurisdiction by which an accepted tenant can be disseised and even disinherited. Something must be wrong with our picture.

One thing wrong with it relates immediately only to the facts of these two cases; but it may affect our understanding of the way in which the requirement of a writ worked for centuries. In neither case was the so-called wrongdoer a mere interloper. The man put out by the countess Amice had been put in by her husband: he had entered with proper warranty. The younger son put out in 1203 had entered claiming as heir of the tenant who had just died. We are not told enough about the supposed *maritagium* to know even of whom he claimed to hold, and cannot speculate about an actual assent to his entry by some lord. But the actual seignorial part in inheritance had been much reduced by mort d'ancestor, which enabled the heir to go in on his own. Once in, even against the lord's will, he was protected by novel disseisin. A mere interloper would not be so protected. Of course he could bring the assize. Anybody could.[2] The question is whether he would win it. It is possible that he would if the lord made his exception of taking by judgment: merely to summon him may acknowledge that he has some tenure. But suppose that the lord, having put him out without any judgment, just allowed the assize to proceed. At any rate unless a long time had elapsed, the recognitors would find for the lord, not because the plaintiff had been disseised justifiably but because he had not been disseised at all. He was never seised. His

---

[1] *Glanvill*, IX, 1:...*nullum seruicium, siue releuium siue aliud, potest quis ab herede, siue fuerit maior siue minor, exigere donec ipsius receperit homagium de tenemento unde seruicium habere clamat.* Cf. IX, 6: ...*non prius de relleuio suo tenetur quis domino suo respondere donec ipse homagium suum receperit...* Cf. also III, 7: warranty established by proving receipt of services.

[2] Cf. the termor; above, p. 22, n. 6.

possession lacked that vestigial element of seignorial assent still necessary.

If therefore the countess Amice had had to do with a mere interloper, she would not have needed her court and would have been unwise to rely on its judgment. She would have allowed the assize to proceed, and explained to the recognitors that the interloper was not seised. But this would have left no trace on the roll: there would just be one more general verdict among the flood. Nothing would identify the defendant as a lord; and indeed, since he did not need a court he need not be one. The 1203 case would have appeared in a guise even harder to identify. We will postulate an adult heir and a mere interloper. Ralph is the lord whose tenant has just died, and in his view William is the rightful heir; but Thomas gets in first. With Ralph's authority William enters and takes the land; and since it is he who has it, it is against him that Thomas brings his assize. William allows the assize to proceed and explains what has happened to the recognitors: they decide that on those facts Thomas was not seised, and so return a verdict that William did not disseise him. The record will be in the commonest of common forms, and will not even mention Ralph's name. He is just a character in the story told to the recognitors, a story which for all the plea rolls tell us the present writer may have imagined.[1] But he has not imagined it. It is the story put in the mouth of his defendant by a writer of about 1240, who includes an assize of novel disseisin among his narrative accounts of various kinds of legal proceeding.[2] His object was to give elementary illustrations of what actually happens in court; and it would be odd if the facts he chose were unusual.

The requirement of a writ, therefore, left untouched the lord's power of control in those blatant situations in which he could properly act without judgment. And since the reality of that control must have vanished slowly like the Cheshire cat, leaving the common law rights of entry by way of grin, it is unfortunate that we cannot hope to recognise it in the plea rolls even at its most

---

[1] It is told expressly, and the lord's court is to be summoned, in *CRR*, II, 168 (court of Odo de Danmartin), *190, 197*.

[2] *Consuetudines Diuersarum Curiarum*, printed in *Select Cases of Procedure without Writ under Henry III*, ed. Richardson and Sayles, Selden Society, vol. 60, p. cxcv on p. cc, a valuable glimpse of the reality behind the clerks' *assisa venit recognitura*...It is rare for the early rolls to disclose even that there was a plaint; see, e.g., *PKJ*, IV, 4059.

real. But that goes to our understanding of the thirteenth century with all those assizes ending in unexplained general verdicts; and this chapter must finish with another look backwards into the twelfth century.

Even allowing for a power of action without judgment, it is still hard to reconcile the requirement of a writ with real seignorial control, and particularly with the clear reality of Glanvill's disciplinary jurisdiction. The lord who can without writ even disinherit his undoubted tenant cannot, as the countess Amice learned, in his own interest put out one he knows is not entitled, and cannot, as the 1203 lord learned, put out one he thinks an intruder in favour of the heir whose homage he has taken. But these results are not to be attributed to the requirement of a writ alone. What has brought it to bear is the assize of novel disseisin. And the situations in which the lord can act without judgment are not to be explained as exceptions to the requirement. They are situations in which the plaintiff is not protected by the assize: he has not been disseised because his physical possession lacked that vestigial element of seignorial assent still inherent in seisin.

As a rule of law, therefore, the requirement of a writ is being applied mechanically by the assize to all cases of seignorial action by judgment except those within the disciplinary jurisdiction. The result may seem capricious; but it is clear. What is not clear is the position before there was any assize. Everybody agrees that the requirement of a writ existed before novel disseisin, but what sense can we give to the proposition? We have imagined a positive rule, existing presumably in the interest of tenants in possession, by which lords' courts are prohibited from acting without royal authorisation. But a rule of that nature requires enforcement; and before novel disseisin there can have been no regular means of enforcement. This difficulty seems not to have been discussed, though it is inherent in a question that has been asked – namely, whether the rule was of customary or legislative origin.[1] A rule imposed by legislation without any means of enforcement seems improbable: the legislative act could be no more than a declaration of custom which it would be desirable for lords' courts to follow.

---

[1] See *Royal Writs in England from the Conquest to Glanvill*, ed. van Caenegem, Selden Society, vol. 77, pp. 223 ff.; D. M. Stenton, *English Justice between the Norman Conquest and the Great Charter*, pp. 26 ff., and the references given by these writers.

Equally improbable, however, is the growth of a custom within lords' courts depriving them of the power to act without external authorisation. Once again, something must be wrong with our picture.

What is wrong can be put only as a hypothesis. In origin, the requirement of a writ was neither legislative nor, in the sense which has been assumed, customary; nor did it need enforcement; nor was it a rule. By nature it was a statement of what a lord's court would not do; and it derived from the internal logic of the lord's court itself, and not from any external policy securing possessors of land. A lord who has seised a tenant, accepted him in the fullest sense, does not go back on his warranty. The tenant may forfeit what had been his unquestioned right by some breach of the conditions of his tenure: that is the source of the disciplinary jurisdiction. But the lord cannot on his own account question the right which he himself gave, nor can he entertain claims by others. This is his man in respect of this tenement, and there is an end of it. And so far as the lord's own court is concerned, there indeed was an end of it. Only the king's writ can open the question.

We have thought of the lord's court as an impartial tribunal prepared to adjudicate on disputes over abstract property rights, but requiring royal authorisation to do so. But the lord's court was not impartial: it was committed to the tenant, bound by his warranty. Nor were abstract rights of property in issue between the parties: the tenant relied upon the lord's warranty; and the demandant claimed another right, equally directed against the lord. Nor was the writ patent cast in the language of authorisation. It did not permit, but ordered the lord: 'do full right' to the demandant.[1] Nor can we dismiss this as the conventional imperative of kings. The order expected disobedience: 'if you do not, the sheriff will'. The sheriff often did, too. For Glanvill and in the earliest rolls default by the lord's court was at least common.[2] In the thirteenth century it became routine.[3] Of course there might be particular reasons for default – for example, that the lord had no court.[4] In such a case nobody expected obedience to the writ's primary command, any more than in the case of the *precipe*. Perhaps it was not often expected. We have interpreted regular

---

[1] e.g., *Glanvill*, XII, 3. Cf. *PKJ*, I, 3551–4.   [2] *Glanvill*, XII, 7.
[3] *Novae Narrationes*, ed. Shanks and Milsom, Selden Society, vol. 80, p. xxxi; *Brevia Placitata*, pp. 1, 41, 126, 153.   [4] Below, p. 69.

defaults in terms of an impartial tribunal disinclined to act. Perhaps the tribunal was immovably partial. So far as the lord and his court were concerned, the tenant had his warranty and was entitled to stay in. They disobey the writ because they must; and the threat with which it ends is carried out. The sheriff takes the case away from the lord's court and brings the king's law to bear. And so it is a correct statement rather than a rule that a tenant cannot be made to answer in respect of his free tenement without the king's writ.

There is hardly any direct evidence for this analysis. But it accommodates the facts, so far as we know them, more easily than does the traditional view. In particular, it answers two questions already posed. The regularity within lords' courts is a form in which the rule could have existed before there was the assize to enforce it. And that regularity depends upon a reason which would not touch cases within the disciplinary jurisdiction, cases which would surely be within any rule imposed as a safeguard for tenants. There are other questions about proceedings within lords' courts. For want of records we may not be able to answer them, but the asking may be suggestive.

On the traditional view, how did warranties work in a lord's court? Suppose a strong case.[1] Half a century ago the then tenant abandoned his tenement and left the district; and it has been believed that he died without heir. Since nobody was doing the services, the father of Ralph, who is now lord, took the tenement in hand; and he and Ralph held it until last year when, perhaps after some final process of proclamation in his court, Ralph granted it to Thomas for homage and service. Now William has turned up claiming to be grandson and heir of the man who went away. He gets a writ patent, on the received view because there is an imposed rule requiring it, and claims the tenement in Ralph's court. Now what happens? Thomas looks at Ralph to whom last year he did homage for this tenement, and claims his warranty. What is he asking for? Does he expect Ralph to take over the defence of the action in his own court? That is not impossible, but it seems odd. And what is to happen if Ralph refuses? Or what is

---

[1] Based on the various claims made by Celestria, wife of Goldhauec of London: (a) *CRR*, VI, *164, 233*, 311; *PKJ*, IV, *4701*; (b) *CRR*, VI, *139*; (c) *CRR*, VI, 142; (d) *CRR*, VII, *22, 27, 76*, 93, 119, *119–20, 183, 247*, 303. Similar cases are mentioned below, p. 165, n. 4.

to happen if he agrees but loses the action? How is Thomas to
enforce his right to *escambium*? And is not a duty upon the lord to
provide *escambium* in such a case itself an odd result to have been
reached by the customs of lords' courts?

On the view of inheritance suggested in this book,[1] the anomaly
in this case is in entertaining the demandant's claim. In the truly
seignorial world, assuming that his grandfather had not been
disinherited by the lord's court for abandoning his tenement and
his service, William had a right to inherit. But it was just that: not
an existing property right good against the world, but a claim that
Ralph as lord should give him the tenement. He comes too late.
Ralph has given it to someone else. When Thomas looks at Ralph
and claims his warranty, he is not making a complicated series of
requests about the conduct of the law-suit, but a single and simple
request: it should be stopped. And so it is. Everybody knew this
would happen, including the demandant; and that is why he got
his writ patent.

What does the writ alter? Unless it induces the lord to work for
some compromise, it cannot alter anything in his court. It cannot
undo the tenant's homage or drain away its force. And so the
sheriff takes the case to the county court, whence it may be
removed to the king's court. In the king's court we can for the first
time hope to see it. But we can hardly hope to recognise it. The
earliest entry of a case that we find is often the election of the
knights of a grand assize, and it recites the mise – that is, the issue
to be put to them. If they are to declare whether Ralph has greater
right to hold in demesne or William to hold of him, we shall not
even know whether the action began as William against Ralph, or
as William against Thomas who vouched Ralph to warranty. If the
voucher was in the county, Thomas may never be mentioned in
the rolls of the king's court. If we are lucky enough to know that
Ralph is Thomas's vouchee, there will still be nothing to tell us
expressly that he is Thomas's lord, still less that William also
claims to hold of him. It is the rarest of accidents for us to know
even that there was a writ patent, let alone to what lord it went.[2]
Perhaps, therefore, it is not evidentially insignificant that in one
or two early cases we know that the demandant's writ patent was
addressed to one who was subsequently vouched to warranty by

[1] Above, p. 41; below, pp. 180 ff.
[2] Below, pp. 67 f., 74 f.

the tenant.[1] In these cases at any rate, for whatever reason, what happened was that William claimed against Thomas in Ralph's court; Ralph's court defaulted of right so that the case was removed; and in the county or the king's court, Thomas vouched Ralph to warranty.

We supposed a strong case for the sake of clarity: the lord reasonably believed that the earlier tenure had come to an end. But the same results would follow if he had consciously passed over the heir to that tenure, or mistakenly accepted the wrong person as heir. The principle applies to any case in which the man in is the lord's accepted tenant. The lord probably accepts a tenant even by taking services; certainly he is not entitled to relief from one succeeding by inheritance without taking his homage or the like.[2] And before the principle behind mort d'ancestor was established, even a tenant taking by inheritance would himself be placed in seisin by the lord. Civil disorders would affect the best regulated lordship; but normally the man in would have the lord's warranty. And it was this warranty which necessitated both the removal of the case from the lord's court and the writ which provided for that removal.

What is to happen if the lord does not warrant the man in? In a world bounded by Ralph's court, there is no difficulty about a claim by William against Thomas in which Ralph and his court believe that William is entitled to the tenement and Thomas is not. There is nothing to stop the court dealing with the matter; and, on the logic here proposed, there is no need for a writ. But it is in such cases that the requirement of a writ, imposed as a rule of law by novel disseisin, differed in scope from the suggested regularity within lords' courts from which that rule grew. The regularity protected only the lord's accepted tenant. But novel disseisin protected seisin in the wider sense we have already seen. The element of seignorial acceptance did not drop away altogether, to leave seisin equated with mere possession: but it now affected mainly the entry with which the possession had begun. The

---

[1] *PRS*, xiv, 124 (Hurton). Once the demandant whom we know to have brought the writ patent to the lord dies, and the voucher is on a new action by his heir; *PRS*, xiv, 121 (Cliueden); *PKJ*, i, *2275*; *RCR*, ii, *140*; *CRR*, i, 233; *CRR*, iii, 326; *CRR*, iv, 195, *244*, *293*; *CRR*, v, 21, *190*, *284*, *298*. And once the lord to whom the writ patent was brought dies, and it is that lord's heir who is vouched; *RCR*, i, *121*; *PRS*(NS), xxxi, 105 (Mara); *CRR*, i, *252*; *CRR*, v, 18, 57.   [2] *Glanvill*, ix, 1, 6; also iii, 7; above, p. 55, n. 1.

countess Amice could have put out a mere interloper, though she would be wise to do it without any judicial process. What she could not do, although she was entitled to have the tenement in demesne, was to act without writ against one properly seised by the then lord, her former husband.[1] In her case, since no writ could bring the matter to her own court, the result was that her court could not act at all. It could have acted if somebody else had claimed to hold the tenement of her. There was no warranty to stop that. But it would have needed a writ. What the rule now requires is indeed an authorisation to act.

In the case of the countess Amice, of course, it would have been coincidence if there was some other claimant. Suppose another case, one in which there is a connection between the lack of warranty on the one side and the claim made on the other. William claims as heir of his father whose second wife held in dower and has lately died; and Thomas is a member of her household who has been managing the tenement and who holds on. If Thomas is her steward or her lover, of course Ralph can put him out and William in; though again he will be wise to do so without any judicial process. Is the case altered if Thomas turns out to be the son of her second marriage? He still has no warranty to stop Ralph or his court dealing with the matter. But, at any rate if he claims that the tenement was not dower but his mother's own inheritance and that he is in as her heir, he is seised within the assize; and the assize will enforce upon Ralph and his court what is now the mechanical requirement of a writ. This was the result reached in the 1203 case, and it surprised the lord: *dicit quod licuit ei hoc facere ut credit sine breui*.[2] Perhaps the seignorial logic, upon which he had acted properly, had only recently been widened by the assize into the mechanical rule.

But the need for a writ is not the end of our question. Suppose that the demandant has a writ, and that the lord's court decides that the man in is not entitled to warranty: is he just put out? So long as there had been only the lord's court, of course he was. But is no initiative now open to him in the king's court countervailing the demandant's writ of right? If not, the unconscientious lord would always do well to reverse his former stance and withhold warranty: the demandant would then recover in the lord's court, and the lord would run no risk of the royal judgment for *escambium*

---

[1] Above, pp. 45 ff.   [2] Above, pp. 53 f.

which might follow upon a removal of the plea. Although there is only one tenement, both parties may have rights against the lord; and the tenant as well as the demandant must be able to compel a royal adjudication on the right he claims.

The action available to him appears to be a forerunner of that which comes to be known as *warantia carte*. In its classical use this is an original writ doing much the same work as voucher to warranty, but in actions in which voucher is not available, or rather in which the court cannot issue its own process against a vouchee. In novel disseisin, for example, the defendant can vouch another, but it is ineffective unless the vouchee is present and warrants of his own accord. The assize will not wait while he is got, still less while his duty to warrant is established. What the defendant should do in such a case is to start a separate action of *warantia carte*: this will not affect the course of the assize, but will enable him to claim *escambium* if it goes against him.[1]

Thinking of royal jurisdiction, we have hardly considered the possible application of this action to claims in lords' courts.[2] And thinking of warranty as a contractual obligation between equals, we have overlooked the seignorial nature of the claim itself. But writ and count are explicit: the party bringing the action always claims that he holds the land of the party against whom it is brought. It must have begun as a claim by tenant against lord, though the early rolls often do not disclose exactly what he is seeking. Sometimes he seems to be facing not a claim to the land itself but a claim by his lord for higher services or for the services owing to the superior lord; and he uses this action rather than some other because he has the proof of a charter.[3] In the very

---

[1] *Novae Narrationes*, ed. Shanks and Milsom, Selden Society, vol. 80, pp. clix ff.

[2] Cf. the discussion in *Select Cases in the Court of King's Bench*, ed. Sayles, vol. II, Selden Society, vol. 57, at p. 12 (reading *adeat* rather than *habeat* for *adheat*). Conversely, consider the effect in the king's court of the king's own warranty. In the case in *CRR*, v, *99, 296, 325*; *PKJ*, IV, *2998, 3045, 3224, 4618, 4657*; *CRR*, VI *73, 100, 143*, 279–80, *388*; *CRR*, VII, *54*, one who has made himself tenant by his own warranty puts forward a charter of Henry II, and makes a proffer to king John *per sic quod warantizet ei terram illam*; the demandant, who also claims to hold in chief of the king, makes a proffer *per sic quod faciat procedere loquelam illam secundum consuetudinem regni*; the demandant's proffer is accepted; and the tenant puts himself on the grand assize with ordinary general mise. Cf. *BNB*, 283; *CRR*, XIII, 573 in which the demandant's admission that the tenant in fact holds under the king ends his case.

[3] Below, p. 128.

earliest rolls he sometimes claims warranty without even mentioning a charter; and quite often, charter or no, there is the bare
claim to warranty with no hint of what has provoked it or what
relief is sought. If some third party is claiming the land, it must be
in proceedings of which we have no record. Perhaps it was in
a court from which we have no record. Perhaps it was in the court
of the lord of whom this tenant claims to hold and against whom his
warranty action is brought.

That the action might play this part is something we are
expressly told only once, and then because of an accident. In
a *warantia carte* brought as late as 1221 against an abbot, there is
difficulty about one who makes himself out to be his attorney: the
abbot is ill, and the appointment has not yet been properly attested.
For this reason the justices send the abbot a message, and the clerk
enrols it: since his warranty is claimed he must not hold a plea
concerning this land in his own court.[1] Two years later the plea in
question itself turns up, no doubt after the required default by the
abbot's court; a third party is claiming the land from the tenant
who had brought the *warantia carte*.[2] The only unusual thing
about the entry of the warranty action is the message. If the action
is in principle against the tenant's lord, is it unusual for it to arise
out of a claim being made in his court? Or is it just that for once
the obvious did not go without saying?

---

[1] *BNB*, 1537; *CRR*, x, 102. For what may possibly be a similar instruction on
behalf of one who has no charter, and whose homage is being refused, see *CRR*,
v, 76 (Monachus).
[2] *CRR*, xi, 1123, *1506, 2066, 2674*; *BNB*, 922; *CRR*, xii, *231*, 1651.

3

PROPRIETARY JURISDICTION

Maitland's picture of the rise of the actions protecting freehold land has a clarity which will never be rivalled. In the beginning there were writs of right, settling as between the parties something we can only think of as the 'ownership' of the land. But these were troublesome, and imposed too great a burden on the demandant when his case was obvious. And so possessory protection was provided: first, novel disseisin and mort d'ancestor, and then, by an extension of the idea, the writs of entry. And since the possessory actions but not the proprietary were proper for royal courts, and since they were preferred, jurisdiction was drawn away from lords' courts into the king's.

It is a compelling picture which seems immediately to fit. Could this be because the society into which it fits is one juristically like ours? Like ours, and like that in which the Roman law grew up, it is a society of equal owners disputing about abstract rights of property. There are lords, of course, but what they have are equally just rights of property. Their dues are charged upon the land, but the land nonetheless belongs to the tenant. Even the right to jurisdiction is valuable for the profits of justice; and the lord has nothing else to lose if a case goes to another court. Against this unchanging background, the same for Henry II as it was to be for Edward I, we have supposed jurisdiction being painlessly transferred as possessory protection is extended. We have even debated, with no sense of possible incongruity, whether the idea of possessory protection was invented a second time by Henry II's advisers or taken from Roman texts.

What seems really to have happened is harder than that for us to reconstruct, and must have been more painful than that for the generations who lived through it. By the time of Edward I the background had indeed changed to conform with our picture. But the process had left stresses which necessitated a resort to legislation unmatched for centuries to come. It was the actions themselves, introduced into a different society, that had initiated this process. They did it by taking away from lords the ultimate control over lands within their lordships, leaving them with the fixed economic rights of our picture. Tenants became owners, subject only to these fixed rights, because lords and their courts lost their power of final decision. But the ownership was bought at a price, the price exacted when any system of law has abstract rights existing in the sky and unaffected by what persons with immediate control are doing on the ground. In the seignorial world a grant or an inheritance as well as the judgment ending a dispute were final decisions of a sovereign body applying the only law there was. In the sense that he had no external redress, a tenant was at the mercy of this body. But so long as it regularly applied its own customs, he enjoyed the certainty which we associate with registered title, and which was long enjoyed by the copyhold successors of unfree tenants: the man accepted was by definition the man entitled. Royal control sought only to keep seignorial courts to their customs. As an inevitable but unforeseeable consequence it destroyed the related certainty. What had been done must now be undone in favour of what ought to have been done. Much of the litigation in the king's courts of the thirteenth century probably consisted not of disputes that would otherwise have gone to lords' courts but of disputes which this generated.

This chapter will consider proprietary disputes within the seignorial framework, especially the so-called writs of right. The name is as good a place as any from which to start because, as names often do in the law, it created an entity. We have seen two entities. The right was a concept of the same nature as ownership. And it was determined in the 'writ of right', a 'form of action' whose unity is shown by the trial by battle which it carried, despite the fact that there were two writs. Let us get the battle out of the way first. We should no longer see a mode of proof as betokening a 'form of action': it betokens only the kind of proposition to be proved. Wager of law is appropriate to certain denials when the affirmative is incapable of proof by document or witness; and battle is appropriate for testing the positive assertion of a witness. Then there is the right. It is true that for Bracton this was a legal concept, though one beyond human understanding: its only property was being different from and somehow higher than seisin.[1] But there is no reason to see either it or the action as an entity before the Great Charter. *Breve de recto* included a writ of dower when it was a patent addressed to the heir; and that has nothing to do with ownership or even inheritance.[2] And in the early rolls it seems never to denote anything but a writ patent. Even Glanvill, in manuscripts of the earliest tradition, captions his *precipe* 'writ of summons' rather than *breve de recto*.[3] The only visible entity is the writ patent ordering a lord to do right to the demandant; and there is no evidence that the right was anything more specific than a right to hold of the lord, however it had arisen.

All discussion, even of mechanics, has therefore proceeded upon assumptions which may be false. If there was a concept protected by a form of action, the writ patent and the *precipe* were a pair; and what was at stake in the choice between them was the lord's right to jurisdiction, when jurisdiction itself meant profits. It is in these terms that historians have asked when each writ was appropriate. Unless new evidence turns up, we may never answer this question for certain, or even know how valid it is. The earliest entry of a case usually tells us no more than that the demandant *petit versus* the tenant the land *ut jus suum*. There is no way of telling whether the claim was first made in a lord's court, removed for default by tolt to the county, and removed again to the king's court by *pone*, or whether it is now first made under a *precipe*. Nor, as we shall see, can we be sure of the terms in which a *precipe* may have been cast.[4] This is our normal situation. In a minute proportion of cases we have the text of the writ: it is enrolled by a nodding clerk,[5] or it is one of the few dozen early writs to survive.[6] If it is a *pone* that we have, then we know that there was

---

[1] See, e.g., Bracton, f. 434 b.

[2] On the writ of right of dower, notice its placing in *Registers*: CA2, CC6, CC6a, R16–18. For *breve de recto* contrasted with the *precipe*, see *Registers*, note following Hib. 4, and *BNB*, 232 (other references below, p. 78, n. 5). But Bracton can speak of *breve...de recto clausum sicut praecipe in capite*, f. 351.

[3] *Glanvill*, I, 6 (Hall, p. 5, note b).   [4] Below, pp. 96 ff.

[5] *PRS*(NS), XXXI, 105, 100–1 (other references above, p. 8, n. 2). Compare the unusual recital of writ, tolt, and *pone* in *RCR*, I, 5 (Ludham): a later entry of this case is in the usual *petit versus* form, *RCR*, I, 76; cf. ibid. *115*.

[6] Lady Stenton's collection of early writs includes a number of writs *precipe*: *PKJ*, I, 3481, 3486, 3487 (entry by gage), 3488 (*de rationabili parte*), 3499, 3506 (entry by gage), 3509, 3522, 3535 (special form, case discussed below, p. 86, n. 2), 3537, 3538 (gage but no *ingressum*), 3541, 3546. It also includes three writs *pone* consequent upon writs patent: *PKJ*, I, 3477, 3500, 3519. But it includes no original writ patent; and it is not clear at what stage in the proceedings, if at all,

a writ patent though not to whom it was addressed. If we are lucky enough to have enrolled a record from the county, that will often tell us whose court defaulted of right; and then we can reconstruct the writ.[1] Otherwise there is only the chance that it will be named. Occasionally in the plea rolls, more often in the pipe rolls but with less certainty of identification, we find mention of a *precipe*.[2] It is more common to find *breve de recto* in the plea rolls; but unless there is other evidence – for example, because the phrase occurs in a county record – it may beg a question to assume that this was a writ patent. And even when we know about the writ, we often cannot tell what the dispute was or what was the tenurial relationship between the parties. Taken all together, the volume of direct evidence about the propriety of the writs is statistically insignificant. But it takes us some way.

It will be easiest to work backwards from what we know for certain. We know, because Glanvill is explicit, that if you have a writ patent at all it must go to the lord of whom you claim to hold, 'not to anyone else, not even to the chief lord'.[3] We also know the position after the Great Charter, which settled an inexorable

such writs reached official custody; *PKJ*, I, p. 20; Hall, *Registers*, p. lxxii f. The earliest actual writ patent known seems to be one of 1219 printed in West, *The Justiciarship in England, 1066–1232*, p. 251; *Registers*, p. lxxi, n. 3. But Lady Stenton prints four cartulary copies; *PKJ*, I, 3551–4. The first three date from 1206, and are discussed below, p. 81. The fourth dates from 1195–97.

[1] (*a*) *PRS*, XIV, 36–7; (*b*) *PRS*, XIV, 121 (Cliueden; full references above, p. 61, n. 1); (*c*) *PRS*, XIV, 124 (Hurton); (*d*) *CRR*, II, 260, 296 (court of Henry d'Oilly; full references above, p. 6, n. 2); (*e*) *CRR*, III, 136–7, *146*; (*f*) *CRR*, V, 45 (court of Milborne Port), 164, *179*, 228–9, *252*; (*g*) *CRR*, VI, *171*, *202*, *208*, 228–31; (*h*) *CRR*, VII, *1*, *218*, *262*, 265–6; cf. ibid. *9*, *26*; (*i*) *BNB*, 40 (a very full account); *CRR*, VIII, *35*, *86*, *145*; (*j*) the cases below, p. 82, n. 3, in which the tenant to the action is also the lord whose court defaulted. In the three earliest of the above cases the language is *falsificata curia*, later it is *probata defalta curie*. Entries on early grand assize rolls may also note the court in which the tenant claimed the assize; *CRR*, I, 5–6 (examples on the second membrane, noted as possibly earlier than others), 10–14 (the sixth membrane). We may learn to whom a writ patent was addressed in other ways: (*a*) *PRS*(NS), XXXI, 105 (Mara; full references above, p. 61, n. 1); (*b*) *RCR*, I, *341*, *374*, 440 (Eston); *PKJ*, I, *2084*, *2467*; *CRR*, I, *159*, *216*; (*c*) *CRR*, I, 48 (Wasseburn'); (*d*) *CRR*, III, 240 (Polstede), *274*; (*e*) *CRR*, IV, 211–12; (*f*) *CRR*, V, 46–7 (recital of proceedings attributed to 1157), *149*; (*g*) *CRR*, V, 93 (Lutre) 113–14, *326*; *CRR*, VI, *403*.

[2] *Precipe* in pipe rolls: Hurnard, 'Magna Carta, Clause 34' in *Studies in Medieval History presented to F. M. Powicke*, pp. 157 ff. *Precipe* so named in plea rolls: (*a*) *CRR*, I, *104*, *272*, *331*, 337 (Puteaco), *338*, 344; (*b*) *CRR*, I, *210*, 360 (Bertram); *CRR*, II, *252*; (*c*) *Lincs.*, 432; (*d*) *CRR*, II, 311 (Rocheford); (*e*) *CRR*, VI, *19*, *57*, 72–3; (*f*) *CRR*, VI, *14*, *23*, 117 (Windesour; possibly referring to *warantia carte*).   [3] *Glanvill*, XII, 8.

rule. With definite exceptions, you must always begin with a writ patent to the lord of whom you claim to hold.[1] If, for example, he has no court, you must still start with him and reach public justice by tolt and *pone* and not directly by *precipe*. Glanvill's undifferentiated *precipe*, indeed, will no longer be issued; and the exceptional cases are now declared in the writ itself.[2] If the lord has waived jurisdiction, the demandant may have a *precipe quia dominus remisit curiam*, which, it should be noted, names the lord. If the lord is the king himself, the demandant must get a *precipe in capite*. And there is a third exception to which we shall come at the end of this chapter.

At what mischief was this provision of the Charter aimed? The oldest and simplest view is that the king was, so to speak, stealing jurisdiction which belonged to lords and which was primarily a source of profit. An important inquiry then established that at least there was a safeguard against this: at the beginning of the plea the lord could come and 'claim his court'. It was therefore suggested that the mischief arose from mistakes: there were situations in which the demandant or the writ-issuing authority might think, reasonably but wrongly, that a *precipe* was in order. The risk of this fell upon the lord, who could guard against it only by constant vigilance; and the intention of the Charter was to transfer the inconvenience to demandants by requiring a writ patent in all but the exceptional cases.[3]

This suggestion assumes that before the Charter the rule really went directly to jurisdiction rather than to writs. There were abstract rules of jurisdiction, for example, that a lord's court could not proceed if the tenant was holding under another lord (which is right), or if the claim was against the lord himself (which seems to be wrong)[4]; and if on these rules the lord had no jurisdiction, it was proper for the demandant to get a *precipe*. A claim of court would be made by the lord if he thought he did have jurisdiction – for example, because the tenant was after all holding

---

[1] *Magna Carta* (1215), c. 34; (1225), c. 24: *precipe* not to issue *de aliquo tenemento unde liber homo amittere possit* (or *perdat*) *curiam suam*. For an early statement, see *PKJ*, III, *639, 640*, 862: *non peciit terram illam in curia domini sui de quo clamat tenere terram illam.*

[2] Clanchy, 'Magna Carta, Clause Thirty-Four', *English Historical Review*, LXXIX (1964), 542.

[3] Hurnard, loc. cit. (above, p. 68, n. 2), which should be read in the light of Clanchy, loc. cit. (n. 2, on this page).   [4] Below, pp. 80 ff.

under him.[1] What the justices did then, on this view, was to examine the substance of the case so far as necessary to apply these rules of jurisdiction. Unfortunately, although the early rolls contain many claims of court, they hardly ever record the decision, let alone the grounds for it; and the only reason noted was that the demandant did not claim to hold of that lord.[2] Glanvill does not mention claims of court in his account of the *precipe*, but gives a full account in connection with the writ patent. A demandant might get a proper writ, but somehow procure the removal of the case without proving default of the lord's court. The lord might make his claim either in the county or in the king's court; and Glanvill says that he will recover his jurisdiction unless default is proved then and there.[3] In this situation, at least, the inquiry seems to have been mechanical: does the demandant claim to hold of this lord, and if so did his court default? These questions could be answered without going into the substance of the case; and there is no evidence that inquiry ever went further.

There is, however, some evidence that the *precipe* might be used as an alternative to the *pone* rather than to the writ patent. In a case of 1207 in which the pipe rolls show that a *precipe* was issued, a lord appears to object that default of his court was never proved.[4] And in 1200 a demandant, who has a *pone* which may be meeting with deliberate delay, proceeds to get a *precipe* before the *pone* is executed. He is in trouble, and both writs are quashed, not because one of them must be wrong but because he has got both at once.[5]

These facts are most simply accommodated by supposing that the principle was always that later affirmed by the Charter. The demandant should begin by applying to his lord. That this initial application must always be by writ may not have been so clear: the preceding chapter suggested that the writ patent began as

---

[1] If the claim succeeded, the case was not transferred: the demandant had to get a new writ; *CRR*, I, *104, 272, 331*, 337 (Puteaco), *338*, 344.

[2] *CRR*, III, 272 (Revel); *CRR*, IV, *48*, 71.

[3] *Glanvill*, XII, 7. Note that it was possible for a demandant to get a *pone* although the case had never formally been before the county: (*a*) *RCR*, I, *341, 374*, 440 (Eston); *PKJ*, I, *2084, 2467*; *CRR*, I, *159, 216*; (*b*) *PKJ*, I, 3093; *CRR*, I, 166; (*c*) *CRR*, IV, 211–12. One way in which this might happen is shown in *CRR*, VII, *1, 218*, 262, 265–6; cf. ibid. *9, 26*.

[4] *PKJ*, IV, *2847, 3166*; *CRR*, V, 91 (Pridias), *97, 206*, 278, *321*; Hurnard, loc. cit. (above, p. 68, n. 2), p. 169, n. 1 (v).

[5] *CRR*, I, *210*, 360 (Bertram); *CRR*, II, *252*.

a factual rather than a legal requirement, and was factually required only against a tenant warranted by the lord. Only the assize of novel disseisin can have turned the writ patent into the necessary authorisation of our received picture.[1] What mattered to a lord was that a claim to be his tenant should at least be put to him. If it was so put, whether by writ or otherwise, and if for any reason he was not going to deal with it, there could be no objection to a demandant compelled anyway to go to the king's court going straight there with a *precipe* instead of by way of the county and a *pone*. The mischief is that demandants choose to go directly to the king's court. That this had become thinkable shows how lords were losing control. Their protest was surely a refusal to concede that, not just an attempt to hold on to the profits of administering a universal justice.

*   *   *

If the right was not a sort of ownership, but just the right to hold of a lord, even the propriety of writs cannot usefully be discussed further in the abstract. We always need to know who is claiming to hold the land of whom. There are four tenurial attitudes which a dispute may assume. If William is always our demandant, and Ralph the lord of whom he claims to hold, then William's action may be: (1) against Thomas, who says that he holds of the same lord, Ralph; (2) against Thomas, who says that he holds of another lord, Humphrey; or (3) against Ralph himself who says that he is entitled to hold in demesne; or (4) against Thomas who says that he is entitled to hold of William himself.

The simplest claim is that by William against Thomas when both claim to hold of Ralph. At least there is no doubt about the writ. On any view William should bring a writ patent to Ralph's court. About what happens there we have little evidence.[2] We have assumed a triangle with Ralph as its apex, and seen the dispute as

---

[1] Above, pp. 57 ff.

[2] Fragmentary glimpses: (*a*) *PRS*(NS), XXXI, 87–8; cf. *PKJ*, II, *79*; *CRR*, I, 72, *93*; *RCR*, I, *240, 269*, 451; (*b*) *RCR*, I, *298*; *RCR*, II, 36 (Curci); *PKJ*, I, *2714*; *CRR*, I, 125, 282, 348; (*c*) *RCR*, I, *262*; *RCR*, II, *44*; *PKJ*, I, *2487, 2748*; *CRR*, I, *442*; *CRR*, II, 112–13; (*d*) *CRR*, I, 58–9; (*e*) *CRR*, I, 59 (court of Arnold de Bosco), *61*?; (*f*) *CRR*, I, 156 (prior of Monmouth); *RCR*, II, *264;* (*g*) *CRR*, I, 296 (court of Tickhill); (*h*) *CRR*, III, 240 (Polstede), *274*; (*i*) *Lincs.*, 1384; *CRR*, IV, *233*?; (*j*) *PKJ*, II, 478, 522; (*k*) *CRR*, IV, 41 (Longo Campo); (*l*) *CRR*, VI, 18 (court of abbot of St Mary's, York); (*m*) *CRR*, VI, 290–2.

merely across the base. Ralph has some property right to jurisdiction, but is not otherwise involved in the dispute between
William and Thomas, which concerns a sort of ownership. But
the logic brought out in the preceding chapter was that of relationships up the two sides of the triangle, with none across the base.
William has a right against Ralph to the tenement, and so has
Thomas, who is actually holding it as Ralph's man. There is no
disputable relationship between William and Thomas: they have
just collided because it is the same tenement, like the victims of
a double booking today. The law-suit decides which of them has
the better right to the tenement, but as against Ralph both rights
may be good; and that is what warranty is about.[1]

If we put ideas like ownership out of our minds and look only
at the law-suit, there is hardly room for doubt about the analysis.
Consider the wording of the writ: it is a command to the lord, not
just to administer justice but to do right to the demandant who
claims to hold of him; and it names the tenant only as keeping
him out of the land. Then consider the count. Again the tenant is
named only as the person who keeps the demandant out. Nothing
at all is said of how he got in, of any past event by which the land
got into the wrong hands. That is no concern of the demandant's.
He sets up only his own right against the lord.

This is most clearly seen in the case of dower, where we know
as well as did the parties at the time what actually happened. The
husband endowed his wife, and then granted the same land to
another tenant. On his death the widow brings a writ patent to the
heir. Her count will go entirely to the endowment, to her own right.
Nothing is said about the grant to the tenant, which is irrelevant
to her claim. And if the tenant brings it up, he does so not in
denial of the widow's claim, but in assertion of an independent
right against the heir. The tenant may, if he chooses, himself deny
the widow's claim by saying that the husband was not seised at
the time of the marriage; and the unspoken basis for his denial
may be that the grant to himself had been made earlier. But usually
he will not himself answer the widow's claim, but vouch the heir
to warrant him on the basis of the husband's grant. The heir may
then deny the grant or, as we shall see in the following chapter,
deny that he is bound to warrant it.[2] If he warrants it, then he may
deny the endowment – for example, asserting that the husband

---

[1] Above, pp. 41 ff., 58 ff.   [2] Above, p. 43; below, pp. 126-7.

was not seised at the time (the basis for which again may be that the grant to the tenant preceded the marriage). Or, as often happens, the heir may agree that he is bound to warrant both sides, with the result noted in the preceding chapter: for the life of the widow she will be entitled to this tenement, and the tenant will be entitled to *escambium* from the heir.[1]

In claims other than dower, the logic is less easily visible partly because the facts are less easily visible. The parties at the time of the action may often not have known what had happened, how and when some ancestor of the demandant had been put out or passed over, so that an ancestor of the tenant got in. It is a point to which we shall come back in the last chapter.[2] But their ignorance was irrelevant. Nothing turned on what had happened, and it was not in issue. The demandant does not try to explain it, or to set up a case as against the tenant. The right he sets up is a right against the lord. His ancestor was seised, as his champion is prepared to prove, and he claims as heir of that ancestor. It does not matter by what malice or mistake some predecessor of the lord contrived to accept somebody else as tenant. If the ancestor was indeed seised, was his man, then the king insists that this demandant shall have his inheritance. The count is not a formal preliminary, a grace to be said: it is the meat itself, and contains all that the action puts in issue.

What William does in Ralph's court, therefore, is to set up his right against Ralph. Nor should we under-estimate a possible personal element. One William about 1192 showed his writ to Ralph's bailiffs, but insisted on waiting some five years for Ralph himself to come home before he would proceed on it; and the court was then in trouble for acting on so old a writ.[3] But it is on Thomas's side that a more immediate personal element may appear. Thomas may answer in either of two ways; and one of them played an important part in the preceding chapter.[4] He too turns to Ralph, the lord to whom he has done homage, and claims his warranty; and if warranty is given, it means simply that William's claim will not be entertained. In Ralph's court that is the end of the

---

[1] Above, p. 43.

[2] Below, p. 182.

[3] *CRR*, I, 59 (court of Arnold de Bosco), *61*?.

[4] Above, pp. 59 ff. Note especially the case at p. 63, n. 2, where a tenant makes a proffer to have the king's warranty, the demandant a proffer that the case should proceed *secundum consuetudinem regni*.

matter, and that is why the writ patent was introduced. The case will be taken away to public justice, and there Thomas will vouch Ralph to warranty. If Ralph warrants, then Thomas will be assured of this or another tenement from him; and Ralph must decide whether or not to concede William's claim to this tenement. But it is still not a claim in the abstract but a claim to hold it of Ralph. And if Ralph chooses to resist it, and to put himself upon the grand assize, the question for the knights will be that between himself and William: whether Ralph has greater right to hold in demesne or William to hold of him. Thomas is not even mentioned in the mise.

But we shall hardly ever recognise such a case on the plea rolls, let alone know how the land is supposed to have got into the wrong hands; and an example which we can recognise may show why this is so. It dates from 1199. The demandant is the younger of two brothers. The elder succeeded to a tenement as heir upon the death of their uncle, but surrendered it to the lord; and the lord then granted it out to the present tenant. The demandant's action is for half of the holding and the underlying proposition is that the tenement is partible, so that the brother could not surrender the demandant's share. He brings his writ patent to the lord, whose court defaults; and before justices the tenant vouches the lord and the lord warrants him. The lord then puts himself upon the grand assize: knights are elected to declare whether the lord has the greater right to hold in demesne or the demandant to hold of him; and the tenant is not mentioned. A day is given at the coming of the justices, and that is the last we hear of the case. But we know so much only through two pieces of luck. One is that the lord, having warranted the tenant, seeks to stop the demandant's case by saying that he has an elder brother alive; and it is the demandant's reply that tells us about the surrender. The other piece of luck is more unusual. None of the five plea roll entries of the case contains any hint that it began by writ patent. That we know only because the *pone* is among the few dozen writs from this period to have been preserved.[1] Even this tells us only that there was a writ patent; and there is still no direct evidence showing to whom it

---

[1] *PKJ*, I, 3477 (the *pone*), *2173, 3086*; *RCR*, II, *135*, 272; *CRR*, I, 314. In one early grand assize entry the warrantor claiming the assize names the tenant who vouched him and discloses that the demandant similarly claims to hold of him; *CRR*, I, 1 (William f. Ralph).

was addressed. But since demandant and tenant both claim to hold of him, it must have been this lord.

What happens in Ralph's court if Thomas's claim to warranty is rejected? In the king's court if a vouchee refuses to warrant the tenant, there is a plea between them. For Glanvill the tenant may prove his case against the vouchee by a battle fought by a suitable witness, a witness to the homage or receipt of services creating the duty to warrant.[1] Do we contemplate a plea of this nature between Thomas and Ralph in Ralph's court, and if so, to what end would it lead? So far as Ralph's court is concerned, surely a decision to warrant Thomas ends the law-suit one way, and a decision not to warrant him ends it the other. If Ralph and his court are proposing to allow William's demand despite Thomas's claim to warranty, Thomas must bring that claim to the king. The preceding chapter suggested that this is an early use of the action which comes to be known as *warantia carte* and to be based invariably upon a charter. We actually see it so used in a case of 1221; but we see it only because of an accident.[2] Normally we do not see it, for the same reason that we do not see the sequence of events when Ralph does warrant Thomas. We have no record of writs patent; and if we see Ralph at all, we can identify him as vouchee but not as the lord to whom the writ first went.

If Thomas claims Ralph's warranty, then, Ralph's court cannot entertain William's demand. Its own logic had always prevented it if it found that Thomas was entitled to Ralph's warranty; and now the king's court will prevent it from making even that finding. There must be a default; and it is the king's court which will enforce both William's right to the tenement and Thomas's right against Ralph on his warranty. The regular defaults of the thirteenth century are therefore explained, and we are left to wonder whether there is any case which Ralph's court can settle. Let us first dispose of a minor possibility, though one that may not have been infrequent. It is of the nature of a modern boundary dispute. A writ patent always recited the service by which the demandant claimed to hold the tenement of the lord. But precedents for the writ, including the writ patent for dower distinguish the case in which the land is claimed as *pertinens* to

---

[1] *Glanvill*, III, 1, 7. Notice that for Glanvill battle is not necessarily ousted by a charter, provided there is a suitable witness.

[2] Above, p. 64.

a tenement already held by the demandant; and it is *pertinens* if it is within the service which he does for that tenement.[1] If that is William's claim, and if Thomas similarly asserts that the parcel in question is by custom part of his tenement, no question is raised about the warranty of Thomas's tenement as such. Perhaps we should anyway not recognise such cases, but they are not in fact common on the plea rolls; and in theory as well as in practice they may have been regarded as appropriate for lords' courts.

But this would be only a special case of a general possibility – namely, that the tenant does not seek to rely upon his warranty but himself undertakes to deny the demandant's right. So long as we think in terms of a dispute over abstract rights of property, this appears as the primary course, and voucher as a mere complication. But on the analysis here proposed, the surprising thing is that the tenant can choose to answer by himself without reference to his warrant; and it is comforting that there is a note of surprise in Glanvill's assertion that this is so. At least it is something that he finds it necessary to say expressly; and what particularly has to be said is that the tenant can put himself on the grand assize without his warrantor.[2] This may suggest a reason. There is a unilateral quality about the logic of a law-suit tried by battle: the demandant's claim is sworn to by his champion, and its truth alone is formally in issue. There is no positive allegation on the other side, nothing more than a denial of the claim. The person making that denial, therefore, appears as a party to the proof rather

---

[1] *Glanvill*, XII, 3. His writ of right of dower has no other variant, only the claim to land as *pertinens* to what is already held in dower, VI, 5; and this is still a prime case in *Brevia Placitata*, where three of five mss have no other (pp. 4, 45, 156; given as a variant at p. 128, not at p. 74). Cf. the references in *Novae Narrationes*, ed. Shanks and Milsom, Selden Society, vol. 80, pp. cv f. to statements about the proper use of the writ of right as opposed to the *precipe* writ *unde nichil habet*: the heir's warranty is a factor which has not been considered. For *pertinens* claims generally, see *Registers*, CA2 (including dower), CC3, CC6a (dower), R18 (dower only); CC44 and R77 are for advowsons, below, p. 78, n. 3. Of the four early writs patent printed by Lady Stenton, not for dower, two are of this kind: *PKJ*, I, 3553, 3554. Plea roll examples of such claims to land: (a) *PRS*, XIV, 2 (Kinton); (b) *RCR*, I, 25–6, *125;* (c) *RCR*, I, 217 (Corbet), *340, 403*; *CRR*, I, 89, *173–4*; *RCR*, II, *82*; (d) *PKJ*, I, *2831*; *RCR*, II, 227 (Witefeld); *CRR*, I, 351, *360–1*; (e) *CRR*, I, 424 (Putehale); (f) *CRR*, II, 275 (abbot of Chertsey); (g) *PKJ*, III, *1596, 2030?*; *CRR*, IV, 95 (abbot of St Benet of Hulme), *177*; (h) *CRR*, VI, 69 (Parles), 309; and many other entries; (i) *CRR*, VI, *11, 12, 51*, 75–6, which shows the special nature of the demand by laying seisin in the ancestor of the demandant's grantor; (j) *Yorks.*, 1117.

[2] *Glanvill*, III, 5.

than as a party to the law-suit itself; and even if the tenant does vouch, the lord may commit the denial to him.[1] But if the tenant claims the grand assize, he does affirm a title in himself: he asks the knights to say which party has the greater right. And since, in the case we are considering, his own right must be that which he would rely on in vouching the lord, it did not go without saying that he could proceed without reference to him.

That his doing so should have become not merely possible but common most obviously reflects the rise of an abstract concept of property in land. But it reflects also the related decline of warranty. What had once been the tenant's title has become a mere ancillary, something that he may or may not have in addition to the new abstract title which he disputes with the demandant, something which he must take special steps to acquire. For Glanvill it seems that the mere receipt of services imposed a duty to warrant;[2] and if so the risk of loss arising from the external enforcement of ancient hereditary claims was cast automatically upon lords. However it had come about that the tenant or his ancestor had been accepted in preference to the demandant or his ancestor, the mere acceptance of this tenant entitled him to compensation from the lord if the demandant won. This was too heavy a burden, and in even the earliest rolls it is apparent that the claim to warranty is being based upon something more than the mere receipt of services; and soon it is nearly always based upon a charter. Unless there is an express undertaking to warrant, even a charter will be insufficient if it records not an original gift but assent to a continuation.[3] And eventually, as grants by substitution become common, warranty is at last detached from tenure itself, and appears as a contractual artefact.

* * *

In the second tenurial attitude which a dispute may assume, William is again demandant, and Ralph the lord of whom he claims to hold; but Thomas, the present tenant, asserts that he holds not of Ralph but of another lord, Humphrey. It is possible that Humphrey is himself lord or tenant of Ralph; but we shall

[1] *Glanvill*, III, 7.
[2] *Glanvill*, III, 7; cf. above, p. 55, n. 1.
[3] On the difference between *concedo* and *do*, see, e.g., *PRS*, XIV, 124 (Hurton); below, p. 132, n. 1.

assume that the two lords are, so to speak, co-ordinate. The situation may have been among the first regularly to attract public justice, but we have hardly any information outside the pages of Glanvill; and he considers it twice. In discussing the writ patent, he expressly tells us that Ralph's court may not hear the plea: *ex necessitate itur inde ad comitatum; et ibi procedet placitum uel in capitali curia.*[1] There, he goes on, both lords must be summoned to hear the plea; and he refers back to his account of warranties, where he insists that the demandant's lord must be summoned as well as the tenant's, and actually made to come.[2]

Since Ralph's court lacks power to hear the plea, it has been supposed that before the Charter William could properly begin with a *precipe*. And since one of Glanvill's discussions comes in his account of warranties, which itself is given in the context of his *precipe* writ, it is at least arguable that he contemplated this. But if the demandant claimed to hold in chief of the king, or if what he claimed was an advowson,[3] a *precipe* would be proper on any view; and these are the facts in two of the handful of cases found in the earliest rolls in which diversity of lordship is squarely raised.[4] In a third the demandant claims to hold of the honour of Gloucester, in king John's hand by his first marriage, the tenant to hold *in capite* of the crown: whatever writ this demandant has, his son, reviving the claim after the Charter and after the honour has come to the Clares, has a writ patent to the earl.[5] In a fourth case the tenant secures a view, although the half knight's fee demanded comprises an entire vill, because *tenet de feodo alio*, the lord of which he names: but the clerk assumes the identity of the demandant's lord to be known, presumably because the writ was patent; and within the single lordship a unit claimed would need no further identification because the peers would know for what land each

---

[1] *Glanvill*, xii, 8.

[2] *Glanvill*, iii, 6–8.

[3] *Glanvill*, i, 3. *Registers*, CC44 and R77 are writs patent for an advowson, but each claims it as *pertinens*; cf. above, p. 76, n. 1.

[4] Claim to hold *in capite*: CRR, iii, *168*, 259 (Welton); CRR, iv, *71*, *148*, *208*; CRR, v, *32*, *98*, *212*, *216*. Claim to advowson: CRR, i, 101 (Alard f. Bernard); RCR, i, 437; RCR, ii, *94*.

[5] The father's claim: RCR, i, *245*, *248*, *256*; RCR, ii, *78*, *196*; CRR, i, *236*, 263 (Kime), 386, *397*, *434*; charters are produced on both sides, and the tenant's title emerges also in other litigation; CRR, vi, 102. The son's claim *per breue de recto et tenere de Comite Gloucestrie*: BNB, 232; CRR, xi, *1114*, *1599*, *2155*, *2773*. For a later case of the same diversity, also probably begun by writ patent, see BNB, 283; CRR, xiii, 573.

homage was done.[1] Lastly there is an invisible case: no record survives of the action between the parties, which may have been pending in the county after default on a writ patent; all we have is a request by the demandant's lord for an inquest to be held between the two lords, and an order that the plea should be adjourned *usque ad adventum predictorum baronum*.[2]

The scarcity of cases is remarkable. The situation cannot have been uncommon; and of course in any number of vouchers by tenants, the vouchee may have been a Humphrey, a second lord of whom the tenant claimed to hold. But only twice in the earliest rolls does Ralph, the demandant's lord, play any visible part. One case is that just mentioned, in which he himself takes the initiative and asks for an inquest between himself and Humphrey. The other concerns an advowson, and both lords are summoned to come if they wish.[3] But even this is a far cry from Glanvill, who thinks it necessary to compel Ralph's presence; and some large change must have intervened. At first sight it may seem a change which did not make much practical difference. Even on Glanvill's scheme Ralph's co-operation was a requirement without which William's claim could not proceed, rather than a benefit to either of them. William stood only to lose from it: if Ralph did not warrant his claim it failed, and there is no mention of compensation from Ralph. Conversely, Ralph did not lose by not coming: unlike Humphrey, he was neither under a contingent liability to find *escambium*, nor was he now in receipt of services which would be lost with his tenant's tenement.

But something more fundamental was at stake. Any action in the right may impose upon the lord a new tenant: that was its original purpose, and that is why the writ patent was directed to the lord of whom the demandant claimed to hold. But are we to suppose that William can bring an action which will make him Ralph's tenant and augment Ralph's lordship without Ralph knowing anything about it, and without the court having heard of Ralph? That would follow if it was proper for William to begin with a *precipe*: unlike the writ patent the *precipe* does not name the

---

[1] *RCR*, II, 31 (Robert f. Walter), *268*; *PKJ*, I, *2505, 2754*; *CRR*, I, *363–4*; *CRR*, II, *100, 104–5*. Discussing the right of a warrantor to the view, Bracton notes that a lord should know for what land he has taken homage and service; f. 377b.

[2] *CRR*, II, 114 (Brause).

[3] *CRR*, I, 101 (Alard f. Bernard); *RCR*, I, 437; *RCR*, II, *94*.

lord;[1] and the count never does. William could presumably make his claim even though he had no lord in mind, gaining a sort of allod until some lord demanded services. Or consider Humphrey's position: unless he claimed his court, would he know even that William did not claim to hold of him, and that his services from this tenement were therefore at stake?[2] Would he, if vouched by Thomas and wishing to claim the grand assize, know whether to frame his mise generally or in the special form denying that William was entitled to hold of him? The case of diversity of lordship is mainly important as another reason for thinking that in principle the position before the Charter was the same as that after it, that the demandant must always begin with some application to the lord of whom he claims to hold.

*   *   *

We turn now to claims in the vertical dimension, and first to that which looks upward: Ralph is holding the land in demesne and William claims that he is entitled to hold it of him. By what writ should William begin his action? If there is a single answer to that question, it is that he should start with a writ patent commanding Ralph to do right to William in respect of land of which Ralph himself deforces him. Only the lord can accept a tenant, and the king can only require him to do so. In a sense this is the prime case covered by the writ patent. But if we think in the modern terms of adjudicating abstract rights and being judge in one's own cause, the conclusion may seem surprising.[3] Particular reasons will therefore be listed.

1. Of only three such cases in which we know that there was a *precipe*, only one carries no suggestion that this was wrong.[4] In another, Ralph seems to deny and William to assert that default of

---

[1] But after the Charter the writ *quia dominus remisit curiam* does name him; *Registers*, CC8 (Latin), R23.

[2] *CRR*, III, *168*, 259 (Welton; full references above, p. 78, n. 4): the tenant claims that he holds of an infant, and *non videtur ei quod possit perdere servitium domini sui* since the demandant *non vocat tenere de eodem.*

[3] On the question whether a lord could be sued in his own court, see Hurnard, 'Magna Carta, Clause 34' in *Studies in Medieval History presented to F. M. Powicke*, at p. 167, and references there given.

[4] *PKJ*, I, 3535, which is the writ itself, and references in note thereto. The claim was based upon a charter, and this may explain the *precipe* writ; below, p. 86, n. 2.

Ralph's court had been proved, which suggests that the *precipe* had played much the part of a *pone*.[1] In the third, Ralph claims his court.[2]

2. There are ten other cases in which the tenant to the action claims his court.[3] Although we cannot be sure in any of these whether the demandant had got a *precipe* or had simply failed to prove default on a writ patent, and although in only two do we know that the claim of court succeeded,[4] it would hardly have been made so often unless in principle it was proper.

3. In the so-called Irish register the first precedent as usual is a writ patent. Unusually, it envisages as its primary case that the lord to whom it is addressed is himself the deforciant.[5]

4. Transcripts survive of three related writs patent issued in 1206, all against the same deforciant. Two of the writs are addressed to him as lord; the third is addressed to another lord. It is worth remarking that plea roll entries of all three cases are in the same *petit versus* form, with no distinction made between them and nothing to show even that the writs were patent.[6]

5. In 1198 a writ patent naming as deforciants the lord himself and a third party is enrolled, probably by mistake. Again other entries give no clue to the nature of the writ.[7]

---

[1] *CRR*, v, 91 (Pridias; full references above, p. 70, n. 4). The evidence for the *precipe* writ is a pipe roll entry.

[2] Another pipe roll case; references in Hurnard, loc. cit. (above, p. 80, n. 3), p. 169, n. 1 (ii), to which may now be added *PKJ*, III, *1499, 1647*. The claim of court by the abbot of Ramsey is at *CRR*, III, 96.

[3] (*a*) *RCR*, I, 429 (prior of Bermondsey); cf. *PKJ*, III, 79; (*b*) *CRR*, I, 102 (Insula), 200, 447, *475*; *PKJ*, I, *2856, 2859, 3038*; *CRR*, II, 28, 72; (*c*) *CRR*, I, 223 (prior of St Augustine's, *recte* Holy Trinity, Canterbury), 238, *329*; *CRR*, II, *35, 181*; (*d*) *CRR*, I, *146, 175, 236*, 276 (prior of Bermondsey); *CRR*, II, *81*; (*e*) PRS, XIV, *11, 20, 32*; *RCR*, I, 2, 87; *PKJ*, I, *2119*; *RCR*, II, *122*; *CRR*, I, 292 (abbot of Ramsey); (*f*) *CRR*, I, 337 (Blundus); cf. ibid. *341, 408*; (*g*) *CRR*, I, 442 (Richard f. Neil); (*h*) *CRR*, III, 197 (Luvetot), *294*; *PKJ*, III, *1442*; *CRR*, IV, *203–4, 248, 256*; *CRR*, V, 26, *198, 212, 271*; *PKJ*, IV, *2974, 3719*; and cases in following note. Cf. (*a*) *CRR*, I, 292 (abbot of Ramsey claiming court *de custodia pueri quam...petit versus eundem abbatem*); (*b*) *CRR*, IV, *3*, 49 (abbot of St Benet of Hulme claims court; the action seems to proceed against him, perhaps as warrantor), *194, 243*; *PKJ*, III, *1929*; *PKJ*, IV, *2620*; *CRR*, V, *201*, 271; there had been a *precipe* writ, Hurnard, loc. cit. (above, p. 80, n. 3), p. 169, n. 1 (iv).

[4] (*a*) *CRR*, I, *68*, 164, 165 (abbot of Faversham); *RCR*, I, 417–18; *RCR*, II, 70; (*b*) *CRR*, VI, 241 (William archdeacon of Buckingham), 286; *CRR*, VII, *9*, 10–11, 24, *48*, 52, 57, 91, *113*.

[5] *Registers*, Hib. 1. The earliest actual writ patent known to survive is addressed to the bailiffs of the deforciant himself; West, *The Justiciarship in England, 1066–1232*, p. 251.   [6] *PKJ*, I, 3551–3; *CRR*, V, 118.

[7] *PRS*(NS), XXXI, 105, 100–1 (full references above, p. 8, n. 2).

6. Another enrolment of the same year is deliberate, and the writs were hybrid and probably forged; but they purported to be writs patent addressed to the lord.[1]

7. No other cases have been noted in which we have the text of such a writ. But in two cases of this tenurial posture the writ is named as *breve de recto*, which at least usually denotes a writ patent.[2]

8. In two cases, one early and one late, a county record tells us that the lord whose court defaulted is the tenant to the action;[3] and this must be so in any case of this posture which went to the county.[4]

9. We have two recitals of claims against a lord in his own court. The vouchee in an assize of 1203 says that he *dirationavit* the tenement in question against his lord by judgment of the lord's court, which he vouches.[5] And a demandant of 1210, against whom the tenant eventually puts herself on the grand assize with special mise claiming to hold of him, alleges that the tenant's father *aliquando eum implacitavit et ei quietum clamavit in curia sua.*[6]

Whether a lord's court would often proceed under such a writ is another question. There was of course no warranty to inhibit it. But if the lord was disposed to entertain the claim at all, he would probably do so without writ. Glanvill, discussing the case of a tenement being held by the lord as an escheat but then claimed by one who makes himself out to be heir, says that he will plead *per misericordiam domini sui uel per preceptum domini regis.*[7] As a matter of fact, therefore, the demandant who got a writ may often have known that the lord's court would default.

We cannot hope to learn even how frequent such claims were. We do not see them until they reach the king's court, and there we shall not often recognise them. Without the writ, there will

---

[1] *PKJ*, II, 113; *CRR*, I, 113; *RCR*, I, *280, 297, 374*; *PKJ*, I, *2265*; cf. ibid. pp. 26–8.

[2] (a) *CRR*, I, 145 (Monachus); *RCR*, II, *197*; (b) *CRR*, I, 102 (Insula), 200, 447; other references to the case are given above, p. 81, n. 3.

[3] (a) *CRR*, I, *409*, 445–6; (b) *CRR*, XI, *1351, 1416*, 1746; *BNB*, 1019. County records are an important source of information about writs patent; above, p. 68, n. 1.

[4] If the *maritagium* was of the usual tenurial cast, the case in *CRR*, I, 12 (Lude) must have begun by writ patent to the demandant's brother as in the case cited above, p. 81, n. 7. For a similar but more explicit mise, see *CRR*, II, *117*, 228–9.

[5] *Northants.*, 869.   [6] *CRR*, VI, 77 (Mauduit), *94, 131–2, 165, 314*.

[7] *Glanvill*, VII, 17. In *PRS*, XIV, 25, a demandant withdraws from a plea against the earl of Salisbury *quousque Requisierit Comitem Inde qui dominus suus esse debet.*

normally be nothing to show that William is claiming the tenement from Ralph to hold it of him rather than of the king or some other lord. The only common indication will come if Ralph claims the grand assize: his mise will be in special form, asking the knights to say whether he has greater right to hold in demesne or William to hold of him. And even then, as we have already seen, it may be that William's action was originally brought against Thomas, who vouched Ralph to warranty in the county or at a missing earlier stage in the king's court.[1]

Equally, of course, we cannot hope often to learn what kinds of fact lie behind such claims. William is not concerned to show how the land got back to Ralph. If his count is true, so that his ancestor was seised as of fee and he is the heir, then he is entitled without more. The likely thing is that after the death of the ancestor named, Ralph or some ancestor of his took the tenement into hand and then, by mistake or otherwise, failed to yield it up to the heir. In principle it makes no difference whether the ancestor died recently or long ago, or whether William is the first heir who could have made the claim or Ralph the first lord against whom it could have been made. Sometimes William relies upon a seisin at the most remote time permissible – namely, in the reign of Henry I. Perhaps his real case rests on events in the anarchy, but other explanations are possible. Twice it was his grandfather who was seised then, and the claim is for virgates: one wonders whether Ralph or his ancestor took them for villeinage, and whether assizes have since shown peer tenements to be free.[2] Once it is William's father who was seised at the death of Henry I, allegedly in fee farm; and since farms could be for life, that may be the real issue.[3]

If the death was recent and the ancestor close, William would normally use mort d'ancestor. Even a father may have died too long ago, as presumably in the fee farm case just mentioned; and exceptionally he may not have died seised – for example, because

---

[1] Above, p. 60. Occasionally the entry of the count shows or suggests that the demandant's claim is to hold of the tenant, e.g., the first case in the next note and that in the note following.

[2] (a) RCR, I, 248, 251; PKJ, I, 2838, 3501 (notes thereto mistakenly attribute seisin to reign of Henry II); RCR, II, 4, 227–8 (Geoffrey f. Richard); (b) PKJ, I, 3551–2 (writs patent addressed to tenant to actions); CRR, v, 118 (no indication either of writ or of tenurial posture). The latter case may arise from a grant of tenanted land taken by the grantee as villeinage.

[3] RCR, I, 44, 100; PRS(NS), XXXI, 75–6. On life farms and for the possibility of confusion, cf. CRR, I, 430 (Kokefeld), below, p. 170.

he left the district and Ralph took the tenement into hand.[1] But the recent death most likely to put William to his claim in the right is that of a more remote ancestor than those who can be named in the assize. We never see this case for certain on the early rolls, but the evidence could hardly be other than circumstantial. Consider the abbot of Evesham whom we see resisting three separate assizes of mort d'ancestor in 1202, and a little earlier meeting a claim in the right by putting himself upon the grand assize with special mise: the knights were to say whether the abbot had greater right to hold in demesne or the demandant to hold of him. All four claims were for virgates in the same Northamptonshire village; and one wonders whether three fathers and a grandfather, as it were, had died seised of tenements which the lord supposed to be unfree.[2] Or consider enrolments without any seisin or descent, which just make William claim against Ralph *sicut jus suum et hereditatem*: once Ralph first claims his court, and then puts himself on the grand assize with the same special mise.[3]

This particular claim by William against Ralph, based upon the recent death of an ancestor outside the scope of the assize, was to figure in interesting argument when the principle of the assize was extended to other relatives by the writs of aiel and cosinage. These were *precipe* writs, and the jurisdictional principle of the Charter was invoked against them.[4] The argument in their favour was one of proof. Like writs of entry, they put the question to a jury; and it was said to be generally inappropriate that such a recent seisin should go to battle or the grand assize.[5] But these were particularly inappropriate for a claim against the lord himself; and the magnates were prepared to approve the new writs only for actions against the lord or somebody who could vouch him.[6] There was undoubted sentiment against battle between lord and man;[7] and since many

---

[1] Above, p. 59, n. 1; below, p. 165, n. 4.

[2] *Northants.*, 604; *CRR*, I, 10.

[3] *CRR*, I, 102 (Insula), 200, 447; other references to the case are given above, p. 81, n. 3.

[4] (a) *BNB*, 1215; (b) *Select Cases in the Court of King's Bench*, ed. Sayles, II, Selden Society, vol. 57, pp. clvi f.

[5] Bracton, f. 281; Hall, *Registers*, p. lxiii, n. 1 and references there given.

[6] In the last four lines of *BNB*, 1215, it is necessary to read either *qui* for *ubi* or *dominus capitalis uocari* for *dominum capitalem uocare*.

[7] For an offer of proof *ut dominus*, see *RCR*, I, 60–1; cf. ibid. 6, 72; *PRS*, XIV, 18–20. For offers *ut versus dominum*, see (a) *RCR*, II, 257 (Baskerville); *CRR*, I, 417, 435; (b) *CRR*, VI, 67 (Mara). These are all appeals in which the parties would themselves fight; cf. Bracton, ff. 81b, 141. In actions in the right

claims in the right ended in a question between them, this may conceivably have played a part in the introduction of the grand assize. How the grand assize itself became infected is another matter: perhaps just as an alternative to battle. The question is how far this sentiment may have been a motive for what happens in the course of the thirteenth century: special mises, by which the grand assize is to decide whether one party is entitled to hold of the other, become steadily less frequent. So far as the upward claim is concerned, aiel and cosinage took some of the load, and seemingly for this reason. There is no evidence that it played a part with the converse downward claim, to which we shall shortly come.[1] That was taken over by writs of entry. But there, as we shall see, jurisdictional propriety worked in the same direction as proof. Not only was a jury appropriate, but the lord was not losing a case which ought to come to his court.

Before leaving the upward claim, two special cases must be mentioned in which we see a little more of the dispute. The first is a curiosity. William claims from Ralph land for which Ralph has taken his homage or given him a charter, but which he has not delivered.[2] On the traditional view of livery of seisin no 'title' can have passed to William; and if Ralph dies, William probably has no claim against his heir, who will not be bound to warrant the gift.[3] In modern analysis the relationship is contractual: Ralph has contracted an obligation and not fulfilled it. Some entries actually apply the language of warranty to these claims, although later dogma has it that only one seised can claim warranty.[4] So

---

battle may have been disliked but was evidently possible: it is offered in *RCR*, I, 44, *100*; *PRS*(NS), XXXI, 75–6 (fee farm), and waged, though for other reasons unwillingly, in *CRR*, I, *409*, 445–6.

[1] Below, p. 88.

[2] Charter: (*a*) *PRS*, XIV, 119 (Alneto); (*b*) *PKJ*, I, *2635*, *2837*; *RCR*, II, 235 (Solariis). Charter and homage: (*a*) *RCR*, II, *109*; *CRR*, I, 202 (William f. Gregory); (*b*) *PKJ*, I, 3490; *RCR*, I, 381; *RCR*, II, 8, 106; *CRR*, I, *116*, 121. Homage: case in n. 1, p. 86, below.

[3] *Glanvill*, VII, 1: *si uero donationem talem nulla fuerit secuta saisina, ex tali donatione nihil post mortem donatoris contra uoluntatem heredis efficaciter peti potest, quia id intelligitur...potius esse nuda promissio quam aliqua uera donatio.*

[4] Actions looking like *warantia carte* may in fact be claims for some of the land comprised in the charter: (*a*) *RCR*, II, 46 (Witchirch); *CRR*, II, *66*; (*b*) *RCR*, I, *303*?; *RCR*, II, 92 (Graue), 229; *PKJ*, I, *2870*?, *3006*?. Actions clearly claiming land may be described as *de placito warantie*: (*a*) *PKJ*, I, 3490; *RCR*, I, 381; *RCR*, II, 8, 106 (both *de placito terre*); *CRR*, I, 116 (*de placito warantie*), 121 (*de placito warantie carte*); (*b*) *PRS*(NS), XXXI, 72 (Lens; *petiit* the land *per cartam*), 73 (*petit quod...warantizet* the land *unde ipse habet cartam*).

immediate is the obligation that William may rely on it even if he or some ancestor had in fact been seised. If, for example, Ralph received the land in wardship with William, taking William's homage as the Assize of Northampton says he should, and later failed to deliver the land up, William would rely upon the homage rather than upon the seisin of the ancestor whose death had occasioned the wardship.[1] If Ralph has indeed accepted William's right, there is no question for his court to decide; and there is some reason to think that the *precipe* writ rather than the patent was appropriate.[2]

The last claim of this tenurial posture arises out of facts to which we shall return more than once. Ralph is the elder son of a father who granted the land to his daughter in *maritagium* or to his younger son William for service; and the claim is by the sister or younger brother against the elder brother, who is heir of the family inheritance and lord of the tenure created by this grant. The obvious question is how, in the demandant's view, the land is supposed to have got back to the heir. Once it was dirty work by the woman donee's husband;[3] and once it was earlier litigation of which the record happens to survive, though it is not even mentioned in the donee's action.[4] But in most cases, and they are not uncommon, we find no clue.[5] When we turn to such grants in the following chapter, we shall see that sometimes there was a constructive delivery so that the land remained with the donor.[6] And both in this case we are considering and in its converse, when

---

[1] *Lincs.*, 248 (homage taken before justices in 1202); *CRR*, VI, 308, 353–4 (claim based on the homage in 1212); cf. *CRR*, VII, 307.

[2] (a) In the case last cited the claim fails because the homage turns out to have been taken for other land than this: the demandant *querat aliud breve, si voluerit; CRR*, VI, 353–4. (b) A claim based as to part of the land upon homage, and as to part apparently upon charters for a term, seems to be described as *per breve de precipe; CRR*, V. 311 (Windesor); *CRR*, VI, 14, 23 (both using language of warranty), 117. (c) The attachment in *PKJ*, 3490 (above, p. 85, nn. 2 and 4) may have been consequent upon a *precipe* writ. (d) The one case noted (above, p. 80, n. 4) of this tenurial posture in which we know a *precipe* writ to have been issued apparently without objection is a case expressly rested upon a charter; *PKJ*, I, 3535, and references in notes thereto.

[3] *RCR*, I, 255, 432; *PKJ*, I, 2270; *CRR*, I, 142 (Castilliun), *184*, *194*; *RCR*, II, 239; cf. *CRR*, II, 34, 75, *181*, *246*, *264*.

[4] The earlier litigation: *PRS*, XIV, 20 (Coldinton, Goldinton), 29. The action against the heir: *PKJ*, I, *2142*, *2459*; *CRR*, I, 163, 342–3, *473*; *CRR*, II, *80*; *CRR*, III, *28*, *204*. For further litigation on the heir's contentions, see *CRR*, VI, 175 (below, p. 137, n. 4).

[5] Examples are listed below, p. 133, n. 7.   [6] Below, pp. 134–5.

the heir sues one claiming as donee, the true question must often be whether the gift was really made or whether, even if it was made, the heir is bound to honour it.

These family gift cases are taken last of the upward claims in order to emphasise an incongruity which they particularly show. The action is begun by writ patent to the heir: once we know this because the writ is enrolled,[1] and once we can deduce it since it was in the county that the heir claimed the grand assize.[2] One of those claims was for one carucate, the other for half a virgate; and at least in the latter it is unlikely that the heir had a court. Perhaps this was the kind of case Glanvill had in mind when he insisted that the writ must go to the lord of whom the demandant claimed to hold and not to anyone else, 'not even to the chief lord'.[3] Then there is the count. If any seisin is recited, and sometimes the clerk seems to omit the obvious, it is usually that of the demandant himself;[4] and if an offer of proof is enrolled, the champion swears to what he himself saw.[5] These are recent facts, not the ancestral seisin under Henry I for which the battle was appropriate and for which, presumably, the grand assize was designed. Indeed, though this is a more general problem, it is hard to believe that the panoply of the grand assize was ever meant for claims to acres. A dispute about a peasant settlement would best have been decided in the lord's court in which the settlement had probably been made,[6] and in which notoriety would reduce such problems of proof. But the writ of right goes to the peasant's heir, and on his inevitable default to public justice. Its logic was not that of an authorisation to the appropriate court to act, but that of an order in a particular case: the lord who had bound himself to a new tenant. The logic of that case was applied indiscriminately; and it made little sense when applied to recent gifts. But it is in the downward claim, to which we now turn, that the misfit is most obtrusive.

* * *

[1] *PRS*(NS), xxxi, 105, 100–1; other references to the case are given above, p. 8, n. 2.
[2] *CRR*, I, 12 (Lude). Compare the mise proposed in *CRR*, II, *117*, 228–9.
[3] *Glanvill*, xii, 8.
[4] See, e.g., the case above, p. 86, n. 4, at *CRR*, I, 163, though the entry of the count is a little confused; and cases in next note.
[5] (a) *CRR*, I, 45, 66–7; (b) *CRR*, II, *117*, 228–9.
[6] Below, p. 115.

The downward claim is the last of the tenurial permutations possible. But, although it is the converse of that just considered, we shall not simply reverse our parties. If there is any chance that the writ should be patent, our demandant must be supplied with a lord. Ralph shall therefore stay in place, this time as undoubted lord of William, who is claiming the land from Thomas; and Thomas will meet the claim by saying that he is entitled to hold it as William's tenant. This way of stating the case brings out an important difference from the upward claim. In the upward claim the tenurial posture was known from the outset, being stated in the writ patent itself.[1] But in the downward claim it will not appear from either writ patent or *precipe* if in common form, and it will not appear from William's count if that too is an ordinary count in the right.[2] So far as the formalities of the action go, William treats Thomas as a mere interloper; and only Thomas's answer discloses the orientation of the dispute. This matters to us in identifying the case in the plea rolls, or failing to identify it. But it must also have mattered at the time in choosing the writ: the choice had to be made before the nature of the dispute had become apparent.

What most often signals the case for us on the plea rolls is that Thomas claims the grand assize with special mise in the converse form to that just considered: the knights are to declare whether Thomas has greater right to hold of William or William to hold in demesne. This form appears in Glanvill, unlike the 'upward' version; and it is more common on the early rolls.[3] Its frequency alone suggests that a substantial proportion of early claims in the right were of this tenurial attitude. But the mise by itself tells us no more about the case, and we are not often able to see much of the underlying facts. They fall into two groups. Probably the smaller, and certainly for our purpose the less important, arises from grants of tenanted land: Thomas asserts that he or his

---

[1] (a) *PRS*(NS), xxxi, 105, 100–1 (full references above, p. 8, n. 2); (b) *PKJ*, I, 3551, 3552; (c) West, *The Justiciarship in England, 1066–1232*, p. 251; (d) *Registers*, Hib. 1.

[2] Occasionally a count seems expressly to claim *in dominico*: (a) *RCR*, I, 271; *PKJ*, I, 2337, 2845; *RCR*, II, 230 (Abruncis); *CRR*, I, 448; *CRR*, II, 16; (b) *CRR*, I, 49 (Bret).

[3] *Glanvill*, IX, 7. It may be even more common than the early rolls show. At least one clerk entered the election of a grand assize on a mise which we know to have been special as though it was general; *RCR*, I, 282, 361 (Baico, Baiocis), 445?; *RCR*, II, 37; *CRR*, I, 162 (mise), 220, 319–20 (election).

ancestor held of Ralph or his ancestor before the latter made his grant to William or his ancestor.[1] If this is true, that grant was of service only, and William's ancestor was never seised in demesne. It follows that William's count is untrue, and that Thomas will raise the real issue by making his customary general denial.

In the more important kind of case, Thomas claims under a grant from William himself or from an ancestor of William's; and William's count is therefore true and the seisin he relies upon is not in dispute. It follows that a grantor or his heir can always make a prima facie case against his tenant, that his count never touches the matter truly in dispute, and that the general denial is to that extent always inappropriate. Sometimes it is avoided: Thomas makes a sort of exception, seeking to cut off William's demand on the ground that William should be his warrant. But if he does this, it is for him to tender proof of the duty to warrant; and he seems never to answer in this way unless he has a charter.[2] Even if he has a charter, he may choose the general issue.[3] If he has no charter, and relies upon a taking of homage, he would have to support his 'exception' by a witness willing to do battle; and since battle is already tendered against him he may as well, and perhaps he must, take the general issue and go to the grand assize. The grand assize with this kind of special mise may indeed be reached in a *de homagio capiendo* brought by Thomas against William: Thomas has the land itself and is trying to compel William to acknowledge him as tenant, tendering proof of an earlier homage; if William resists, claiming himself to be entitled in demesne, Thomas may go to the grand assize as though William had brought a writ of right.[4] Even in the normal case in which the litigation is started by William's writ of right, it is no doubt

---

[1] In descending order of clarity: (a) PRS(NS), XXXI, 76 (Theobald Walter); (b) RCR, I, 266, 292, 308, 427 (Sine Averio); PKJ, I, 3504 and note thereto, 2557; RCR, II, 17-18, 113; (c) PRS(NS), XXXI, 106 (abbot of St Mary's, York).

[2] (a) PRS(NS), XXXI, 81 (Macun); (b) CRR, IV, 114, 133, 148-9, 252. A record from the court of Tickhill makes a tenant identify warrant and charter: *dicit quod habuit inde warantum et nominatim cartam* of the demandant's elder brother; CRR, I, 296.

[3] Yorks., 287 (full references above, p. 12, n. 1). In CRR, IV, 214, 304, the Templars argue that one claiming to be their tenant needs a charter even to entitle himself to the grand assize; cf. below, p. 92.

[4] (a) PRS, XIV, 135-6, 120; CRR, I, 70; RCR, I, 371, 382, 437; RCR, II, 33, 140; (b) CRR, III, 81, 191-2; (c) PKJ, III, 997; CRR, IV, 19; (d) BNB, 53; CRR, VIII, 65, 145, 232-3, 339. In Gloucs., 1495, it is the lord who gets to the grand assize, because he is in fact in seisin; below, p. 172, n. 5.

commonly preceded by Thomas's tendering his homage and
William's refusing it. And victory for Thomas on William's writ
of right may be marked in the same way as victory in his own
de homagio capiendo: the case will end with William taking his
homage in court.[1]

The reality of any action in the right lies in the question the
grand assize is to consider; and in this case that question has two
features of importance to us. The first is mechanical. Although
considerations of proof lead the tenant to take the general issue,
the substance of the matter is a confession and avoidance: yes,
this is the demandant's inheritance of which his ancestor was
indeed seised, but then the ancestor made this grant. This will
have a consequence which we shall for the moment postpone: the
demandant who knows what the tenant is going to say may wish
to go straight to the real issue by himself attacking the validity of
the grant. But when we speak of grants at the time of the earliest
rolls, we raise the second important feature of the knights'
deliberation; and this concerns the terms in which they were
thinking. If we defy the wording of charters and equate a grant
with our own once-for-ever transfer of ownership, we shall see the
knights as making a purely historical inquiry: did title pass? But
that is our question, not yet theirs. What they knew was not ownership but a renewable relationship; and they had to ask not just
whether it had been validly created, but whether it had been
renewed or whether the tenant was now entitled to have it renewed.
As always we must be willing to take the mise literally: has
William greater right to hold in demesne or Thomas to hold of him?

This will become particularly relevant when in the following
chapter we turn to consider dealings with land. In particular, it
will enable us to accept the reality of what must otherwise seem
unenforceable customs limiting the grants that a man could make,
especially by way of gift to members of his family.[2] The real
question was not whether the grantor could give, but whether his
heir would be obliged to renew, to warrant the gift. As with the
upward claims, family gifts lie behind the largest single group of
these downward claims in which the rolls give any glimpse of the
facts. Typically William, as heir of the family inheritance, is
claiming land given by his father or grandfather to a younger son;

[1] *CRR*, I, *34*; *RCR*, I, 329 (Baldric f. Baldric); cf. first case in preceding note.
[2] Below, pp. 121 ff.

and Thomas, who either is himself the younger son or is the younger son's heir, puts himself upon the grand assize claiming to hold of William. But before doing so he makes assertions not only about the circumstances of the gift itself, but also about things that have happened since, such as that homage was done by the donee's heir or to the donor's heir.[1] These tell us more than we usually learn about the facts of the dispute and therefore, as we shall see, about the law. But their importance for the present discussion is in warning us once again how much of both may be lost within an issue to the grand assize.

Outside the field of family gifts there are many early actions in the right which we can identify as being of this downward kind, usually because of the special mise, but of which we can learn no more. The common dispute is probably the same: William has just succeeded to his inheritance, and is claiming land which Thomas will say was granted to him by William's ancestor. And usually the ancestor who is supposed to have made the grant will be the one on whose seisin William has counted. But in situations in which the tenure was still seen as a renewable relationship, this would not always be so. In a case which first appears in 1203 a layman claims land from a religious house, which puts itself upon the grand assize with special mise. The demandant counts upon the seisin of his father, but this does not accord with a note left for us or for the knights by a kindly clerk: *sciendum* that the house claims under a grant in alms from the demandant's great-grandfather.[2] If we think of him as being supposed to have transferred ownership, we can see nothing but a muddle. But if we think of him as having undertaken a charitable subscription, which was renewed through two generations, we can see the demandant as just seeking to discontinue this charge upon what remains his inheritance.

Such a case is exceptional in the same way as the family gift: the heir's duty to warrant is not automatic. But the main assumptions hold good even in the case of the ordinary seignorial relationship created by a grant for full service. This is indeed William's

---

[1] (a) RCR, I, 344, 350 (Robert f. Neil; younger brother recovers from elder in novel disseisin); PKJ, I, 2285; CRR, I, 310 (elder brother claims in the right, younger alleges homage); (b) CRR, IV, 181, 193–4, 258–9; CRR, V. 14. See generally below, pp. 138 ff.

[2] CRR, II, 171, 282; CRR, III, 75, 94, 122, 122–3. Cf. the seisin attributable to an heir as warrant of dower, below, p. 145, n. 4.

inheritance, and Thomas can have no title except William's warranty. Consider once more the countess Amice, having taken control of her inheritance upon the dissolution of her marriage. She summoned her husband's grantee to answer *quo waranto* he held, and put him out by judgment of her own court. He recovered in novel disseisin because he had not pleaded willingly and the proceedings were without writ.[1] But he was not entitled to her warranty. She was wrong in procedure, but not in substance. What she should have done was to bring an action in the right of the kind we are now considering; and it would not have been heard in her own court. Other early entries seem to show lords doing just that. Consider the abbot of Waltham in 1199 claiming plots, of which the largest is six acres, from some twenty separate tenants.[2] What is going on? We get some picture from his remitting those of his claims which concerned 'old enfeoffment'; and these nse of this appears from a claim for fifteen acres made by the Templars in 1206. Their tenant seeks the grand assize with special mise, and they resist because, they say, he relies upon 'new enfeoffment' and they never grant land except by charter.[3] These sound like lords who still feel entitled to make their tenants show their tickets, even though they can no longer do it in their own courts. The abbot of Savigny, also in 1206, does so in pregnant language: each of five separate virgaters is to answer *quem ingressum habeat*.[4]

It has already been said that '*ingressum*' is a word lying in the mouth of an English rather than a Roman *dominus*, of a lord and not just an owner.[5] Consider the long wrangle in the thirteenth

---

[1] Above, pp. 45–6.

[2] *RCR*, I, *324, 346, 423*; *RCR*, II, *78–9*; *CRR*, I, *149, 154*.

[3] *CRR*, IV, *214*, 304. Cf. the case above, p. 48, n. 1: terre-tenants facing *quo waranto* inquiries on an escheat mostly produce charters from the dead tenant-in-chief, but one says he held *de veteri tenemento et de antiqua tenura*; *Lincs.*, 482.

[4] *CRR*, IV, 124; a sixth is to say *quid juris clamat*, ibid. 71. Cf. ibid. 136, where a half-virgater is to answer for services. One of the five had earlier recovered in mort d'ancestor from a third party, who had objected that he was a villein but produced no suit; *Northants.*, 382; and although the abbot is not mentioned in that entry, the preceding entry shows a plaintiff in novel disseisin, who may also be one of the five, asserting that he ought to hold freely of the abbot; ibid. 381. In such cases the lord may well be contending that the tenements are unfree; consider *CRR*, IV, *64*, 127 (Malduit), *159*, *202*; *CRR*, V, 29, *112*, 198–9; for litigation between this lord and other tenants, cf. *Lincs.*, 1316, and the case above, p. 82, n. 6.

[5] Above, p. 47.

century over a lord's right to prevent or complain of a sub-infeudation made by his tenant. Could he claim that the tenant's grantee *iniuste ingressus sit feodum suum*? Bracton used those words to deny the possibility.[1] But lords nevertheless procured legislation to protect at least their incidents, and the same language is used in the preambles. *Cum dudum provisum fuisset quod viri religiosi feoda aliquorum non ingrederentur...*, says the statute of Mortmain, referring to the Provisions of Westminster.[2] The famous opening phrase of the statute which finally dealt with the problem is seldom quoted as far as its verb: *Quia emptores terrarum... de feodis magnatum...in feodis suis sunt ingressi...*[3] We have managed to miss altogether the seignorial overtones of '*ingressum*'; and indeed by the late thirteenth century they remain distinct only when it is a lord paramount speaking of his tenant's tenant. When a lord uses the word of one he does not accept as his immediate tenant, Bracton has taught us to hear only a Roman or a modern proprietary claim, the claim of an 'owner' against one who had purely physical 'entry' commonly through a wrongful 'alienation'. We have forgotten that the alienation was generally a downward grant, and so have not noticed that the claim was generally a down-ward claim of the kind that we are now considering. Our picture of the writs of entry has lost its important dimension.

The outline of the development is clear. The first stage is re-presented by the countess Amice, the downward claim being made without writ in the lord's own court. If the requirement of a writ was originally a statement of fact about lords not going back on their warranty, it did not avail those whom they did not warrant. The countess's *quo waranto* became improper when novel disseisin turned the factual statement into a mechanical rule. This produced the second stage, in which the claim is begun either in the court of the lord paramount by writ patent or in the king's court by *precipe*;

---

[1] Bracton, f. 46b.

[2] Stat. *De viris religiosis*, 1279, referring to Provisions of Westminster, 1259, c. 14: *Viris autem religiosis non liceat ingredi feodum alicujus sine licentia capitalis domini, de quo scilicet res ipsa immediate tenetur.* Cf. Petition of the Barons, c. 10: *Item petunt remedium, quod religiosi non intrent in feodum...*

[3] Stat. *Quia emptores*, 1290. Cf. the Chester ordinance of 1260 printed in Plucknett, *Legislation of Edward I*, pp. 108–9: *nemo in feodo alterius aliquem feoffet, nec aliquis alterius feodum ingredi presumat per feoffamentum...* Cf. also the king's ordinance of 1256 about alienations by tenants-in-chief, *Calendar of Close Rolls, 1254–6*, p. 429: *ad dampnum nostrum gravissimum...est manifeste quod quilibet ingreditur baronias et feoda que de nobis tenentur in capite...*

and for the moment we shall not ask which. Usually the tenant claims the grand assize with special mise, as we have seen, and the detail of the dispute is lost to us.[1] But an unusually explicit enrolment of 1202 will give us our bearings in between the countess Amice and the writs of entry. William counts on the seisin of his mother. Thomas says the land was given to his father by William's father with the consent of William's mother, and then goes on to claim the grand assize with special mise.[2] In the third stage, the question there put to the knights would have been raised directly by a writ of entry *cui in vita*, just as the countess Amice's claim would have been made by *cui ante divortium*; and the case would have gone directly to the king's court.

This outline leaves open two questions, and they may be connected. When William's downward claim is made by writ of right, should it be patent or *precipe*? And how did the *precipe* writs of entry come into being? For the first question the evidence is sparse, but the answer seems clear: William should begin with a writ patent directed to his lord, Ralph. This seems to be correct for one special case – namely, the action based on a disclaimer;[3] and Glanvill expressly states it in another – namely, the purpresture.[4] And by a lucky chance we know in one case on the rolls which ended with this kind of special mise that the action had been in Ralph's court: some mishap after the writ of peace provoked a complaint which was enrolled.[5] But even if there were no specific pointers, the conclusion would follow *a priori*. Until the tenant answers, nobody formally knows the orientation of the dispute. For all William can tell, Thomas may claim to hold of Ralph. Even if Ralph's court ought not to determine the downward claim, that is where it should first be made.

But although this conclusion seems clear, it does not seem sensible. Unless we postulate a time when any grant made by

---

[1] We may learn more if the tenant makes the 'exception' that the demandant should be his warrant, and produces a charter from the demandant's ancestor: in the cases above, p. 89, n. 2, the underlying dispute concerns the capacity of the ancestor or the genuineness of his grant.

[2] *RCR*, II, *65*; *PKJ*, I, *2901*; *CRR*, I, *239*, *406*; *CRR*, II, *78*; *Lincs.*, 207, 225, *1138*. Cf. *CRR*, VII, *175*, 296 (Mauluvell), where the demandant's case is that he made a grant while out of his mind.

[3] *Novae Narrationes*, ed. Shanks and Milsom, Selden Society, vol. 80, p. lxi.

[4] *Glanvill*, IX, 13: *dominus…placitabit in curia capitalis domini per breue de recto.*

[5] *CRR*, V, *156*, 224–5, 237.

a tenant had to be approved by his lord,[1] Ralph's court is an inappropriate tribunal for the dispute between William and Thomas. To Ralph, of course this is William's inheritance. Whether Thomas is entitled to hold as William's tenant is a question not for Ralph's court but for William's; and when it arises the other way round, with William in possession and Thomas making the upward claim, it is William's court to which it goes.[2] If we have understood the development rightly, indeed, the downward claim was first made in William's court. Not only was the poor countess Amice substantially in the right: the procedure she adopted was in principle appropriate. What caught her, and indeed caught the law itself, was a juristic accident. There is now a dogmatic rule requiring a writ; and the writ available is inappropriate to the case. The writ patent did not take shape as an authorisation by which lords could exercise 'proprietary' jurisdiction: it was an order to the lord to accept the demandant as his tenant.[3] Formally, therefore, it was appropriate for the upward and the horizontal claim; but it never made sense when William was making the downward claim against Thomas, and his right as Ralph's tenant was not in dispute.

This feature of the tenurial topography is relevant to the evolution of the writs of entry, but it is not a complete explanation. Mr Hall's work on entry *sur disseisin*, for which Maitland saw a sudden legislative authorisation, should warn us that the evolution may have been slower and less distinct than we have supposed.[4] Nor is it just a matter of the earliest writs being issued as a special favour and for special payment. There is a pre-natal history within the writs of right: what demandants first pay for is an inquest upon a special issue. The point is tellingly made in a case of 1203, which begins with three angry sisters bringing what looks like a variant form of mort d'ancestor: was their brother, whose heir they are, seised on the day he took to his death-bed? From other entries we can make out their real grievance. Near the end of his life the brother married a woman whose claim to dower the sisters are also contesting, and granted this land for homage to some relation of hers, the present tenant. The tenant says the brother was healthy

---

[1] Below, pp. 115 ff.   [2] Above, pp. 80 ff.   [3] Above, pp. 58 ff.
[4] Hall, 'The Early History of Entry sur Disseisin', *Tulane Law Review*, XLII (1968), 584; Pollock and Maitland, *History of English Law* (2nd ed.), II, pp. 64 f.

at the time, eating and drinking and riding; and at a later date the matter would clearly have been settled in a writ of entry *dum non compos mentis*. But the writ the sisters have got is quashed. *Non est de assisa regni*, says one roll austerely, but another is more informative: *talis jurata non solet fieri nisi emersisset de brevi de recto. . .et habeant breve de recto si voluerint*.[1]

How would such a jury emerge from a writ of right? Let us use the later language of pleading to analyse the action the sisters should have brought. They must count on the seisin of their brother, knowing that this is a ritual because the fact is not disputed. Even if the tenant does not seek formally to repel the claim on the ground that the sisters should warrant him, his answer is in substance a confession and avoidance: he admits the brother's seisin, but claims to hold of the sisters by virtue of the grant. The invalidity of that grant, the true ground of the sisters' claim, is in principle a replication to that; and a jury will emerge if they are allowed to stake the case upon the special issue: did the tenant have *ingressum* otherwise than *per* the brother who granted it to him *dum non fuit compos mentis sue*? We do not know whether there was such an unrecorded dialogue, or whether the demandant would propose his issue immediately after his count. Nor do we know exactly what was in his mind, or in that of the court. He might feel that the general issue would be misleading; and sometimes he may even have stated the *ingressum* only to ensure that it was not overlooked by the knights.[2] But usually he sought to avoid the grand assize altogether, and for this several arguments of principle were open to him: these are recent facts for which the grand assize is generally inappropriate; it is particularly inappropriate because, if the tenant is right, they are lord and man;[3] and anyway his own hereditary right is not in issue. But the only argument the clerk recorded, indeed the only evidence we usually have that he was asking for a special issue, is a proffer of money. In the

---

[1] The sisters' action against the grantee: *CRR*, II, *251*, 253 (Mara). The dower action: *CRR*, II, *227*, *251*, 287–8. Other mentions of writs *contra assisam regni*: (*a*) *CRR*, I, *95*; *CRR*, VII, 348 (Sifrewast); *CRR*, III, *120*; (*b*) *CRR*, I, *390*, 439 (earl Patrick); *PKJ*, I, *3400*; cf. *CRR*, I, *422*; *PKJ*, I, *3470*. For a claim in principle like that of the sisters, and expressly *per breve de recto*, see below, p. 97 at n. 1. For death-bed gifts, etc., see below, pp. 121 ff.

[2] For a verdict in which, unusually, the knights give reasons, explaining an *ingressum* by seignorial action, see *CRR*, IV, 58–9 (full references above, p. 6, n. 2).

[3] Above, pp. 84–5, on proof between lord and man.

end, whether to forestall any possibility of a general issue on the right, or whether to cut off the roundabout writ patent, tolt, and *pone*, he came to make his proffer earlier and have the issue formulated in the writ.

Our difficulty is that even this may be indistinguishable on the plea roll. In 1218–19 a claim was brought on the same basis as that of the three sisters: the demandant alleged *ingressum* through his mother *dum...jacuit in lecto mortali de egritudine qua obiit*. It looks so like a writ of entry that the clerk himself must have been struck, and he made a note in the margin: *per breue de recto*.[1] The problem is most strikingly displayed in cases which begin with an *ingressum* and end with the downward grand assize.[2] The grand assize might seem to show that the *ingressum* was not in the writ; but if Bracton is to be believed, this is not so. He says that issue may be taken in the right even on a writ of entry, if the demandant has counted in the right.[3] The possibility that this learning itself grew from a misunderstanding at least brings out the slippery nature of the evidence: Bracton, like ourselves, may have been too ready to assume that an *ingressum* in the roll was also in the writ. We will take a clear case, and see what makes it clear. In 1204 a bishop of London claims something as part of his barony, so it is anyway likely that the writ was a *precipe*. He makes a normal count in the right, relying on the seisin of his predecessor on the day Henry I died; and we are lucky that this is not abbreviated as *ut jus suum etc.*, but enrolled in some detail. Then follows the *ingressum*, though we cannot tell whether it was tacked on to the count or provoked by something said by the tenant: *et in quam ...nullum habet ingressum nisi per predecessores suos, qui alienare vel dare nichil potuerunt ab episcopatu nisi in vita sua...* And then

---

[1] *Yorks.*, 1127; *CRR*, VIII, *80*. Cf. *CRR*, IV, 268 (Eustace f. William); *CRR*, V, *11*, *32*, where *per breve de recto* is in the body of the entry.

[2] Cases other than those specifically discussed: (*a*) *RCR*, I, *278*, *405*; *CRR*, I, 122–3 (demandant claims to hold of king so presumably *precipe*), 188; (*b*) *CRR*, IV, 229, 236 (Crevequor; this *op. se* entry suggests that the *ingressum* was here in the writ), *286*; *CRR*, V, 108, *195*; (*c*) *CRR*, XIII, 162, 1518, *1978, 2674*; *BNB*, 323; (*d*) the case below, p. 158, n. 1. For a case in which the *ingressum* (essentially *cui in vita*) is alleged after the tenant has proposed the grand assize, see *CRR*, III, *59, 204, 223, 224, 233, 274, 296, 297*; *CRR*, IV, 34–5, 56, *118–19, 146–7, 169*.

[3] Bracton, ff. 326–326b, where, however, he also contemplates a writ of right, a count *de iure suo per descensum*, and then *si tempus probationis permiserit, in fine post descensum bene poterit descendere ad ingressum per haec verba: et unde talis non habet ingressum nisi per talem cui etcetera...* Cf. *Brevia Placitata*, pp. lxxviii f.

comes another piece of luck: the words '*et offert etc.*' show that the *ingressum* was by way of proffer for a jury, neither just for the information of the knights nor included in the writ. Finally, we are lucky in having another enrolment, some two years later, which sounds purely in the right: no *ingressum* is mentioned, and the tenant ends by seeking the grand assize with special mise.[1] But what could we have made of it if there was only the first enrolment, and if that had omitted the proffer and abbreviated the count? By chance, that is what survives from an apparently similar dispute of 1203. A canon claims land *sicut jus prebende sue de Stafford' et in quam non habet ingressum nisi per Ailmerum Presbiterum, qui ei terram illam dedit et eum inde feffavit injuste*...The tenant says he should hold of the demandant, as did his predecessors of the demandant's predecessors, and goes to the grand assize; and we just cannot tell what the *ingressum* clause represents.[2]

It follows that we equally cannot tell when the *ingressum* takes the form of a known writ of entry. In 1202 a tenant goes to the grand assize with special mise on a claim which reads as though it was made by writ of gage *ad terminum qui preteriit*.[3] Perhaps it was, but we must not assume it: in 1206 a demandant is said to claim *sicut jus suum per breve de recto, et in quas non habet ingressum nisi per* a gage[4], and in 1200, although the writ is not named, there is a full count in the right alleging seisin on the day Henry I died, followed by an allegation of *ingressum* by gage and a proffer for a jury thereon.[5] Another case of 1200, in which again we cannot tell whether the gage was in the writ, may suggest an explanation of these cases which end in the grand assize. The tenant seeks to put himself on the assize, and is refused on the ground that he admits the gage and has no sufficient proof of a subsequent grant in fee

[1] *CRR*, III, 181; *CRR*, IV, 74–5, *139*. The tenant's case seems to rest upon tenure *a conquestu Anglie*, the grant being only a confirmation of this.

[2] *CRR*, II, *223*, 229 (prior of St Thomas's, Stafford), 233, *281*. Cf. the claim based on a predecessor's 'loan', apparently not formulated with an *ingressum*, in *CRR*, VI, *276*, *282*, 309 (Neville).

[3] *PKJ*, II, 785. Cf. *CRR*, I, 119–20, *186*, where battle is offered on similar facts; the parties figure in other interesting litigation, below, p. 117, n. 4.

[4] *CRR*, IV, 268 (Eustace f. William); *CRR*, V, *11*, *32*; the tenant prays age, and the demandant *reliquid breve illud...et vult perquirere utilius breve*.

[5] This litigation began with a defective writ of gage: *RCR*, I, *231*, 306 (Garwinton), 312; *PKJ*, I, *2619*; *RCR*, II, 46–7 (*sine die quia breve non est de cursu*), 58. Then the second action was commenced: *RCR*, II, *128*, *281*; *CRR*, I, 158, 220. Cf. *Staffs.*, 61 (Adam f. Randolph), *168*, where the gage looks just as though it is in the writ, but there is a proffer.

on which he relies.[1] Compare this with one last example of a case which does get to the grand assize, this time beginning with *ingressum* through a husband, essentially *sur cui in vita*. In 1202 Henry son of Joel claims land *ut ius suum*. *In que non habent ingressum nisi per predictum Joelem patrem suum qui nichil iuris habuit in terra illa nisi per Biatricem matrem suam cuius hereditas terra illa fuit*. Before going to the grand assize, the tenants assert that the grant was by Joel and Beatrice jointly, and that Beatrice took homage after Joel's death, and Henry himself after Beatrice's death.[2] Certainly in these last two cases, and possibly in the other *ingressum* cases in which the grand assize is claimed, the *ingressum* is not so much denied as confessed and avoided; and this may be why the special issue was resisted.

Cases ending in the grand assize have been segregated only for clarity. They emphasise the association between '*ingressum*' and the downward claim as evidenced in the special mise. And they militate against the assumption, to which we cling in defiance even of Bracton, that writs of entry were a creation fundamentally distinct from writs of right: we see 'forms of action' where our sources are preoccupied only with proof. But the immediate lesson applies to all *ingressum* cases: what looks on the plea rolls like a writ of entry may not be. Confident identifications have been made.[3] But, while the enrolment of words of proffer and the like often shows that an *ingressum* was not in the writ, the rolls themselves hardly ever show that it was.[4] The best chance lies in the verbal

---

[1] *PKJ*, I, *2710*; *CRR*, I, 188 (Gaie). Proof could be difficult in such cases; *Gloucs.*, *1387*, 1477.   [2] *Beds.*, 101.

[3] e.g., *RCR*, II, 168; *PKJ*, I, 3157, and editorial discussion at pp. 19, 74 ff.

[4] Occasionally the *ingressum* appears in a formal *optulit se* entry, and this may suggest that it was in the writ: (a) *CRR*, III, 40 (Laurence f. Reginald): (b) *CRR*, IV, *229*, 236 (Crevequor), *286*; *CRR*, V, 108, *195*. But cf. *CRR*, VI, 97 (Hostiarius), where an *optulit se* in debt gives detail one would expect only in the count. The following are cases not otherwise here mentioned in which it is more or less clear that the *ingressum* was not in the writ. Proffers: (a) *PKJ*, I, *2474*; *CRR*, I, 159 (Rivere), 324; (b) *CRR*, I, *115*, *122*, *153*, 156 (Querendon), *290*, 357–8, 410, 412, *467*, *468*; (c) *CRR*, VI, 41 (Heriet), *122*, 233 (essoin *de malo lecti*), 246 (proffer increased), *293*, *312*; (d) *CRR*, VI, 46–7, *101*; (e) *CRR*, VI, *197*, *258*, 393–4. No proffer by demandant recorded, but *ingressum* alleged after an ordinary count in the right: (a) *CRR*, II, 50 (Margaret f. Basilia); (b) *CRR*, VII, 7 (Henry f. Adam; essoin *de malo lecti*), 27, 102, *121*, 260–1 and, less clear, (c) *CRR*, III, *32*, 290 (Sine Averio; essoin *de malo lecti*); *PKJ*, III, 1191; *CRR*, IV, 129, *169–70*, 227. The *ingressum* may be provoked, with or without a proffer, by an offer of battle or grand assize when the parties are of one stock: (a) *PRS*, XIV, *21–2*, *56*; *RCR*, I, 22–3, 26; *PRS*(NS), XXXI, *110*; *PKJ*, I, *3361*, *3422*; for

comparison of twin enrolments. In 1200, for example, such a pair both begin with the words '*Preceptum fuit...quod reddat*' and are identical to the end of what must be a recital of the writ, even making the same grammatical mistake which is pleasingly noted by the editor in one but not in the other; and thereafter they differ.[1] But few cases are so clear: small discrepancies render the comparison inconclusive even when the approximation is closest.[2]

If anything, indeed, comparison of related enrolments tends to reduce the number of cases in which it is likely that the *ingressum* was in the writ, because an enrolment including a contrary indication such as words of proffer may infect others which in themselves could represent writs. Consider claims made on the same basis by the same lady against three separate tenants in 1202. The first could unhesitatingly be read as a writ of entry *cui in vita*.[3] Of the second there are two enrolments: one in itself seems equally clear; but in the other the *ingressum* is stated in different language and the tenant offers battle.[4] And in the third of her claims the demandant makes a full count in the right ending with the required tender of battle; and this is followed by a proffer for a jury to say whether the tenants have *alium ingressum uel aliud juris* than through her husband.[5] The likelihood is that even the first of her

related litigation, see below, p. 146, n. 2; (*b*) RCR, I, 358–9; *PKJ*, I, *2129, 2516, 2763*; CRR, I, *222*. A claim of court suggests that the *ingressum* was not in the writ, where the *ingressum* shows that the demandant does not claim to hold of that lord; CRR, IV, 60 (abbot of Missenden), 123, 141–2, 221–2. Good illustrations of the general difficulty are claims by Gilbert de Gant based upon dispositions supposed to have been made by earl Simon, the husband of Gilbert's cousin Alice who inherited the barony but died without issue soon after the earl: (*a*) against Gilbert de Lacy, CRR, III, 295; (*b*) against the prior of Sempringham, CRR, III, *175, 232*; CRR, IV, 126–7, *166, 195*; (*c*) against Ralph de Bruiera who vouches Renfrey f. Roger, CRR, III, *263, 301, 334, 347*; CRR, IV, *10, 40,* 42–3, especially p. 42, n. 2.

[1] CRR, I, 182, 249–50, *294, 452, 476*.

[2] Sometimes the clerk may be abbreviating the terms of a writ: (*a*) Lincs., 215, 1154; (*b*) CRR, VII, *36,* 85, 122–3, *277?*, 282 (but this third enrolment has a puzzling addition). A change of word may be harder to explain, CRR, VII, 46 (Robert f. Gilbert; *dimisit*), 108 (*invadiavit*), *133*; especially when abbreviation must also be postulated, CRR, III, 92–3 (*dedit*), 114 (*tradidit*). Sometimes it seems unlikely that the two enrolments were composed from the same text, CRR, VII, 106 (Windlesores; essoin *de malo lecti*), 107, *218–19*, 231.

[3] Lincs., 484.   [4] Lincs., 268, *1099, 1108,* 1127.

[5] Lincs., *246, 262, 1101, 1111, 1128,* 1177, *1205*. Consider also parallel claims based upon the same *ingressum* by a dead father upon land which his two sons have divided between them: (*a*) CRR, II, *171, 245*; CRR, III, 82 (Ramescumbe), *333*; CRR, IV, *106, 232, 301*; (*b*) CRR, II, *171*; CRR, III, 37–8, 242–3; CRR,

claims was by writ of right, and looks like a writ of entry only because of clerical abbreviation.

What we can learn about from the rolls, then, is the rise of the practice by which demandants sought to formulate their case in terms of the tenant's *ingressum*. What we cannot learn about is the inclusion of that formulation in the writ. We cannot date the writs of entry from this source, and they are probably later than we have thought. The best evidence would be actual writs themselves, but few survive from this early period. Of the eighty odd printed by Lady Stenton only three are relevant and they all concern gage.[1] Then there are Registers. The two earliest printed in the Selden Society volume, probably dating from the 1220s, each gives two writs of entry only: *ad terminum qui preteriit* and *cui in vita*.[2] The absence of other forms has seemed surprising in the light of the plea rolls;[3] but it may be the rolls that are misleading.

We are not necessarily turning away from the question of chronology if we take one last look at the reason of the thing. Why did the writs of entry develop? We may have been misled by the rolls into antedating them because we have thought in terms of possessory protection and transfer of jurisdiction, and have seen the writs of entry as following on from novel disseisin and mort d'ancestor almost by way of extension. It is a view which leaves little room for special issues in writs of right; and the evidence of the rolls requires the question to be put differently. Why did it become the general practice to write the *ingressum* into the writ itself? At least a part of the answer is probably the Great Charter. For these downward claims the writ patent was needed, but by a juristic accident and inappropriately. The question which feudal principle required to be put to Ralph's court was whether William was entitled to be Ralph's tenant; and when William makes his downward claim against Thomas that is not in dispute. The Charter meant only to safeguard the principle. It caused the disappearance of Glanvill's undifferentiated *precipe*.[4] *Precipe* writs

iv, *86*. The principal enrolment in the first has only a proffer to show that the *ingressum* is not in the writ, and hides most of the facts disclosed by the principal enrolment of the second.

[1] The writs are printed in *PKJ*, I, pp. 350–418, and *PKJ*, III, pp. xi–xii. The relevant three are *PKJ*, I, 3487, 3506 (both formulated with *ingressum*), 3538 (which should be compared with *Glanvill*, x, 9).

[2] *Registers*: Hib. 25, 26; CA 11, 12.   [3] Hall, *Registers*, pp. xlii f.

[4] Clanchy, 'Magna Carta, Clause Thirty-Four', *English Historical Review*, LXXIX (1964), 542 ff.

were now supplied with clauses explaining why the matter could come directly to the king's court: the land is claimed *in capite*, or the lord has waived his jurisdiction. The proliferation of the writs of entry looks like a part of this process. The *ingressum* equally shows why the case need not be put to the lord: it is not about the demandant's relationship with him.

4

GRANTS

Any study of early grants is subject to confusion. One cause is their diversity: the royal control which so quickly standardised litigation was slower to eliminate variations between customary arrangements, and a transaction unthinkable in Northamptonshire may have been commonplace in Norfolk. Another is the uneven survival of evidence. The grants most systematically preserved were those made by fine and those involving religious houses, and inferences may not apply to private grants between laymen. But the greatest difficulties are in our own minds. A modern deed of grant is the actual disposition; and if we remember livery of seisin at all, it is as a formality to be evaded. But charters were evidence, and the actual grant was made in a context not recorded, commonly, it seems, in a court.[1] This links with the most intractable of our assumptions. We suppose a once-for-ever transfer of something like ownership; and whether or not the grantee can likewise pass that ownership on by his own voluntary act, we see it as passing on his death to his heir as by a modern rule of intestate succession. Conveyance, inheritance, litigation: for us these are distinct processes transferring or determining abstract rights. The ancient reality, preserved into later times only in the formalities of copyhold, saw all three as preliminaries to what mattered: the lord's acceptance of this tenant.

Our assumptions have allowed us to speak of alienability without always distinguishing between substitution and subinfeudation. And when we have made the distinction, we have either reduced it to a lawyer's technicality or assumed the early possibility of substitution without the lord's consent. Plucknett's view of *Quia emptores* exemplifies both: it was a conveyancing act 'with the modification of the *habendum et tenendum* clause of deeds as its immediate object'[2] and in permitting substitution against the lord's will it was declaratory of what had existed for some time.[3]

---

[1] Below, pp. 115–16.   [2] *Legislation of Edward I*, p. 106.   [3] Ibid. p. 104.

Apparently, indeed, it had existed since the beginning of Henry III's
reign: of an admittedly obscure provision in the Charter of
1217 he observes that 'the lord already seems unable to resist
having a corporate tenant thrust upon him'.[1] It is the gist of
this book that in his view of the actions and of the ideas behind
them, Maitland did not sufficiently reckon with the feudal
dimension. But he reckoned with it in connection with grants,
and his chronology is not Plucknett's. Early substitutions, he
observes, are found in fines. 'As regards modes of conveyance less
solemn than a fine, had it not been for Bracton's distinct assertion,
we should probably have come to the opinion that a new tenant...
could not be forced upon an unwilling lord.'[2] We shall return to
Bracton's assertion: it may be less distinct than we have supposed,
and *Quia emptores* correspondingly more important.[3]

Glanvill has a problem. If one recovers land by a concord made
in court, from someone who has already paid relief for it, does he
have to pay relief again? Glanvill is uncertain of the answer;[4] but
what matters is the case in which the question arises. He does not
ask whether relief is due from a private grantee by substitution.
That was not a thinkable transaction without the lord's acceptance,
for which payment could naturally be asked. Of course this is not
stated: the unthinkable never is. But it is assumed throughout the
book, coming nearest to the surface over the marriage of heiresses,
when again the general assumption is emphasised by the particular
problem. Relief cannot be demanded from a second or subsequent
husband,[5] and this needs saying because the lord's consent is
necessary to any marriage. It does not matter that the marriage is
not the first, in which case a relief has already been paid, or that
the lady is only heiress-presumptive, in which case no relief is yet
due. The lord must consent 'lest he be forced to receive homage
for his fee from an enemy or some otherwise unsuitable person';

---

[1] Ibid. p. 95, discussing *Magna Carta* (1217), c. 43; (1225), c. 36. For the
interposition of a religious house between tenant and lord, see *Gloucs., 1368,
1450, 1531*: finding himself *grauatum de duro dominio* of the lord, the tenant
reddidit ei terram illam et homagium suum per sic quod illam daret to the house;
the lord did so; and the house remained in seisin for a day or two before regrant-
ing to the tenant to hold of itself. The lord may have been deceived about the
intention, but the substitution of the house as his tenant was by surrender and
admittance and in no way against his will.

[2] Pollock and Maitland, *History of English Law* (2nd ed.), I, p. 345.

[3] Below, pp. 152–3.   [4] *Glanvill*, IX, 3.

[5] *Glanvill*, IX, 4.

and the ultimate sanction is disinheritance.[1] The assumption is the same as that behind the writ patent: only the lord's acceptance can make a tenant.

But of course it was the point of the writ patent that the lord could be compelled to accept a tenant; and this is reflected in the other facet of Glanvill's problem. It arises over a fine because by fine a tenant can be imposed upon the lord.[2] Fines form too large a topic for this book; but we must not think of an early resort to collusive litigation as a conscious device, or suppose that the purpose was to gain just evidential security. Fines appear to have been common in seignorial courts; and a fine made in the lord's court was not in principle different from a charter of feoffment made by the lord and witnessed by his court. Whether or not in settlement of a dispute, any rearrangement of rights required acceptance by the lord and the community within which the rights existed. And so long as there was only the lord's court, the acceptance was conclusive: if William surrenders his tenement to Ralph who then admits Thomas in William's place,[3] or if the same result is reached by concord between William and Thomas in Ralph's court, all parties are as secure as their world allows. But this depends upon that supreme authority which Stenton saw in seignorial courts sanctioning such transactions,[4] and the security is gone when the court is no longer sovereign. If the king's law may later upset the arrangement with a writ of right at the instance of William's heir, Thomas may wish to bar the heir's

---

[1] *Glanvill*, VII, 12.

[2] Pollock and Maitland, *History of English Law* (2nd ed.), I, p. 345. Fines to hold of the chief lord are commonly silent about his consent, e.g., Hunter, *Fines*, II, pp. 7, 8–9 (where the presence and consent of a tenant is noted), 12–13. But sometimes his presence is recorded: (*a*) ibid. p. 59; (*b*) *CRR*, v, *63, 156, 163, 175,* 231 (Mora); and once the court requires his acknowledgment before passing the fine, *PKJ*, I, *2801, 2852*; *RCR*, II, *223*; *CRR*, I, 367–8 (a tenant and 24 men owing service are also to come, all *in adventu justiciariorum*). One lord apparently (pronouns uncertain) sues his tenant for making a fine *eo absente*; *PKJ*, II, *954,* 974, 1044, *1208*; *CRR*, III, *44.* Another simply disseises him; *CRR*, II, 44–5. But it is said to be lawful to make a fine *salvo jure capitalis domini*; *RCR*, II, 139 (Furnivall; traces of the earlier proceedings in that case also survive, *RCR*, I, *104, 111*; *PKJ*, I, *2525*; *RCR*, II, *14, 40*; *PKJ*, II, *1165*). And one fine to which the lord was not a party still apparently imposed on the grantee a requirement that he should consent to any further disposition; *CRR*, II, 97 (Warenne), *122,* 133, *224*; *CRR*, III, *24,* 24–5.

[3] For charter examples, see *Charters of the Honour of Mowbray, 1107–1191,* ed. Greenway, nos. 290, 333.

[4] *The First Century of English Feudalism* (2nd ed.), pp. 51 ff.

claim in the jurisdiction in which it exists: it is substantive assurance that he seeks when he concludes his transaction with William in the king's court rather than in Ralph's. Nor is Ralph entirely the loser by this. If he accepts Thomas in William's place on his own authority, and William's heir has Thomas put out on the king's authority, Thomas will turn to the king and compel Ralph to find *escambium*. From the beginning it may have been inevitable that the lord's loss of control would be complete. But that was a century and a statute away from Glanvill, for whom the lord's will could be overridden only by direct resort to the king's court.

Assumptions seem to be unchanged in the earliest rolls, and must be sought in what is not said. Take dower, for example. The logic of the widow's action against a grantee from her husband depends upon the grant being by subinfeudation.[1] But the nearest we get to an express statement is a formula with which the tenant sometimes answers: 'I am not your husband's heir and hold nothing of him.'[2] It would be a poor answer if substitutions were common. In fact they are rare on the rolls; and some that we do find are there for security rather than because of any dispute.[3] Consider an entry of 1207. William brings a writ of right against Ralph, relying on the seisin of his grandfather; and if everything was done properly, it would have been a writ patent to Ralph himself which reached the king's court by tolt and *pone*. In the king's court the following things happen: Ralph recognises that William is entitled to hold of him; William thereupon concedes all his right in the land to Thomas to hold of Ralph; Ralph now recognises that Thomas is entitled to hold of him; the court adjudges seisin to Thomas; and Thomas does homage to Ralph.[4] This is a surrender and admittance at second hand; and probably Ralph had no court. But powerful fears must have prompted so elaborate a conveyance for eight acres.

The few actual disputes involving substitutions nearly always

---

[1] Above, pp. 43 and 72–3.

[2] (a) RCR, I, 80 (Robert f. Roscelin); (b) RCR, II, *38*; PKJ, I, *2507*; CRR, I, *158*, 160 (Boliton), *324* (there are many entries of claims against other tenants).

[3] Cases not otherwise here discussed: (a) PRS(NS), XXXI, 106 (Rollesbi); (b) CRR, I, 372–3; (c) Lincs.-Worcs., 909 (note that the writ of *warantia carte* supposes tenure between the parties, whereas the charter recorded shows a substitution).

[4] CRR, v, *4*, 34 (Thomas f. Alexander).

mention something which shows the lord's acceptance.[1] Sometimes we are told it was done in the lord's court,[2] and perhaps this is generally to be understood. In one case, involving a grant by substitution from father to younger son, the witnesses to the relevant charter are named in the enrolment; and they were probably members of the lord's court.[3] This was shown by Stenton to be so when the same arrangement was made in another lordship sometime before 1140.[4] Except for mysterious goings-on in East Anglia, the lord's participation can be taken for granted.

Even when the lord consents in advance to a substitution, giving his tenant an express power to assign, he seems still actively to accept the assignee. In one case the substituted tenant produces not only the charter by which the lord gave his original tenant the power to assign, but also a second charter by which the lord confirmed the substitution of himself and acknowledged the taking of his homage.[5] Another case deserves a longer look. There are three relevant brothers, in order of seniority William, Henry, and Thomas; and in 1205 William as heir claims land which had been Henry's and is now in the possession of Thomas. This is a pattern we shall meet again; and if Henry had got the land from their father, William would have been excluded and Thomas entitled by the rule against being lord and heir. But Henry had got it from a stranger lord, who had granted it to him with power to assign to

---

[1] Cases not otherwise here discussed: (a) *CRR*, III, 281–2 (verdict showing that on death of tenant lord *reddidit* tenement to heir *sicut jus suum*, and heir at once sold to third party who *devenit homo* of the lord; full references below, p. 117, n. 4); (b) *CRR*, IV, *181, 209, 231, 294*; *CRR*, V, *23, 58, 142, 143–4* (tenant *resignavit et quietum clamavit ad opus* of religious house; but since we cannot tell whether or not the claim itself is 'upward', this may represent just a surrender without an admittance); (c) *RCR*, I, *282, 294–5*; *RCR*, II, *73, 239*; *PKJ*, I, *2353, 2716*; *CRR*, I, 150 (Catesclive; confirmation of lord); (d) *CRR*, VI, 180–1 (charter by which religious house confirms land sold by former tenant, makes new grant of other land; it is produced on a voucher in litigation of which many entries survive); (e) *CRR*, I, *172, 193,* 240–1, *270* (royal confirmation of a substitution in chief; much associated litigation survives); (f) *Lincs.-Worcs.*, 256 (lord knew of grant and sought to uphold remainder).

[2] *Lincs.-Worcs.*, 898, where we learn how the conveyance was made only because the circumstances have to be explained. Cf. the grant made in the court of king Henry II recited in *PKJ*, I, *2037, 2400*; *CRR*, I, *129, 178–9, 455*; *CRR*, II, *70, 83*.

[3] *CRR*, VII, *338*; *RCR*, II, 88–9; *PKJ*, I, *2973*; *CRR*, I, *179, 180, 226*; cf. F. M. Stenton, *The First Century of English Feudalism* (2nd ed.), Appendix, no. 7, pp. 263–4, a composition in the court of earl Ferrers also witnessed by William Pantulf.   [4] Stenton, op. cit. p. 55.

[5] *PKJ*, IV, *3018, 3106*; *CRR*, V, *190, 299*; *CRR*, VI, 147–8.

anyone except men of religion. Thomas's case is that Henry had
assigned to him, giving him the land to hold of the lord; and the
issue is whether this gift had been completed.[1] William says that
Henry had died or entered religion seised, and that Thomas
*nullum saisinam vel introitum habet in terram illam nisi per capitalem
dominum, qui eum in saisina posuit.*[2]

But the case suggests more than that the lord put the assignee in.
Why did Henry take his grant in that form? Bracton has a theory
that powers to assign were invented for bastards, who will have no
heirs if they die childless so that ordinary grants will escheat.[3]
If this is true, our case is not an example: William's claim as heir
shows that Henry was indeed childless but not a bastard. But if
we put a sort of collapsible ownership out of our minds, and think
instead of relationships, we can imagine Henry and the bastard
asking the same question: who will warrant this land after my
death? Henry clearly did not want William to get his land, and
may have had Thomas in mind from the outset. If he made
a downward grant to him, it would be William to whom Thomas
would later look for warranty, and two dangers would arise: if
William himself later died childless, Thomas would be hit by the
lord-and-heir rule; and, more serious, we shall see that the
warranty of an elder brother was not something to which one
could look forward with confidence.[4]

Whether or not powers to assign later played a part in increasing
the frequency of substitution, they are rare in the early rolls.[5] And
some of the few examples found seem to be there for security. The
preoccupation with warranty is particularly clear in two entries in

---

[1] Cf. Bracton, f. 20b on gifts to bastards with power to assign: *si in vita sua
terram assignaverit hora congrua et tempore competenti...valebit assignatio et
donatio quamvis heredes de corpore suo defecerint...*

[2] There were in fact five brothers, and Henry seems to have made similar
gifts to two others, one of whom apparently granted over to the abbey of
Thornton Curtis; *CRR*, III, *185*, *323-4*, *330*; *PKJ*, III, *1546*, *1674?*, *1874*, *2101*;
CRR, IV, *60*, *76*, *135*, *138*, *153*.   [3] Bracton, ff. 12b, 20b.

[4] Lord and heir: below, pp. 139 ff. Grant to younger son or younger
brother: below, pp. 133 ff.

[5] Plea roll examples not here specifically discussed, in all of which a charter
is either enrolled verbatim or summarised: (*a*) *CRR*, V, 202–4; (*b*) *Lincs.-Worcs.*,
530; (*c*) ibid. 556; (*d*) *Gloucs.*, *517* (grantee *capellanus*); (*e*) ibid. 635 (grantee
presbiter); (*f*) ibid. 639; (*g*) *BNB*, 804; *CRR*, XV, 553. Charters: Douglas, *The
Social Structure of Medieval East Anglia*, Oxford Studies in Social and Legal
History, vol. IX, Appendix I, no. 65, p. 258; *Charters of the Honour of Mowbray*,
1107–1191, ed. Greenway, no. 335 (*possit dare cui fratrum suorum voluerit ad
tenendum de me et heredibus meis*).

which the object seems to have been to make sure of the future warranty of the grantor's heir apparent. Once he is improbably joined in an altogether improbable action.[1] And once, after a warranty action between grantee and grantor in which the charter is enrolled verbatim, the clerk adds a note: *sciendum* that the grantor's heir *presens fuit et predictam warantiam concessit*.[2] These are not owners anxious about warranty as an ancillary to their ownership, but parties to an arrangement trying to provide for a change of parties.

This had been true also of an ordinary grant mentioning heirs rather than assigns: the heir became entitled by force of the lord's acceptance of himself, not by force of the grant to his ancestor. It is therefore no surprise that we find substitutions using the language of inheritance. Instead of asking his lord to accept a substituted tenant now, the present tenant may try to 'make' an heir for the lord to accept after his death. This may be what the unlucky Henry wanted to do in the case of the three brothers just discussed. But, as that case illustrates, royal justice has made the position of the natural heir extremely strong, indefeasible if the original tenant dies seised.[3] One tenant, old or ill, retired into the abbey from which he held his land. According to them he surrendered his tenement. But still *suscepit ut heredem* another, whom the abbey later put out; and against his ensuing claim they set up not only the surrender but also a fine they have made with the natural heir.[4] In another case, the lord eventually co-operated, taking the homage of one whom his original tenant *constituit heredum suum*; but he did so only after a law-suit in which the natural heir warranted.[5] So long as there was only the lord's court, this arrangement had presumably been effective and land to that extent devisable. It is royal interference that has subjected it to the will of the natural heir as well as of the lord.[6]

---

[1] *CRR*, v, 233 (Harebi).

[2] *CRR*, IV, 136–7 (*licebit...assignare...cui voluerit, et eciam, si voluerit, viris religiossis*).

[3] Cf. *Glanvill*, VII, 1: *Potest itaque quilibet sic totum questum suum in uita donare sed nullum heredem inde facere potest...quia solus Deus heredem facere potest, non homo.*   [4] *CRR*, I, 265, 267 (Tokeville), 421.

[5] *PRS*(NS), XXXI, 80 (Criket); *CRR*, II, 183, 204. Note the language used by the lord (lady): she admits that she *dedisse* to the original tenant and *postea concessisse* to the 'constituted' heir; but in fact she warranted him against a third party, and had to find *escambium*.

[6] Cf. *Glanvill*, VII, 1: *Posset tamen huiusmodi donatio in ultima uoluntate alicui facta ita tenere si cum consensu heredis fieret et ex suo consensu confirmaretur.*

Describing a concord in the court of earl Ferrers between 1162
and 1166 by which the heir of a tenant passed his right of succession
to a younger brother, Stenton picked out the underlying assumption: the lordship was a self-contained unit, and its court had
final authority to sanction such a rearrangement.[1] Yet in the early
rolls, only a generation later, lords' courts seem regularly to sanction
only one departure from the natural course of inheritance, and
that is an acceleration. A living tenant resigns in favour of his heir,
whose homage the lord takes. Once the phrase *heredem constituit*
is used;[2] and if the beneficiary happens to die first it can alter the
devolution of the inheritance.[3] Usually it makes no difference
except to this father and son, and we shall consider the arrangement
for its own sake with other family gifts at the end of this chapter.
But it is appropriately mentioned last in a survey of early substitutions, because it marks the point of their greatest constriction.
Acceptance by the lord and his court had always been necessary.
It ceased to be sufficient when the heirs of the old tenant could in
the king's court seek the ouster of the new. Only the substitution
of the heir himself was invulnerable and remained frequent. And
we shall see that in some sense it was from this that, in the
thirteenth century, a new freedom of substitution was to grow.[4]

*   *   *

In turning to subinfeudation we must not suppose that we are
turning from one conveyancing mechanism to another. So long as
the tenurial relationship mattered in peoples' lives the two were
quite different; and in any given situation the one would be
natural and the other not. Except at the humblest level, subinfeudation would no doubt be the more frequent. No doubt also

---

[1] *The First Century of English Feudalism* (2nd ed.), pp. 51–4. In the early rolls
only two references have been noted to such arrangements between the sons of
a mesne tenant. In one the elder *resignavit...et remisit* to the younger *totum jus
et clamium quod habuit in hereditate patris sui*; *CRR*, VII, *190, 288, 321, 322–5*
(the part played by Gilbert Foliot, bishop of London, places the supposed
transaction before 1187). In the other the concession was apparently made by
the son of the elder son, conceivably in settlement of a *casus regis* dispute: *omne
jus quod habet in terra illa concessit sibi in curia comitis Britannie*; *CRR*, I, *72*
(full references above, p. 71, n. 2). But such arrangements were made in the
king's court, especially over Anglo-Norman inheritances: (*a*) *CRR*, V, *189–90*;
(*b*) *CRR*, VI, *397–9*.   [2] *CRR* I, *363* (Burnes).
[3] *Casus regis;* below, p. 147.   [4] Below, pp. 152–3.

some desired substitutions would fail to gain the lord's consent, which was not just a matter of persuasion or payment: the splitting of a tenement, for example, might be unacceptable. But substitutions still seem unnaturally rare on the early rolls, perhaps avoided for fear of that ineradicable hereditary claim in the king's court. Suppose a situation in which the parties would desire a substitution, and in which the lord would not object. The grantee may still apprehend a claim by some heir of the grantor, and the lord a consequential claim for *escambium*. One safeguard is for the parties themselves to go to the king's court and entrench their arrangement in a fine. Another is for the grantor to take his grantee's homage. This creates a warranty which will descend to keep his heirs out. But the cost is an artificial tenure with an artificial lord who may have no court, and with services that *ex hypothesi* are also artificial in the sense of not being desired. Artificiality is hard to detect in legal records, and we shall not see it in individual cases. But the difficulties which the king's law had finally to face in *Quia emptores* were to an unknown extent of its own making.

The principal questions about subinfeudation have long been asked, though sometimes in the misleading terms of 'restraints on alienation'. This supposes an owner whose prima facie freedom is being restrained, and our grantor is not an owner. Ralph granted land to William, and undertook in the grant that William's heirs should have it after him. William now makes a similar downward grant to Thomas. How far is the interest of Thomas under the second arrangement subject to the interests of Ralph and of William's heirs under the first?

We shall take first the interest of Ralph, the lord, and begin by asking exactly what it was. The answer is not simple. At the end of the thirteenth century, *Quia emptores* treats William's grant to Thomas as affecting only the incidents due to Ralph on William's death. If William has granted the land to Thomas for nominal services, and then dies leaving an infant heir or no heir, it will be the nominal services which come to Ralph by wardship or escheat instead of the land itself.[1] This was not new in 1290, but it was probably occurring more often. A grant for reduced services had once been a gift; and there had been limits on the proportion of

---

[1] The preamble to Stat. *Quia emptores*, 1290, refers to lords as losing escheats, marriages, and wardships. For explanation, see Plucknett, *Legislation of Edward I*, pp. 102 f.

his land that any individual could give away.[1] Even when these disappeared, there remained a natural limit to the overall loss sustained by lords: few people give most of their wealth. But by the late thirteenth century, the William who reserved nominal services was not necessarily making a gift to Thomas. He was often a vendor taking a capital payment; and Ralph might lose from any kind of disposition.

But of course the change finally accepted by *Quia emptores* was not just that land was being sold for money. Land has been reduced to a form of property, and the parties to the tenurial transaction have been reversed. The tenant is now owner of his tenement. The lord has only a *jus in re aliena*, having as its valuable components the services and incidents; and, especially if the services were long ago fixed in money, the incidents may be the more important. But the incidents had come into existence in a world in which it was the lord who was buyer. He was paying for desired services by an allocation of land; and the incidents provided only that the pay should be at his disposal if there was nobody immediately able to do the services. The theory of that earlier world is still reflected in Bracton's treatment of the problem finally settled by *Quia emptores*. He has no sympathy for the lord. The loss is *damnum absque injuria*; and he can no more complain of his tenant making such a grant than of his leaving an adult male heir, and so occasioning the fixed relief instead of some richer incident. For Bracton the incidents are still just incidental profits: the lord has a right to whatever does accrue, but no right that anything shall accrue. His entitlement under the tenurial bargain is to the services; 'and so let him take what is his and be gone'.[2]

It is therefore no surprise to find, as we move backwards from *Quia emptores*, that the incidents are not the only concern of earlier provisions about subinfeudation. *De viris religiosis* mentions services and escheats in that order.[3] The Chester ordinance of 1260, made familiar by Plucknett, is enrolled without reasons.[4] But the royal ordinance four years earlier, controlling subinfeudation by tenants-in-chief, may be emphasising the services in putting them second: *wardas et escaetas amittimus et barones nostri...adeo*

---

[1] Below, pp. 121 ff.   [2] Bracton, ff. 45b–46.

[3] Stat. *De viris religiosis*, 1279. The Provisions of Westminster, c. 14, specifies no mischief. The Petition of the Barons, c. 10, mentions wardships, marriages, reliefs, and escheats but not services.

[4] Plucknett, *Legislation of Edward I*, pp. 108 f.

decrescunt quod servicia nobis inde debita sufficienter facere nequeunt unde corona nostra graviter leditur.[1] And lastly there is the earliest provision of all, that of the Charter of 1217: *Nullus liber homo decetero det amplius alicui vel vendat de terra sua quam ut de residuo terre sue possit sufficienter fieri domino feodi servicium ei debitum quod pertinet ad feodum illud.*[2] The only loss envisaged is in the tenant's ability to do his services. The contrast with *Quia emptores* is complete.

What is not yet complete is our explanation. The economic change explains why the incidents grew to be the more important part of the problem. But it does not explain why *Quia emptores* does not even mention the services which, though they had declined relatively, were still important to lords at every level. The reason for that is legal: the services due from William to Ralph cannot be impaired by William's grant to Thomas. If they are not done, Ralph will distrain on the land. It may be Thomas's chattels that he takes, and therefore Thomas who is in fact compelled to do the services; and Thomas may then have a claim against William for acquittance, which he can enforce by the action of mesne. But none of this concerns Ralph, who raises his service from the land itself. It is not that the services are not important, but that they are not a problem. Yet they had been a problem. The earlier legislators do not see the services as a property right which Ralph can always raise from the land itself, but as an obligation which Ralph must enforce against William; and William will be unable to discharge it if he parts with too much, especially if his grant to Thomas is gratuitous or for a lump sum instead of for full services.

This change is another aspect of one already mentioned. In the thirteenth century distress by chattels became an independent remedy, a form of self-help by which a lord could raise his dues directly from the land. But it began as something quite different. William's dues were an obligation which Ralph would enforce in his own court; and distress by chattels was no more than a stage in the customary process of that court.[3] What we now need to know, therefore, is the effect in Ralph's court of William's downward grant to Thomas. In 1204 Thomas brings novel disseisin against Ralph, who makes his exception of due process for arrears due from William. The proper steps are elaborately warranted

[1] *Calendar of Close Rolls, 1254–6*, p. 429.
[2] *Magna Carta* (1217), c. 39; (1225), c. 32.   [3] Above, p. 10.

by Ralph's court, including offers to William and his relations to
replevy. Thomas admits that the land is of Ralph's fee, but claims
to hold it of William for homage and service. This is not itself an
answer, and he is amerced for a false claim *quia satis constat quod
non fuit in curia*. But what could he have done in Ralph's court
where, in his own name, he had no standing? It is conceivable that
mere notice of his holding would make it improper for Ralph's
court to act. But that result, although imaginable after the introduction of the assize, is unlikely to have been reached by the
customs of lords' own courts: any subinfeudation would then
gravely imperil the services. What Thomas could more probably
have done is to replevy on William's behalf. Indeed, it looks as
though the king's court is giving him one more chance to do this:
although he has lost his assize, a day is given on which he is to
produce his warrant, namely William.[1]

This is a starting-point from which the classical position could
intelligibly have developed in the thirteenth century. But although
factual pressure may extend to Thomas, the thrust of Ralph's
proceeding is to enforce a personal obligation upon William. When
distress becomes a 'real' remedy, for example, it may be levied
anywhere in the fee: but another case tells us in passing that a lord
ought to be distrained at the place where he holds his court.[2]
Ralph is looking to William; and the mischief of William's grant
to Thomas lies in the depletion of William's resources.

This much at least is clear from the provision of 1217, which
orders, like Canute, that the mischief shall not happen: William is
not to give away too much. But that only raises what for this book
is the important question, and one which it will not completely
answer. What change has brought the matter on to the legislator's
agenda? There must have been some loss of seignorial control, but

[1] *CRR*, III, 133–4; note that this is one of the Devon cases mentioned above,
p. 7 at n. 3, as particularly illuminating. For an under-tenant saying that he is
disseised by the lord for a failure by the tenant, see *RCR*, II, *207*; *CRR*, I, *136*,
177–8, 343, 458; *CRR*, II, *61, 277*; *CRR*, III, *75*. For a taking of the chattels of
an under-tenant by way of distress, see (*a*) *CRR*, I, *123*, 408 (Roger f. Alan);
(*b*) the later pair of cases in *BNB*, 158; *CRR*, X, 317. Cf. Bracton, f. 217: *si
distringat tenentem tenentis sui, licet feodum suum, cum tenens suus qui medius est
sufficiens habeat dominicum*.

[2] *CRR*, VII, *25*, 41 (Punchardon), *48*. In a much later case, *BNB*, 1207, an
under-tenant actually argues that the lord should have distrained on the *capitale
mesagium* of the tenant: the lord is eventually held liable on the ground that the
under-tenant himself had other chattels which should have been taken before
his crops were arrested.

what? A simple answer would be that novel disseisin has after all deprived Ralph of his means of enforcement to the extent of William's grant to Thomas. But the 1204 case suggests otherwise, and the explanation seems too drastic.

A more familiar possibility is that William's grant had once required Ralph's consent; and since this would have been enforced by Ralph's own court, the change would again be due to novel disseisin. This is at least consonant with the legislative evidence. The ordinance of 1256 required the king's licence, and if the grantee of a tenant-in-chief entered without it, the land was to be taken into the king's hand.[1] Mortmain worked on the same principle.[2] As to charters, they do not often recite the lord's consent to a subinfeudation; but silence cannot be conclusive on a matter that would have gone without saying. This is indeed illustrated by a relevant disclosure in the plea rolls. Two or three entries show subinfeudations at the humblest level being made in the court of the grantor's lord and attested by a charter of which he is the main witness. What is unusual about these is a combination of circumstances which leads to the lord's court being offered as proof.[3] Nothing is usually said of how or where a grant was made, and chance has given us a glimpse of the normal. But the normal thing is not that subinfeudations are made in the court of the grantor's lord, but just that grants are made in courts. Other chances in the rolls show all kinds of grants made in lords' or in public local

---

[1] *Calendar of Close Rolls, 1254–6*, p. 429. But the Charter shows that the king had not regarded himself as bound by the principles behind novel disseisin and mort d'ancestor; and it may be argued that if he had ever had the power of licence there would have been no need to revive it. On the novelty of the 1256 ordinance, see Bean, *The Decline of English Feudalism*, pp. 66 ff.; Turner, 'A Newly Discovered Ordinance', *Law Quarterly Review*, XII (1896), 299. See also the last sentence of *Glanvill*, VII, 1, and Mr Hall's note thereon, ibid. p. 185.

[2] Stat. *De viris religiosis*, 1279; Plucknett, *Legislation of Edward I*, pp. 96 ff.

[3] (a) *PKJ*, I, *2710*; *CRR*, I, 188 (Gaie): demandant alleges entry by gage; tenant admits, alleges subsequent grant in fee, proffers charter sealed only by the lord, *et preterea producit sectam vivarum vocum*, which the case next cited suggests would be men of the lord's court; (b) *RCR*, I, 341 (Seredust); *RCR*, II, 72–3; *PKJ*, I, *2600, 3092*: demandant alleges entry *ad terminum*; tenant seemingly asserts that that transaction itself was a grant in fee and done in the lord's court, proffers charter bearing the seals of the lord and of the demandant; the lord and his court are to be summoned; (c) case cited above, p. 100, n. 5: demandant alleges entry by a voluntary *custodia*; tenant says it was a sale in the lord's court; (d) *CRR*, XI, 154; *BNB*, 234; demandant alleges gage made in county court; tenant alleges quit-claim in his own court. For similar disputes, though with nothing to show that the transaction had been made in a court, see: (a) *Gloucs.*, 1427; (b) ibid. 1470; (c) ibid. 1477.

courts;[1] and custom would put any rearrangement to the peers
who would attest and uphold it. Our grantors of acres had no
courts of their own; and even at that level these entries are far
from showing a requirement of consent. Sometimes indeed we
learn of a grant made without even the lord's knowledge. In 1202,
for example, Thomas brings novel disseisin against Ralph's
seignorial officers, who say that the tenement is William's and they
took it into Ralph's hand because William has joined the king's
enemies. But Thomas says and an inquest finds that William had
taken Thomas's homage for it a full year before leaving England;
and at least so far as the assize is concerned Ralph and his men are
bound by this.[2]

More direct indications in the rolls would have to be either
assizes against lords who had acted in their own courts against
their tenants' unlicensed grantees, or actions brought by lords in
the king's court. Assizes are not found, but we might not recognise

---

[1] Concords in lords' courts are frequently mentioned in the earliest rolls, and
usually there is no telling whether or not they were in settlement of genuine
disputes: (a) RCR, II, 36 (Curci); CRR, I, 282, 348 (full references above,
p. 71, n. 2); (b) CRR, II, 112–13 (full references in same note); (c) RCR, I, 294,
362, 440–1; RCR, II, 83–4, 216; CRR, I, 134–5; (d) RCR, I, 238, 239, 241, 289,
333; RCR, II, 14, 237–8; CRR, I, 254–5, 281; (e) CRR, I, 364–5 (also related
references above, p. 26, n. 4); (f) CRR, I, 185 (court of Malmesbury; full
references above, p. 51, n. 3; note that Manasser Bisset died 1177, ceased to be
steward of the king's household c. 1170); (g) PRS, XIV, 119 (court of earl Simon);
RCR, I, 221; CRR, I, 70, 222; RCR, II, 55, 269–70; PKJ, I, 3085; (h) CRR, I
225, 447–8, 453 (note that non fuit lis inter eos per aliquod breve sed per voluntatem
utriusque); cf. CRR, II, 1; PKJ, II, 940, 1041; PKJ, III, 383; (i) CRR, I, 400
(court of bishop of Rochester), 458 (per concordiam...et per licentiam domini...
et non per judicium curie). Undoubted transactions in lords' courts, other than
those above, p. 107, nn. 2 and 3, p. 110, n. 1 and below, p. 146, nn. 3 and 4:
(a) PKJ, II, 440; (b) Northants., 663 (surrender and admittance between persons
wrongly taken to be villeins); (c) CRR, IV, 16 (recital of quit-claim in halimote
and portmote); (d) CRR, IV, 311 (archbishop's court at Gillingham); (e) CRR,
IV, 317 (court of St Edmund's abbey); CRR, V, 97; (f) Lincs.-Worcs., 841 (a case
which shows the court acting as a register of title). Transactions in county or
other local courts: (a) PKJ, I, 3161; RCR, II, 170, 214–15; (b) RCR, II, 260
(abbot of Eynsham; quit-claim in county attested by charter of sheriff);
(c) Northants., 496; (d) CRR, III, 131, 134–5, 138; (e) CRR, III, 128, 332–3;
(f) CRR, V, 261 (Welle); (g) CRR, VI, 81–2; (h) CRR, VI, 232–3, 275; (i) CRR,
VI, 143–4, 197, 250, 299; (j) CRR, VI, 305–6, 349; (k) CRR, VI, 359 (Merston);
(l) Yorks., 100; (m) Lincs.-Worcs., 923; (n) BNB, 985; (o) BNB, 754; CRR, XV,
145.

[2] Northants., 390, 483, 601. Similar facts no doubt lie behind many cases
concerning escheats. Consider PKJ, IV, 4477; CRR, VI, 342, 351–2: quo waranto
ipse intrusit se against one who claims by grant in ligia potestate from dead tenant
as reward for past service (on which see below, p. 122).

them. One entry seems to show a lord putting out a religious house to whom his former tenant had made a grant; but we learn this only because the usual *ita dissaisiuit eum* is followed by a *sciendum* concerning a new tenant to whom the lord had then given the land.[1] Actions by lords are found, but nearly always in special circumstances which militate against the existence of a general principle.[2] In one curious case the need for consent had been specially imposed by a fine.[3] And there is a group of cases in which Ralph sues William for granting and Thomas for entering land which William held of Ralph; but the sting is not that the grant was made without consent, but that Thomas is Ralph's own lord.[4] This is said to be to Ralph's disinheritance, and it is possible that his entire interest was in theory extinguished. But an example in 1221 expresses the matter in a way which brings us back to Ralph's perennial preoccupation: *posuit feodum suum in manum capitalis domini sui ubi ipse non potest distringere feodum suum pro seruicio ei debito.*[5]

More clearly relevant are two other cases in which lords proceed against their tenants' grantees. But they seem to be not late applications of an established principle but precursors of the provision of 1217: the mischief is being faced, rather uncertainly, by individual plaintiffs. In 1212 one Adam has granted to a prior some or all of his holding of half a knight's fee in Lincolnshire. Although tenure may not have cut very deep, this was evidently a subinfeudation: the land is described as not held *in dominico* by Adam but given *in elemosinam* to the prior. It was, however, not a pure benefaction. Adam had needed money to buy himself out of the king's prison and had raised it by selling this land to the

---

[1] *PKJ*, ii, 430: this was an urban tenement, and the tenurial nature of the gift in alms is not clear. Another possible case is *CRR*, i, 161 (Trevet); *RCR*, ii, 191. An undoubted case, but much later, is *BNB*, 1248, where the lord expressly based himself on *Magna Carta* (1217), c. 39. See below, p. 119, n. 3.

[2] (a) *CRR*, v, 94–5; (b) *CRR*, vii, 161, 197–8.

[3] *CRR*, ii, 97 (Warenne), 122, 133, 224; *CRR*, iii, 24, 24–5.

[4] (a) Mesne sues tenant for selling to lord: *CRR*, ii, 208 (Haia), 262. Mesne sues lord for land *quam emit ad exhereditacionem suam*: *CRR*, ii, 288; *CRR*, iii, 180, 227, 281–2, 296; *PKJ*, iii, 1381, 1582; cf. possibly related litigation, *CRR*, iii, 184, 234, 261, and for the parties, *PKJ*, i, 3546; the case itself is mentioned in Plucknett, *Concise History of the Common Law* (5th ed.), p. 540; (b) *CRR*, iii, 178, 187 (Crevequor); (c) *Northants.*, 357; (d) *PKJ*, iii, 1632; *CRR*, v, 42, 51, 53, 77–8, 78–9; (e) *CRR*, vi, 186, 217–18; (e) *CRR*, i, 283, 295 (Pokebroc), 341 (much litigation centres on these parties; see especially *RCR*, ii, 84); (f) *Lincs.*, 1348 (probably an example, though confused; cf. above, p. 28, n. 1).

[5] *Gloucs.*, 26, 173, 191.

M L F

prior; and this has enabled the prior to get a royal confirmation of the grant. Moreover, the grant imposed upon the prior the obligation of doing *servicum quod ad tantam terram pertinet*; and although the obligation was owed to Adam rather than to Adam's lord, there is no intention to impair the lord's services. The lord however brings parallel actions, one against the prior *quare ingressus est...sine assensu*, and another against Adam *quare ipse vendidit...sine assensu*. Adam warrants his grant to the prior, explains the circumstances, and says that he is not in fact in arrear with his service, and what is more, a clear foreshadowing of 1217, that he has retained enough of his holding *unde ipse facit ei plenarie servicium*. The lord admits that he is up to date, denies that he has retained enough to support the service, and introduces a new point: *perdens erit de homagio et warda, cum acciderit*. But this is an afterthought: the action is about the services and Adam's ability to do them. It is adjourned without a decision.[1]

The other case dates from 1203, and concerns land in Warwick-shire held of the lord, himself in fact a prior, by one Henry. Henry has granted what seems to be the whole of it to an abbot at farm, for a term having nine or ten years to run. But the limited nature of the grant may not be known to the prior when he starts his action: it looks as though he came to distrain upon Henry and found the abbot's men in possession. His complaint is against the abbot: *sine assensu et voluntate ipsius prioris intrusit se in feudum ipsius prioris contra consuetudinem rengni...ita quod servicia que terra illa ei debet a retro sunt ei et non potest illa habere propter illam intrusionem*. The damage is elaborated in a second entry: Henry does not pay his relief or do his services, and the prior *non potest eum distringere per predictum feodum propter libertates predictorum monachorum*. The words '*per predictum feodum*' probably denote any distress on this land rather than a taking of the land itself;[2] and the '*eum*' shows that the distress frustrated is seen as distress of Henry himself. There is a difficulty about enforcing Henry's obligation *propter libertates monachorum*. What those were we can only speculate. Perhaps there was a special immunity from distraint; perhaps, if distraint was process of the lord's court, a difficulty arose from the liberty against being impleaded elsewhere than in

---

[1] *CRR*, VI, *240, 247, 276, 315*, 342–3; *PKJ*, IV, *4520*. Adam's need of money may have been an aftermath of *Lincs.*, 810, 815.

[2] Cf. the language of *CRR*, I, *123*, 408 (Roger f. Alan).

the king's court; or perhaps some general immunity was thought to flow from the Constitutions of Clarendon. There is probably some connection with a writ which existed early in the thirteenth century and then disappeared: *ne vexes abbatem contra libertates*.[1] Whatever its exact nature, the lord's difficulty flows not just from the grant but from an immunity in the grantee. And the judges, in telling him to brave it, perhaps hope that their own problem will go away: *Preceptum est priori quod capiat se ad feodum pro defectu servicii, si voluerit, donec videatur si quis ei inde maleficium fecerit*.[2]

Although themselves needing more explanation, which others may be able to give, these cases explain features of the provision of 1217. Despite its general terms, it was applied only to grants to religious houses, perhaps only in alms.[3] The special difficulty about distraining them, whatever it was, was more easily caught hold of than the indeterminate obstruction caused by any grant.[4] Even so confined, the provision was ineffective.[5] It did not occur to the legislator, any more than to the justices of 1203, that anything was needed beyond leaving lords to enforce it for themselves. His assumptions were of a world which novel disseisin was rapidly changing. Another assumption from that world must lie behind the lord's claim in 1203 that the abbot had entered *contra consuetudinem rengni*. What are we to make of a custom that gives rise to just two cases, and is reasserted in ineffective legislation? Is it

---

[1] *Registers*: Hib.37a; CA56; both writs say that the liberties are enjoyed *per cartas predecessorum nostrorum regum Anglie*. The privilege against being impleaded otherwise than before the king or his justices is described by Bracton, f. 332b as *quale habent templarii et hospitalarii et plures alii*, and he refers to *Lincs.-Worcs.*, 980; an early example is *CRR*, I, 23 (Ruffus); *CRR*, VII, *330*. It is tempting to suppose a connection with Stat. Westminster II, 1285, c. 33 against erecting crosses in tenements *ut tenentes per privilegium Templariorum & Hospitalariorum tueri se possint contra capitales dominos feodorum*: forfeiture was provided as in the case of mortmain.

[2] *CRR*, II, *226, 282*; *CRR*, III, 69–70. For the sense of betaking oneself to one's fee, cf. *CRR*, v. 78–9 (full references above, p. 117, n. 4): *recongnoscat se ad feudum suum et seisiat illud in manum suam*. For possible examples of a lord so taking because of a grant in alms, see above, p. 117, n. 1. For objections by an heir to grants *viris religiosis*, see *CRR*, VII, 322–5 (full references above, p. 110, n. 1).

[3] *BNB*, 1248, referred to by Bracton, f. 169b: both speak of gifts in alms, as does *Calendar of Patent Rolls, 1232–47*, p. 234. But at f. 168b Bracton speaks of any gift *viro religioso* which does not leave the feoffor enough to support his services. See generally Bean, *The Decline of English Feudalism*, pp. 42 ff. Note the context of Bracton's discussion: will the assize lie against the lord?

[4] For an example, see *BNB*, 273; *CRR*, XIII, 423, *728*.

[5] Witness the statute *De viris religiosis* and its forerunners; above, p. 112, n. 3.

that some ancient rule has ceased to be obeyed? In a sense, perhaps it is.

A custom is something that happens before it becomes a rule.[1] It is well known from charters that grants to religious houses were often confirmed by the grantors' lords. Since religious houses figure disproportionately in the charter evidence, it is worth saying that the same appears from the plea rolls. The king confirms all kinds of grants. Other lords occasionally confirm their tenants' grants to laymen. But it is their tenants' grants to religious houses that lords most regularly confirm. Why? At the level of detail, the lord is accepting a possible loss to himself. Later the loss anticipated would be of incidents, but now his concern was with his services: and however his power to distrain his own tenant was seen, the effect of his confirmation was to exempt the land concerned. This is stated by Bracton in connection with grants in free marriage.[2] These were confirmed much less regularly than grants in alms; and Bracton's passage may reflect a time at which the proposition would make no sense in connection with alms, because the grantees had an independent immunity from distraint. Because of this immunity, lords find themselves at the beginning of the thirteenth century suffering this same loss from grants which they have not confirmed; and hence their complaints.

If we equate confirmation with consent, it looks indeed as though tenants are for the first time disobeying a rule requiring the lord's consent for any grant to a religious house.[3] But to put the matter in that way is to think of the tenant transferring a sort of ownership. Perhaps the underlying change is that the tenant is beginning to think of himself as having a sort of ownership which he can transfer. Before royal control, and in particular before mort d'ancestor allowed an heir to feel that he entered in his own right rather than under a grant to himself from the lord, no tenant could think that he had something which he could by himself give for ever to an institution which would last for ever: of course the lord must join in. His confirmation would not just add some marginal advantage to a self-sufficient gift. The gift was

---

[1] Cf. the rule that a tenant need not answer for his freehold without writ, above, p. 58, and the changing nature of inheritance, below, pp. 180 ff.

[2] Bracton, f. 21b (but printed at p. 78 in Woodbine edition). He deduces that the confirmation may waive *pro tanto* the lord's right to services from his own tenant.

[3] Cf. Pollock and Maitland, *History of English Law* (2nd ed.), I, pp. 340 ff.

unthinkable without it. What has changed is the thinkable. Now
the tenant has a title which he can transfer on his own, and there
may be marginal loss to the lord. And so we find lords beginning
to propound the custom as a rule: *sine assensu et voluntate...
intrusit se in feudum...contra consuetudinem rengni.*

The effect of such interior changes are not easily grasped, either
by historians or by those affected at the time. All that lords or
legislators could see was a new danger to services. Any subinfeudation might impede distress and, if for less than the land
owed, would reduce the tenant's resources. Yet they sought to deal
only with the most tangible case on both counts, the grant in alms,
and that ineffectively. This is probably because there is yet another
respect in which the problem was a new one for lords, and the
same interior change is responsible. So long as William had only
a title for life he could give only for his life. Even if he gave to
Thomas and undertook that he and his heirs would warrant
Thomas and his heirs, that created only an obligation; and when
the time came William's heir would have to decide whether to
honour it or not. In making that decision, he and his court would
have to consider his other obligations: to William's widow, to
William's other grantees, and above all the overriding obligation
to Ralph. Ralph in 1217 faces a nebulous and somehow new
problem because William's heir is losing that discretion. Now the
king's court will make him honour Thomas's grant, even if it
leaves him too little in demesne to support Ralph's services. Royal
control is creating a sort of ownership, which in this as in every
other respect is incompatible with a system of truly dependent
tenures.

* * *

It is no doubt because the lord's interest was not a problem,
certainly not a problem for the king's court, that it is not mentioned by Glanvill. But he does discuss the heir's interest, giving
detailed rules about the extent to which grants may be made to his
disinheritance.[1] There is a general prohibition of death-bed gifts,
which are vitiated by a presumed turmoil of mind. Subject to this,
there is unlimited power to give land which the grantor has himself
acquired, except only that he must not altogether disinherit his
own children if he has any. But the gifts that can be made from

[1] *Glanvill*, VII, I.

inherited land are limited to what Glanvill describes as a certain or a *rationabilis* part.[1] The grantees mentioned are religious houses in alms, daughters and other women in *maritagium*, bastard sons, and strangers *in remunerationem seruicii sui*. This last may refer to a reward for past service; and, if so, Glanvill's discussion is all about gifts, and does not touch grants for full service which do not diminish the heir's resources.[2] Lastly, because younger sons are so often favourites, gifts to them are altogether forbidden; but this like all the other restrictions may be overridden with the heir's consent.

These rules are cast in terms of what a donor may do, and Glanvill is praised for venturing into substantive statement. But the most businesslike of English legal writers might not have relished this. He does not clearly explain, at first sight does not explain at all, how his rules are brought to bear; and in the end they perished because they could not well be enforced in the king's courts which he is discussing. But their end was neither quick nor distinct.

In the plea rolls, the obvious thing to look for is enforcement by action, with the heir seeking to retrieve what his ancestor had given away. It will be convenient to begin with the one rule that survived. The writ of entry *dum non compos mentis* enforces the principle behind Glanvill's prohibition of death-bed gifts. We saw in the preceding chapter that writs of entry were the form finally taken by 'downward' claims made first by *quo waranto* in the grantor's own court and then by writ of right in the court of his lord. What we might expect to find on the earliest rolls, therefore, is the grantor's sanity being raised in a writ of right brought by his heir; and we are largely disappointed. Express assertions of insanity by demandants are rare.[3] But implied denials by tenants

---

[1] The word is perhaps best translated as 'rightful'.

[2] Thorne, 'English Feudalism and Estates in Land', [1959] *Cambridge Law Journal*, 193, esp. at 207. Such gifts were no doubt often made by persons nearing death, and in the rolls they are attacked on that ground: (*a*) *PKJ*, IV, *4477*; *CRR*, VI, *342*, 351–2; (*b*) *Yorks.*, 342.

[3] (*a*) *RCR*, I, *313*, *411*; *RCR*, II, *36*, *186*; *CRR*, I, 89 (Bocland: in this earliest appearance the heir casts his claim in terms of intrusion, and the tenant *defendit vim et injuriam*), *127*, *233*, *257* (*defendit jus suum*, produces charter and confirmation of chief lord; heir *dicit quod si donum illud et cartam eis fecit, hoc fecit in infirmitate sua unde obiit*), *300*, *375*, *422*, *441*; (*b*) *Yorks.*, *1127* (which one could take for a writ of entry were it not for a marginal note: gift *in lecto mortali* and *dum fuit sub virga...viri sui*); *CRR*, VIII, *80*. For the assertion made by a widow claiming in dower, see *CRR*, IV, *289*, *298*, *300*; *CRR*, V, 6 (Rocheford); for it made by a lord claiming escheat, see first case in preceding note, also cast

are common. One who relies on a grant often asserts that it was made *in ligia potestate*. This phrase is roughly equivalent to the Roman *sui juris*, so that, for example, a *cui in vita* allegation may be rebutted by saying that after the husband's death the widow confirmed the grant *in ligia potestate*.[1] But it usually rebuts a suggestion of mental incapacity;[2] and in this phrase, as in the frequent assertions that land granted was the grantor's own purchase[3] or that his heir consented to the grant,[4] Glanvill's rules seem to haunt the law as ineffective ghosts. Grantees and their successors allege compliance, but nothing visibly turns on it: we do not see the heirs of grantors getting the land back on the ground that the rules were broken. Either the assertions are reminiscences of what

in terms of intrusion. If there was no effective livery, the heir can recover in mort d'ancestor: (*a*) *BNB*, 45; *CRR*, VIII, *2*, 7–8, 186; (*b*) *CRR*, X, *38*, 254–5; *BNB*, 144. In *PKJ*, IV, *3193*; *CRR*, V, 272 (Bigot), *296*, the tenant seems to have countered an assize with *warantia carte*. But if seisin was delivered, mort d'ancestor is no remedy even if the recognitors expressly find it was a death-bed gift: *Lincs.-Worcs.*, 341. Cf. *Beds.*, 86, and the case above, pp. 95–6.

[1] (*a*) *RCR*, II, 168; *PKJ*, I, 3157, and fine printed ibid. p. 76; (*b*) *CRR*, III, *175*, *232*; *CRR*, IV, 126–7, *166*, *195*; (*c*) *BNB*, 671; *CRR*, XIV, *184*, *846*, *1423*, 2311. Cf. the widow's charter enrolled at *CRR*, V, 12–13: *post obitum . . . mariti mei in viduitate et propria potestate mea*. The phrase is used also of other kinds of legal incapacity: (*a*) *Northants.*, 482 (husband's acquisition *in ligia potestate* contrasted with *maritagium* given with his wife); (*b*) *CRR*, IV, *114*, *133*, 148–9, *252*; cf. ibid. *61*, 126, *217* (contrasted with having taken habit of religion); (*c*) *CRR*, VIII, *27*, *156*, 357–8; *BNB*, 114 (contrasted with being disseised by king).

[2] For this contrast expressly made, see (*a*) *CRR*, V, 6 (Rocheford; full references above, p. 122, n. 3); (*b*) *PKJ*, IV, *4477*; *CRR*, VI, *342*, 351–2; (*c*) *CRR*, VII, 138 (Andeville); (*d*) *Lincs.-Worcs.*, *560*, 657, 785; (*e*) *BNB*, 255; *CRR*, XIII, *16*, 192, *349*; (*f*) *CRR*, XIII, *1626*, *1922*; *BNB*, 354; cf. *CRR*, XIII, 1467; *BNB*, 318. But the common thing is that a grant, generally within the family, is said to have been made *in ligia potestate* without recorded explanation or contradiction, e.g., (*a*) *CRR*, IV, 23–4 (full references below, p. 135, n. 4); (*b*) *RCR*, II, 134 (William f. John; full references below, p. 148, n. 1); (*c*) *CRR*, VII, 117–18 (below, p. 148, n. 2); (*d*) *CRR*, I, 359 (Geoffrey f. Warin; full references below, p. 151, n. 5); (*e*) *CRR*, I, 45, 66–7 (below, p. 133, n. 4).

[3] The last two cases in the preceding note are examples. Others: (*a*) *CRR*, I, 310 (Robert f. Neil, full references above, p. 91, n. 1); (*b*) *RCR*, I, *242*, *345*, *420*, 438 (Bosco); *PKJ*, I, *2350*; *CRR*, I, *146*; (*c*) *RCR*, II, 88–9 (full references above, p. 107, n. 3); (*d*) *CRR*, II, *183*, 248 (Cocus). Cf. the occasional allegation that a grantor *venit in conquestu Anglie*; *CRR*, II, 301–2; *CRR*, III, *71–2*, *229–30*, *306*, *315*.

[4] (*a*) *PRS*(NS), XXXI, 100–1 (full references above, p. 8, n. 2); (*b*) *RCR*, II, 202–3; *CRR*, I, 330–1, *466*; *CRR*, II, *30–1*; (*c*) *CRR*, VI, 140–1, *186*; (*d*) *CRR*, VII, 280–1; (*e*) *CRR*, IV, *181*, 193–4, *258–9*; *CRR*, V, *14*; (*f*) *CRR*, VII, *14*, 48–9; (*g*) *CRR*, VI, *197*, *258*, 393–4 (consent to confirmation of tenant's gift in alms). The same effect may be achieved by the heir confirming the gift when it is made: (*a*) *CRR*, I, 309, 317 (Amundeville; full references below, p. 135, n. 1); (*b*) *CRR*, III, *131*, 134–5, *138*; (*c*) *Lincs.-Worcs.*, 822–3.

would once have mattered in the heir's own court, or they matter now in a way we do not see.

What we most obviously do not see are questions within the general issue. To a downward claim by an heir against his ancestor's grantee, as the preceding chapter noted,[1] the tenant could either plead specially that the demandant should be his warrant, or he could put himself on the grand assize with special mise. The latter was the more common, and led to a verdict for which reasons are hardly ever given; but if the case turned upon a grant, the knights must have considered its validity. Two relatively late cases show us what might happen. In 1214, to a count upon the demandant's own seisin, the tenant pleads a grant from the demandant himself for which he has a charter, *et preterea* offers to put himself on the grand assize as entitled to hold of the demandant. Had the case gone that way, we should know no more. But the demandant admits the charter and tells his story. At the time *non fuit potens sui nec scivit sensum suum*, and the tenant, who is his uncle, had him in his sole care; and he seeks an inquest *si carta illa facta fuit tempore predicto vel in potestate sua*.[2] In the language of a case already considered, and also turning on a grant while incapable, the issue has 'emerged' from a writ of right.[3] Usually it was left to the knights. In 1218–19 it emerged and was bundled back again. Whether or not after inquiry in his own court, the first move of the grantor's heir was to disseise the tenant, who recovered in the assize. The heir now claims in the right, counting on the seisin of his grandfather. The tenant produces the grandfather's charter and claims that the heir should warrant him. The heir says that if his grandfather made the charter it was *in infirmitate sua unde obiit* and seisin was delivered by the grandfather's wife; and to this the tenant simply claims the assize with special mise. There is reason to think that the court was being specially careful over this case; otherwise the enrolment would probably have been as blank as most which end in the grand assize.[4]

---

[1] Above, p. 89.

[2] *CRR*, VII, *175*, 296 (Mauluvell). Cf. what seems to be a similar abuse in *RCR*, II, *81*, *129*, 146 (Musele).   [3] Above, pp. 95–6.

[4] *Yorks.*, 353 (the assize), 198, 287, 1115. The case is discussed by the editor, ibid. pp. xxviii f. The objection that the demandant had an elder brother whose son is living appears to be made by the court, and may reflect a new attitude to the *casus regis*. A much later case similarly shows the capacity of a grantor being put to the grand assize in a special mise; *BNB*, 671 (full references above, p. 123, n. 1).

We now turn to claims based on Glanvill's rules about quantum: some gift was permissible, but the heir attacks this as excessive. No writ of entry evolved, perhaps because the claim itself disappeared too early, perhaps because it resisted formulation. But in early writs of right it is visibly the point in dispute more often than the mental incapacity of the grantor. Twice it is even made the basis of attack on a settlement reached in the king's court.[1] Once a mere cousin of the grantor tries to recover, not denying the grant but demanding judgment whether *potuit dare totam terram suam ad exheredacionem heredum suorum*. Since it was the grantor's own purchase, Glanvill would have allowed the claim only to an heir of his body, but it seems to be arguable in 1207.[2] Less surprising are brothers trying to recover *maritagium* given to their sisters to their own disinheritance. The sisters evidently accept the proposition of law: they assert that their fathers had died seised of other land.[3] One such case suggests that the rules about quantum may be the basis of more claims in the right than we can see. Issue is joined on the sister's assertion that the father had had other land, but she had earlier sought the grand assize.[4] If the case had gone to the knights, they would surely have asked the same question and decided the case accordingly; and we should know the decision but not the question.

A conscientious clerk in 1221 seems to show us just this happening. He first wrote an entry in common form recording the election of a grand assize to say whether the tenant had greater right to hold of the demandant than the demandant to hold in demesne, then recording the verdict of the knights that the tenant had indeed greater right to hold of the demandant, and then the judgment thereon. In all this there is nothing to show who the parties were or what it is all about. But then he inserted an interlineation making the verdict read: the tenant has greater right to hold of the demandant under the gift *in maritagium* which the demandant's

---

[1] (a) *CRR*, VI, 134–5 (for another aspect of this case see below, p. 175, n. 4); (b) *BNB*, 1054; *CRR*, XII, 266; cf. *CRR*, X, 236, 248.

[2] *CRR*, V, 47–8, 139, 182, 227: we know it was the grantor's purchase, because the tenant produces the charter under which the grantor held; it conferred a power to assign, which he seems not to have used. *Glanvill*, VII, 1: *si nullum heredem...ex corpore suo procreauerit, poterit quidem ex questu suo cui uoluerit partem quandam donare siue totum questum hereditabiliter.*

[3] (a) *RCR*, I, 276; *CRR*, I, 87 (Coueleia); *PKJ*, I, 2294, 2343, 2833; cf. *RCR*, II, 237; (b) case in next note.

[4] *CRR*, VI, 68, 167, 201 (Walda), 208, 274, 397; *CRR*, VII, 23.

father made to his daughter, the tenant's mother; and this tells us more than we often know about a case which goes to the grand assize. The interlineation itself, however, was probably put in only to make sense of something very rare, a memorandum at the end of the entry: *sciendum quod idem* demandant *cognouit donum factum matri ipsius* tenant *et petiit judicium si possit dare medietatem*.[1] A request for *judicium* is usually made to the court: but since the case was before the grand assize this may have been addressed to the knights themselves, and can at most have been a request for judicial direction. Glanvill contemplates their finding facts from which the court may deduce the greater right;[2] but this never appears on the roll, which always records a general verdict. Whether Glanvill's rules were applied by the court or by the knights, and we must not assume that they were uniform all over England, it seems certain that they were largely brought to bear in the grand assize and therefore out of our sight. And it follows that they may lie behind entries which, if they refer to the grant at all, appear to record a dispute about whether it was ever made.[3]

So far we have discussed only actions by the heir to recover what his ancestor had given away. These are easy to understand, and perhaps misleading, because they fit our own ideas. Was the grant made at all? Was it vitiated by mental incapacity? Was it of more than the grantor had power to give? Our questions are about the past event, which either passed a sort of ownership or did not. But Glanvill's rules also come up in actions which are expressed to be about the present. These are actions by the grantee against the heir claiming warranty; and they do not fit our picture even of the procedural framework. We attribute to the action claiming warranty the same role as the traditional voucher: a third party is claiming the land, and the present tenant wants to secure *escambium* from his grantor if he loses. Of the warranty actions raising Glanvill's rules, the only examples consonant with this arise from a claim to dower made against the grantee by the grantor's widow. This claim is itself warranted by the heir, and the question is whether he must also warrant the grantee.[4] In 1199 the heir is

---

[1] *Gloucs.*, 981; cf. ibid. 1212, showing the demandant held in chief, so action probably started by *precipe*.   [2] *Glanvill*, II, 18.

[3] Tantalising hints are sometimes given, e.g., *CRR*, I, *186*, 343 and n. (Bacun; *sicut jus suum* in one roll, *sicut illas quas pater ejus qui exheredator ejus fuit dedit ut noscitur ei injuste* in another: this demandant was making many claims for small parcels).   [4] Above, pp. 43 and 72–3.

obliged to warrant both sides in several of the widow's claims against no less than eleven grantees. On the sixth he admits that the charter was made by his father, but says he had held only a quarter of a knight's fee and gave away so much that too little remains for the heir to do the king's service. The widow got her dower, but we do not know whether the heir was obliged to warrant the tenant.[1] If yes, he would have to find him *escambium* for the life of the widow.

But even in this context we are reminded that warranty was not just incidental to other claims, and not just about *escambium*. In 1211 a widow demands dower from a grantee, who again claims the heir's warranty; and the heir pleads that if the charter was indeed made by his father it was on his death-bed. The grantee seeks an issue on this, but accidentally defaults. The widow therefore gets her dower from the grantee, and there is an end of her action. But the grantee still pursues his claim for warranty; and it is not halted by his admission that he had lost the dower action through his own default and not that of the heir.[2] This was surely a bar to his claim for *escambium* for the life of the widow. But on her death a larger question would arise: was the land originally in dispute to come back to the heir in demesne or to be held of him by the grantee?

Less easy to understand are other claims to warranty by the grantee resisted by the heir on the basis of Glanvill's rules. In none does it appear that a third party is claiming the land from the grantee, and the grantee is probably countering some action by the heir himself:[3] but what? Consider a claim for warranty brought by

---

[1] *RCR*, I, 406–9, especially the claim against Pelham at 408; *RCR*, II, 6. In *BNB*, 944, a dower action raises the same objection not as between husband's heir and husband's grantee, but as between grantee's heir and grantee's grantee: *pater suus uendidit terram suam totam ita quod parum ei remansit de hereditate patris sui*; it is not considered, because the grantee himself had denied the marriage. This widow was claiming against several tenants, but their vouchers all seem to lead back to the same grantee: *CRR*, X, *137*, *146*, 235, *241*, *246*; *CRR*, XI, *804*, 1157, 1671, 2079.

[2] *CRR*, VI, *121*, 149 (Nereford), *186*, 218, 303, *365*; *PKJ*, IV, *4473*, *4579*.

[3] It may be some action against the grantee's tenant. In *Gloucs.*, 26, 173, *191*, the heir seems to be claiming the land itself, and resists the claim to warranty on two grounds: that the sub-tenant is his own lord (above, p. 117); *et petit judicium si pater suus potest dare medietatem tocius hereditatis sue*. In *Lincs.-Worcs.*, 560, 657, 785, the heir is probably taking rent directly from the sub-tenants: the grant was by his father to his sister, and he resists the claim to warranty on the ground that it was made *in lecto suo mortali* (above, p. 123, n. 2). Cf. *RCR*, I, 427 (Fulk f. Theobald; full references below, p. 133, n. 1): religious house

a grantee in *maritagium* against the grantor's heir. The heir admits his father's charter, but says it reserves the service of only an eighth of a knight whereas he holds the land for a quarter: *et petit considerationem curie utrum potuit terram illam dare per minus servitium quam terra debet.* The grantee denies that the land owes more than the eighth of a knight, and wants this put to the peers of the fee.[1] Our usual situation is reversed. We are told exactly what facts were in dispute and what the relevant law was; and we can even see the rules at work in their context. What we are not told is what has provoked the grantee's action, or what relief he is seeking. There seems, however, to be only one realistic possibility: the heir has been distraining for the larger service.

Two of our assumptions must be displaced for this. One is among those inherent in 'the forms of action' – namely, that the choice of writ is always governed by the factual nature of the dispute; and the proper form for a tenant distrained to do excessive services is *ne vexes.* But the choice of writ is sometimes governed by proof. *Ne vexes* is appropriate if the tenant has nothing special showing the rightful services, *de fine facto* if they were fixed by fine, the warranty action, if, as here, he has a charter.[2] And our assump-

---

claims rent granted by father of heir who says *inter alia* that his father gave more than a third *tocius terre sue; et petit inde considerationem curie utrum warantizare debuerit hujusmodi donationes.*

[1] *RCR*, I, *227, 301; RCR*, II, 90 (Ruffus).

[2] In connection with *de fine facto*, the proposition is obvious; *Novae Narrationes*, ed. Shanks and Milsom, Selden Society, vol. 80, p. clxxxiii. Plea roll examples concerning just the services between the parties: (*a*) *RCR*, I, 295 (Witefeld, *de placito finis facti*); *CRR*, I, 142 (*de placito servitii*); *RCR*, II, *81,* 239; (*b*) *CRR*, I, 380 (Kime; *de placito finis facti*), 394 (*vexabat eum exigendo... contra finem factum*); cf. *CRR*, V, 30. Concerning the services due to a superior lord: (*a*) *CRR*, V, 188 (Hose); (*b*) *CRR*, V, 240 (Lindon), *268; CRR*, VI, 22. Note that for Bracton the question whether warranty is conferred is simpler in the case of a fine than in the case of a charter; f. 389. In connection with *warantia carte* the proposition is less obvious, partly because of our preconceptions about this action and partly, no doubt, because the distraints would normally be stopped by production of the charter in the lord's court or in the county. Plea roll examples concerning just the services between the parties: (*a*) *CRR*, II, 3 and 47 (prior of St Bartholomew's; *de placito warantie carte*), 7 (*de placito vexacionis contra cartam...vicecomes interim faciat deliberari averia ipsius prioris*), 53 (*quare vexat...contra cartam*); (*b*) *Lincs.*, 258 (*de vexatione...contra tenorem cartarum*), 275 (*de warantia* cancelled, replaced by *quare uexat*); (*c*) *Lincs.*, 265; (*d*) *Lincs.*, 429a (both these clearly *warantia carte*; sheriff ordered *non permittat ipsum... inde uexari per illum uel per alium pro eius defectu*); (*e*) *CRR*, IV, 221, 268–9; (*f*) *Gloucs.*, 557; (*g*) *Yorks.*, 241; (*h*) *Yorks.*, 255; (*i*) *BNB*, 804; *CRR*, XV, 553 (power to assign; plaintiff is assignee). Concerning acquittance: (*a*) *RCR*, I, *340; RCR*, II, *43, 75*, 131–2; (*b*) *CRR*, VII, 320 (Overton); (*c*) *Gloucs.*, 1134. Bracton,

tion that *ne vexes* was a particular remedy goes with another: that distress was a particular entity. It was not. Distress was part of the process of the lord's court; and what the tenant is here countering is a claim made by the lord in his own court. For Bracton, as we have seen, a dispute about the quantum of the lord's return will be seen as touching the right and so needing a writ; and the writ will take it out of the lord's court.[1] But that has not yet happened at the time of Glanvill or the earliest rolls. The lord's court may proceed without writ. But the tenant may ask the king's court to intervene, and that is what he seems to be doing here.

What then are we to make of claims to warranty which somehow turn on Glanvill's rules but which do not concern quantum of service? All we know is that a grantee demands warranty on the basis of a charter, and the grantor's heir resists on the ground that it was a death-bed gift.[2] The grantee must be resisting some action of which we are not told, and it seems extravagant to postulate an independent dispute with some third party: the heir himself must be doing something. But before asking what it was, we may take our bearings by recalling the possible course of events if he brought an ordinary 'downward' action in the right claiming the land itself. The grantee could either put forward his charter by way of 'exception', seeking to bar the action on the ground that the heir should warrant him, or he could go to the grand assize claiming to be entitled to hold of the heir.[3] But these same issues can be reached in actions brought against the heir by the grantee. If he can produce only the testimony of peers that the ancestor took his homage, he will bring *de homagio capiendo*; and if the heir answers by claiming to be himself entitled in demesne, the grantee can go to the grand assize with the same special mise.[4] Behind that curtain we could not see Glanvill's rules even if the heir relied upon them; but it is worth remarking that one such action arises out of a gift to a younger brother.[5] If, on the other hand, the grantee

---

ff. 399–399b, gives both uses of the writ, but records the opinion of some that if it is the lord himself who distrains the tenant should use *ne vexes*.

[1] Above, p. 31.

[2] *RCR*, I, 157–8 (damaged but gist clear), 168. Cf. *PKJ*, IV, *3193*; *CRR*, V, 272 (Bigot), *296*, where the tenant's *warantia carte* is evidently in response to a mort d'ancestor by the heir.

[3] Above, p. 89.

[4] Examples above, p. 89, n. 4.

[5] *PRS*, XIV, 135–6 (full references in same note).

has a charter, he will bring the warranty action: and hence our cases.[1] It is the heir's reliance on Glanvill's rules that makes us particularly suspect this use of the action; but it may lie behind many unexplained demands for warranty.

So much for the conceptual place of these warranty actions, and indeed of *de homagio capiendo*: but what is their place in the practical scheme of things? What has happened to send the grantee to the king's court, and what is the meaning of the remedy that he seeks? The heir is to warrant him, but this cannot be in the traditional sense relating to a third party's claim; and as to the land itself, the grantee already has that. No satisfying answer is possible in terms only of those parts of the framework which survived into later times. Like other actions, the action claiming warranty was first to control the doings of lords' courts. Our heir is typically a new lord who has lately succeeded. He has taken the homage of his men or otherwise formally accepted them: but he rejects this grantee. That is what has sent the grantee to the king's court with his warranty action or his *de homagio capiendo*. But what does he fear? What does the rejection matter to him? When his holding of the land itself comes to be entirely protected in the king's court, it will matter little: the taking of homage or the like by the heir will be a ceremony; and warranty itself will matter only against third parties. But warranty had been the tenant's only title; and then to be rejected would be to lose the tenement. The countess Amice had lately taken control of her inheritance; and when her husband's grantee could not show that he was entitled to her warranty, she put him out. His assize taught her that she could not do that in her own court unless he pleaded willingly; but we saw that this may have been a new consequence of novel disseisin.[2] A lord could still without writ put out a tenant who would not do as much service as his own court judged to be due;[3] and in principle the cases are indistinguishable. Even if a rejected tenant knew that the lord could no longer put him out, he would still feel that he lacked the only title there was. The king's court cannot yet declare him an abstract owner: all it can do is to make the lord's court accept him. That is what this warranty action and *de homagio capiendo* are about.

---

[1] It seems that *warantia carte* eventually came to do the remaining work of *de homagio capiendo*; *Novae Narrationes*, ed. Shanks and Milsom, Selden Society, vol. 80, pp. clviii f.   [2] Above, pp. 45–6.

[3] *Glanvill*, IX, I; above, pp. 26, 31–2.

An entry of 1201, in which the underlying question probably had nothing to do with Glanvill's rules, gives what may be a direct glimpse of a lord's court playing this central part. One John seems to be facing a *quo waranto* in the court of earl Ferrers; but all we can see is his claim in the king's court that the earl should warrant him land granted by Robert, ancestor of the earl, to Colsuan his cook, predecessor of John. There is no saying whether it was as cook that Colsuan was predecessor; but since John has a confirmation from another Robert, we can probably identify the grantor as the earl who died in 1139. The question, therefore, is whether this earl is bound by a grant made sixty years earlier and renewed by his ancestors since. John wants this decided in the king's court; but he loses his nerve and hence the value of the case. The earl's attorney reports that *comes fecit inquiri per homines suos utrum debeat warantizare terram illam vel non, et ipsi dederunt ei intelligi quod non debet warantizare.* This would once have been the conclusive decision of such a question, and John presses the matter no further: *reddidit terram...in misericordiam comitis.*[1]

In that framework Glanvill's rules make sense. There was no ownership to pass or not by a valid or invalid grant. The ancestor made an allocation from his inheritance, and undertook as a matter of obligation that he and his heirs would maintain it. When he died, his heir had to decide whether to honour that obligation, or rather his court had to decide whether the circumstances were such that he was not bound to honour it. Glanvill summarises customs governing that decision; and he does after all have a procedural discussion showing how they are brought to bear. It is very short: the heirs of donors are bound to warrant gifts rightly made.[2]

It is because that framework vanishes that Glanvill's rules mostly vanish. They depend upon a relationship which requires renewal. Renewal by the grantor's heir becomes meaningless when his own court can no longer give effect to an adverse decision. Now he can proceed only under the king's writ; and whatever may be happening within the grand assize, the writs of entry will show him in the end as attacking the initial validity of a once-for-all grant. But the applicability of Glanvill's rules is not the only reason

[1] *CRR*, II, *13*, 16–17. For another and similar glimpse see *CRR*, I, 258 (William f. Oliver).
[2] *Glanvill*, VII, 2.

for seeing the renewable relationship as still real at the time of the
earliest rolls. Even lay grants for full service are often renewed or
confirmed by heirs; and the confirmation of an heir was worth
having even though he would normally ensure that his own charter
did not itself create any new obligation to warrant against third
parties, but merely assented to a continuation of the tenure.[1] But
the grants most regularly confirmed by heirs, whether at the time
the grant was made[2] or at the time the heir succeeded,[3] are grants
from which some question may still arise between heir and grantee,
gifts to church or family particularly governed by Glanvill's rules.

*   *   *

Many disputes in the early rolls can be seen to arise out of gifts
within the family, and there must be many more in which even that
fact is hidden – for example, within the grand assize.[4] A father
wishes to provide for a younger son, a daughter, or a bastard; or
he wishes his heir to have his land in his own lifetime. How does
he make his gift, and what may go wrong?

There are common factors, including allegations that the gift
was made *in ligia potestate* or from the donor's own purchase or
with his heir's consent.[5] These go to the validity of an undoubted
attempt to give. But possibilities in the family situation can bring
the fact itself into dispute. One is often associated with the
suggestion that it was during the donor's last illness: a charter is
said to have been fabricated by another member of the family
using the donor's seal. Once an heir questions his father's gift to

---

[1] Plea roll cases about *do* and *concedo*: (*a*) *PRS*, XIV, 124 (Hurton); (*b*) *PKJ*,
IV, *2720*; *CRR*, V, 105–6; (*c*) *Gloucs.*, 1459. Examples of usage: (*a*) case above,
p. 109, n. 5; (*b*) *CRR*, I, 155 (Traci); (*c*) *CRR*, I, 317 (Morba); (*d*) *CRR*, III,
188, 286, 318 (Waspaill); *CRR*, IV, 3.

[2] Examples above, p. 123, n. 4.

[3] Gifts to religious houses: (*a*) *CRR*, I, 155 (Traci); (*b*) *CRR*, II, 51 (Maskerell),
54–5; (*c*) *CRR*, IV, 314–15. Gifts in *maritagium*: (*a*) *CRR*, I, 142 (Castilliun; full
references above, p. 86, n. 3); (*b*) *CRR*, I, 317 (Morba); (*c*) *CRR*, II, *166*, 268
(Ludesdon); *CRR*, III, *48*; (*d*) *CRR*, III, *188, 286*, 318 (Waspaill); *CRR*, IV, 3.
Gift to younger son: *CRR*, VI, *5*, 85 (Russel). It is rarely possible to be certain
whether a confirmation was an independently evidenced consent at the time of
the gift, or was given later: some cases in this note may therefore belong above,
p. 123, n. 4 and vice versa.

[4] Consider *Gloucs.*, 981, above, pp. 125–6. Without the clerk's additions to
his original entry in common form we should not know even that the dispute
arose from a gift in *maritagium*, let alone that it turned on the size of the gift.

[5] Above, p. 123.

a religious house on the grounds that it was too large, and also that his sister, a nun at the house, *familiaris patri suo fuit, et sigillum suum habuit ad libitum suum*.[1] More often the favourite with access to the seal would be supposed to have used it for his own benefit.[2] Most often the heir accuses his mother or stepmother of concocting a gift to a younger son *quem plus dilexit*.[3] One lady indeed is supposed to have kept and used the seal long after her husband's death, and perhaps she had put the younger son in seisin then.[4]

This case introduces a larger difficulty both for donees and for us. The younger son claims from the heir on the basis of a gift from their father *tanquam adquisitio sua, quam in ligia potestate dedit ei pater suus pro homagio suo. . .et unde vestitus fuit et saisitus*. The *vestitus* allegation is rare, and must be intended to emphasise the *saisitus*.[5] Emphasis was here called for. The heir could not be bound unless seisin had passed:[6] but he now has the land, and no explanation is offered. Disputes arising out of family gifts are often of this posture. The person claiming under the gift is demandant, and the heir is somehow in possession.[7] Very rarely the claim itself

---

[1] *RCR*, I, *232*, 427 (Fulk f. Theobald), *433*; *RCR*, II, *63*, *209*; *PKJ*, I, *2621*; *CRR*, I, *168*, *181*. Cf. *BNB*, 255; *CRR*, XIII, *16*, 192, 349.

[2] (a) *PRS*(NS), XXXI, 81 (Macun); (b) *BNB*, 332; *CRR*, XIII, *2045*, 2107 (arising from power to assign). Cf. *CRR*, III, *128*, 332–3.

[3] *CRR*, VII, 138 (Andeville). Cf. *Northants.*, 638.

[4] *CRR*, I, 45, 66–7. For a wife supposed to have delivered seisin after her husband's death, see *Yorks.*, 287 (full references above, p. 124, n. 4).

[5] See Milsom, introduction to Pollock and Maitland, *History of English Law* (2nd ed., reissue 1968), pp. XXXV f. Although Glanvill does not have *uestitus* in his counts on the *precipe* for land (II, 3) or advowson (IV, 6), he does have it in his count on a writ of right of dower (VI, 8). It is occasionally found in the rolls, e.g., *CRR*, V, *111*, *304*, 310 (Romayn): *unde mater ipsius. . .fuit vestita et saisita et in custodia* of the tenant's father. Cf. *CRR*, IV, 23–4 (full references below, p. 135, n. 4): *quam terram pater suus ei in legia potestate sua dedit et in saisinam misit*, but it had then been returned to the father.

[6] *Glanvill*, VII, 1; above, p. 85, n. 3.

[7] Other claims under a grant to a younger son or younger brother: (a) *RCR*, I, *371*, *404*, *434*; *PKJ*, I, *2311*; *CRR*, I, 143 (Lec); (b) *RCR*, I, 438 (Bosco; full references above, p. 123, n. 3); (c) *CRR*, II, *176*, 184 (Tanu), *237*; *CRR*, III, *35*; (d) *CRR*, II, *183*, 248 (Cocus); (e) *CRR*, IV, 23–4 (full references below, p. 135, n. 4); (f) *CRR*, VII, *14*, 48–9; (g) by inference *PRS*(NS), XXXI, 85–6. Claims under a grant in *maritagium*: (a) *CRR*, I, 163, 342–3 (full references above, p. 86, n. 4); (b) *PRS*(NS), XXXI, 100–1 (full references above, p. 8, n. 2); (c) *CRR*, I, 12 (Lude); (d) *CRR*, I, 75 (Nuers; full references above, p. 6, n. 3); (e) *CRR*, I, 142 (Castilliun; full references above, p. 86, n. 3); (f) *CRR*, II, 117, 228–9; (g) *CRR*, V, *83*, *87*, *155*, 194 (Muncell), *295*; (h) *CRR*, VI, *270*, 288 (Lovingdon). See also *CRR*, VII, 121, 177 (Warenne).

shows how he came to get back,[1] or we find out by chance from another case;[2] but usually there is no indication.

One possibility is that donors wished to provide for their children after their own deaths without relinquishing present control. Livery would be formal only; the donor would die apparently seised; and the heir would enter on that basis. The early rolls sometimes show a father acting as *senescallus et custos* for his son. Twice he is defendant in novel disseisin, and pleads seignorial action by judgment of the son's court: in one he describes himself as *dapifer* of a lordship which had come to his son by marriage;[3] in the other he had himself given the fee to his son.[4] Whether or not the land originally came from his father, a son might genuinely entrust it to him on going overseas or the like.[5] But sometimes we are expressly told of a gift with the land being immediately handed back. Two kinds of case are found. In one, when the donee is usually the heir, the gift is by substitution and, as we shall see, often made in the lord's court;[6] and the land is at once returned to the father as steward[7] or as farmer[8] or *ad se sustentandum*.[9] In the other, the donee is a daughter for whom the father wishes to provide a marriage portion although no marriage is now in prospect;[10] and after the gift she places herself in her father's wardship. One such entry is particularly full: *saisinam habuit in vita patris sui, et postea consilio amicorum suorum posuit se in custodiam patris sui et post discessionem ejus posuit se similiter inde*

---

[1] (a) CRR, I, 142 (Castilliun; full references above, p. 86, n. 3; husband of donee in *maritagium* returned it to heir); (b) CRR, II, *183*, 248 (Cocus; youngest brother *commisit in custodiam* to eldest on whose death middle brother entered); (c) CRR, VII, *14*, 48–9 (on death of younger son to whom mother gave land, heir of elder son entered: heir of younger treats this as wrongful taking in wardship as though under age, but heir of elder is in fact denying the gift).

[2] Above, p. 86, n. 4.

[3] CRR, III, 62 (Revell), *129, 129–30, 138, 146, 149.*   [4] *Northants.*, 782.

[5] (a) RCR, I, *254*; PKJ, I, *3009*; RCR, II, 77 (Stokes), 220; PKJ, III, 815–16; (b) CRR, II, *235*, 242, 278–9; CRR, III, 27; (c) CRR, III, 234 (Berking; mother *custos* for crusader); (d) CRR, VII, *316*; *Gloucs.*, 257; (e) BNB, 984. Land entrusted to brothers: (a) CRR, II, *183*, 248 (Cocus); (b) *Lincs.-Worcs.*, 981; (c) *Gloucs.*, 200.   [6] Below, pp. 146 ff.

[7] (a) CRR, III, 129 (Ostricer; gift to heir, father remaining *ut senescallus*); (b) CRR, VII, *316*; *Gloucs.*, 257 (gift to younger son, father remaining as *custos*); (c) CRR, IV, 104 (Manneston; full references below, p. 151, n. 8; gift in *maritagium*, father holding thereafter *per balliam*).   [8] CRR, III, 6–7.

[9] CRR, VII, *142–3*, 200 (Daneville). Cf. the *convencio* in BNB, 36.

[10] Below, p. 145. Even on an immediate gift in *maritagium* there may be no sufficient livery if donor and donees establish a common household; CRR, VII, *121*, 177 (Warenne).

in custodiam of the heir against whom her claim is now brought.¹
The same must have happened when the donee was under age.² But
few cases are explicit. Even when the passing of seisin is the point
in dispute, it may be left to the grand assize.³ Only once, in an action
against the heir by a younger son based upon a gift from their
father, is issue joined on the father having died seised *ut de feodo
an sicut de custodia per manus* of the younger son.⁴

Formal delivery therefore explains some cases in which the
donee sues the heir; but it is questionable whether it explains them
all. Another conjecture will be offered, because it depends upon a
practice which may be of general importance, the converse of a gift
by the father who makes formal delivery but remains in actual control. He delivers without meaning to give, physically allocating land
to members of the family by way of allowance but not passing any
title. This may be what Glanvill, in his discussion of mort d'ancestor,
means by *commendatio*.⁵ On the rolls the noun used is '*ballia*',⁶

¹ *CRR*, I, 309 (Amundeville), 317, *378*; *PKJ*, I, *3243, 3271, 3364*; *CRR*, II,
42. Similar cases: (*a*) *Northants.*, 685, *748*; (*b*) *CRR*, XIII, *2178*; *BNB*, 342; and
possibly (*c*) *Lincs.*, 477. Cf. *Lincs.-Worcs.*, 636, *782*, below, p. 145, n. 7.
² Cf. *RCR*, I, 438 (Bosco; full references above, p. 123, n. 3), where a younger
son claims by gift from his father and says that after the father's death he and the
land were taken into wardship by the father's lord. In *Lincs.*, 1335, a father failed
to give to his infant son because he remained in seisin; and since the son was
a bastard he could take nothing.
³ *CRR*, VI, *5*, 85 (Russel).
⁴ *CRR*, III, 257, *321–2, 339*; *CRR*, IV, 23–4; *PKJ*, III, *1497, 1658*; cf. *CRR*,
III, *213*, 239, *244*. Cf. the issue reached in *RCR*, I, *254*; *PKJ*, I, *3009*; *RCR*, II,
77 (Stokes); 220; *PKJ*, III, 815–16: the heir's case probably rests upon a supposed
se demisit by the father who held thereafter as *senescallus et custos*.
⁵ Glanvill, XIII, 11: *si concedatur antecessorem illum cuius saisina petitur habuisse
inde qualem qualem saisinam sed per ipsum tenentem uel per aliquem antecessorum
eius, ueluti in uadio uel ex commendatione uel alia huiusmodi causa, eo ipso remanet
recognitio illa...*
⁶ (*a*) *RCR*, I, 358–9 (full references above, p. 99, n. 4; to brother); (*b*) *RCR*,
II, 220; *PKJ*, III, 815–16 (full references this page, n. 4; to father); (*c*) *CRR*,
I, 424 (Furnivall; see also above, p. 105, n. 2); *CRR*, II, *31, 66, 74*; (*d*) *CRR*, II,
235, 242, 278–9; *CRR*, III, 27 (to father); (*e*) *CRR*, IV, 58–9 (full references above,
p. 6, n. 2; apparently to farmer); (*f*) *CRR*, III, 182 (Scrouteby; probably to
brother), *231, 282*; (*g*) *CRR*, IV, 4, 46 (Cusinton; to brother; demandant reopens
matter by writ of right, 106 and later references); (*h*) *CRR*, IV, 104 (Manneston;
full references below, p. 151, n. 8; back to father who had given in *maritagium*);
(*i*) *CRR*, IV, *142*, 255–6, 300–1 (by doweress); (*j*) *PKJ*, III, *2259, 2479*; *CRR*, IV,
268, *269*; *CRR*, V, 28–9 (to doweress until proper dower can be delivered);
(*k*) *CRR*, V, 218–19, *271*, *300* (to brother); (*l*) *CRR*, VI, 41 (Heriet; full references
above, p. 99, n. 4; to son); (*m*) *Gloucs.*, 1018 (king grants escheat *ad se
sustentandum in seruicio suo quamdiu ei placuit...sicut de ballio*); (*n*) *CRR*, VIII,
120, 215–16; *BNB*, 87 (to brother for life); (*o*) *BNB*, 283; *CRR*, XIII, 573 (by

with '*committere*',[1] '*commodare*'[2] or '*concedere*'[3] as verbs; but the
phrase which most often suggests such an arrangement is '*ad
se sustentandum*'. References are not frequent; but this may reflect
not its infrequent use so much as its non-legal character; and
when it does appear, it is as the accompaniment of something
which does have legal consequence. When a father's gift to his son
was in issue, it was necessary to explain that his possession thereafter was only *ad se sustentandum*.[4] Conversely, a father might be
unwilling to give out-and-out on the marriage of his eldest son;
but he could make an allowance *ad se sustentandum*,[5] and agree
that the bride should be endowed from the land so advanced. If
the son died before the father the endowment *ex assensu patris*
would be of legal effect, but not the allowance itself. In such cases,
indeed, the creation of a 'legal' tenure would attract the rule against
being lord and heir, to which we shall come;[6] and this would be
disastrous. It is in that context that Bracton mentions the gift *ad se
sustentandum*; and for him the important point is that homage is

king to serjeanty tenant); (*p*) *BNB*, 95; *CRR*, VIII, 238, 290–1 (full references
below, p. 149, n. 5; mother to son); (*q*) *CRR*, XIII, 709 (full references above,
p. 47, n. 3; by king); (*r*) *CRR*, XV, 131; *BNB*, 750, 857 (by king, first *ad
voluntatem suam*, then *ad sustinendum in servicio suo*).

[1] (*a*) Northants., *167*, *205*, 541, 541a (*in warda ut filio et seruienti suo*); (*b*) *CRR*,
I, 266 (Bouda), *270*, *339*, *381–2*, *395* (to brother *custodiendas*); (*c*) *CRR*, II, *183*,
248 (Cocus; to brother *in custodiam*); (*d*) *CRR*, II, *225*, *241*, 275–6 (to lord's
steward *custodiendam*); (*e*) *CRR*, IV, 58–9 (full references above, p. 6, n. 2;
to farmer); (*f*) *PKJ*, III, 855 (to abbot *in custodia* with son and heir); (*g*) *CRR*,
VII, *142–3*, 200 (Daneville; to father *ad se sustentandum*); (*h*) *Lincs.-Worcs.*, *609*,
654, *750* (father *se demisit* in favour of infant son, *custodiam ipsius commisit* to
maternal relation); (*i*) *Lincs.-Worcs.*, 981 (to brother *custodiendam*); (*j*) *CRR*,
VIII, *120*, 215–16; *BNB*, 87 (to brother for life); (*k*) *BNB*, 754; *CRR*, XV, 145 (to
one *ad custodiendum ad opus* of infant younger son to whom father had given
land); (*l*) *BNB*, 984 (to father *custodiendam*). Cf. Douglas, *The Social Structure
of Medieval East Anglia*, Oxford Studies in Social and Legal History, vol. IX,
App. I, no. 6, p. 225: father *se demisit* to son, and says *non possum manum mittere
in predictis terris...nisi per commissionem* of son.

[2] (*a*) *RCR*, II, 26 (Hubald; to bastard elder brother *pro miseria sua*); (*b*) *CRR*,
VI, *276*, *282*, 309 (Neville; unexplained).

[3] (*a*) *CRR*, VI, 143–4, *197*, *250*, 299 (life concession to bastard uncle); (*b*) *BNB*,
566; *CRR*, XIV, 1473, *1506* (to mother and her present husband, *misericordia
motus...pro uoluntate sua et ad sustentacionem ipsorum...non habuerunt seisinam
aliquam nisi de gracia*). Cf. Bracton, f. 277.

[4] (*a*) *CRR*, VII, *142–3*, 200 (Daneville); (*b*) *BNB*, 566 (in preceding note,
where it is alleged that the mother *se demisit* in favour of the son). Cf. the
convencio in *BNB*, 36.

[5] (*a*) Northants., *167*, *205*, 541, 541a; (*b*) *PKJ*, III, 997; *CRR*, IV, *19*; (*c*) *CRR*,
II, 213–14. Cf. the puzzling *CRR*, VII, *93*, 226 (Alrecumbe).

[6] Below, pp. 139 ff.

not taken.[1] His verb is '*concedo*'; and whether or not we can suppose a connection with the failure of that word in charters to carry warranty,[2] we can legitimately see a permissive arrangement

Allowances of this kind could play a part in law-suits, most obviously among the facts considered by a grand assize, without appearing on the record.[3] There are, for example, many claims by heirs against members of the family claiming by gift; and they must have got in somehow.[4] But the arrangement may also help to explain the converse case that we were considering: the person claiming under the gift is demanding the land from the heir, and does not say how the heir got it back. Perhaps he just took it back when the donor died, on the basis that this had been only an allowance from the donor.

Put like that, the dispute sounds purely factual: gift or allowance? But the difference would not be clear-cut in a world in which a grant was itself a renewable allocation; and we have seen that it is into such a world that Glanvill's rules fit. Consider his statement that a father cannot easily give any part of his inheritance to a younger son without his heir's consent.[5] In practical terms, what does he mean? If he had a substitution in mind, he could mean that the lord would not easily agree for fear of a later claim in the king's court by the heir. But he is talking of subinfeudations; and in that context he can only mean that the father cannot easily ensure that his heir will honour the gift. It is an allocation which

[1] Bracton, f. 277: *sive* should presumably be read as *sine*.

[2] Above, p. 132, n. 1.

[3] Consider *CRR*, VI, *71, 127, 172* (Craucumbe), *223, 243, 277, 352*; *CRR*, VII, *31*.

[4] Arising out of gift to younger son or younger brother: (*a*) *PRS*(NS), XXXI, 81 (Macun); (*b*) *CRR*, I, *310* (Robert f. Neil; full references above, p. 91, n. 1); (*c*) *RCR*, II, 88–9 (full references above, p. 107, n. 3); (*d*) *CRR*, I, 359 (Geoffrey f. Warin; full references below, p. 151, n. 5); (*e*) *CRR*, IV, 34–5 (full references above, p. 97, n. 2); (*f*) *CRR*, IV, *181*, 193–4, *258–9*; *CRR*, V, *14*; (*g*) *CRR*, VI, *5*, 85 (Russel); (*h*) *CRR*, VI, *191*, *224*, *245*; *CRR*, VII, 20 (Monacus), *140*, *197*. Arising out of gift in *maritagium*: (*a*) *CRR*, I, *296* (from court of Tickhill); (*b*) *CRR*, III, *188*, *286*, 318 (Waspaill); *CRR*, IV, *3*; (*c*) *CRR*, V, *132*, 137 (Tresgoz), *163*, *231*, 244, *247*; (*d*) *CRR*, VI, 144 (Ebroicis; Orenga was presumably the tenant's mother, not the demandant's), *171*, *194*, *339*, 367; (*e*) *CRR*, VI, *26*, 95–6, 175 (Roppesle; see also above, p. 86, n. 4), *176*, *240*, *246*, *312*. There is of course no mystery when the heir formally pleads that too much was given; see the cases above, p. 125, nn. 3 and 4.

[5] *Glanvill*, VII, 1: *non poterit de facili preter consensum heredis sui filio suo postnato de hereditate sua quantamlibet partem donare.*

the heir is not bound by the custom of his own court to renew, an allowance indeed. And when the question is removed to the king's court, which will be by writ patent to the heir if it is he who has the land,[1] by the heir's 'downward' claim[2] or the younger son's *de homagio capiendo*[3] if the younger son has it, it can only go to the grand assize. The knights will declare whether the heir has greater right to hold in demesne or the younger son to hold of him; and this result is all we learn. But so long as the rule has any force, the mere finding that the father gave cannot determine their verdict: they must consider whether the land came to him by inheritance or purchase, what other land he had, whether the heir consented at the time, and whether he has anyway taken the younger son's homage for this land.

Assertions that homage was taken are a particular feature of cases arising out of a gift to a younger son or younger brother. If it is the donee who claims from the heir, he can say no more than that the gift itself was for homage.[4] If the claim is by the immediate or a later heir of the donor, the tenant claiming under the gift may allege the taking of homage at every devolution on either side;[5]

---

[1] *PRS*(NS), xxxi, 105, 100–1 (full references above, p. 8, n. 2).

[2] Examples above, p. 137, n. 4. In *RCR*, i, 350; *CRR*, i, 310 (Robert f. Neil; full references above, p. 91, n. 1) the heir began by disseising his younger brother who got back by the assize and so put the heir to his 'downward' claim in the right. Cf. *BNB*, 754, *CRR*, xv, 145, where the heir himself was in Ireland when his father died, and his lord took all his lands into hand *sicut in custodia*, including what the father had elaborately given to a younger son.

[3] *PRS*, xiv, 135–6 (full references above, p. 89, n. 4): the original gift was by an elder to a younger brother; this *de homagio capiendo* is brought by the son of the younger against the son of the elder, who claims to be entitled in demesne and puts himself on the grand assize with special mise; when he defaults he is described as *petens*; he eventually takes homage in court.

[4] (a) *CRR*, i, 45, 66–7; (b) *CRR*, i, 143 (Lec; full references above, p. 133, n. 7).

[5] (a) *PRS*, xiv, 135–6 (above, n. 3; the tenant alleges homage by his father to the donor and apparently by himself to the donor; his action is to compel its taking by the donor's son); (b) *CRR*, ii, 137 (Eddingeton), *302* (claim by heir's widow in dower against younger son donee, who alleges homage to donor and then to heir); (c) *CRR*, ii, *2, 42, 84, 128, 173*, 206–7 (younger son donee alleges homage to donor and then to heir); (d) *CRR*, iv, 187–8 (full references below, p. 142, n. 1; heir of eldest son against one warranted by youngest; land had been given by father to middle son, and youngest alleges homage to father and then to eldest); (e) *CRR*, iv, *181*, 193–4, *258–9*; *CRR*, v, *14* (heir of elder son against heir of younger, who alleges gift by father with elder's consent to younger and homage by younger son to father, then by younger son to elder son, then by this tenant to elder son, then by this tenant as younger son's son to this demandant as elder son's son).

and sometimes he will end by saying that he himself has done homage to this demandant.[1] What is the function of these assertions?

Homage had been the most powerful bond there could be between lord and tenant; and one of the mystical forces it brought into play was that which barred the lord from claiming the tenement for himself so long as the force lasted. Heritability itself seems to have grown from the process by which it lengthened out to affect another generation. The details may be irrecoverable: but suppose a stage at which this tenant's homage protects him for his own life, even though the original lord dies; he will still do homage to the lord's heir, because that will later compel the lord's heir to accept his own heir.[2] Between strangers in blood, the process may be complete at the time of the earliest rolls. Between brothers, it looks as though the heir is always entitled unless there is a recent homage to keep him out. So far as the court of the donor and his heir is concerned, a benefit to a younger son can be no more than an allowance. Only an external force can bind the heir; and homage is seen as invoking an external force, an older and more absolute one than the rules of the king's court. Perhaps the force was understood to make the son a stranger; and in earlier times it may somehow have put him outside the family for the purpose of inheritance.[3]

For Glanvill, it still has disconcerting effects on the devolution not of the inheritance itself but of the portion granted to a younger son.[4] The homage needed to keep the donor out as lord also keeps him from inheriting if on the ordinary canons he happens to be heir of the grantee; and within the family he often will be. Suppose a grant for homage and service made to the middle of three brothers, who dies childless but survived by the other two. So long

---

[1] (a) Case last cited; (b) CRR, I, 310 (Robert f. Neil; full references above, p. 91, n. 1). Cf. BNB, 754; CRR, xv, 145.

[2] Thorne, 'English Feudalism and Estates in Land', [1959] *Cambridge Law Journal*, p. 193 at pp. 200–1.

[3] Among the puzzles about forisfamiliation is its tenurial bearing. Maitland supposed a subinfeudation; Pollock and Maitland, *History of English Law* (2nd ed.), II, pp. 292–3, 438, n. 3. But *Glanvill*, VII, 3, contemplates the forisfamiliation of an elder son; and his word 'assignet', together with the discussion immediately following (below, p. 147, at n. 6), may indicate a substitution. Bracton's allusions, ff. 6b, 64, do not help. It is suggested below, p. 151, that gifts to younger sons may first have been commonly by substitution.

[4] *Glanvill*, VII, 1, on the rule against being lord and heir.

as there are heirs there can be no escheat,[1] and the question is who
will inherit. If the grant was made by a stranger, of course it will
be the eldest brother.[2] If the eldest brother himself made the
grant, however, the homage keeps him out, and the youngest
brother will inherit.[3] If the grant was made by their father, either
from his own purchase or with the consent of the eldest brother,
the eldest may possibly be able to hold until the lordship descends
to him on the father's death; but then, if not at once, the land will
again go to the youngest brother.[4] If he in turn dies childless, but
survived by the eldest brother and his two sons, it will be the
younger rather than the elder of these who is eventually entitled.[5]

   Glanvill, having just stressed the difficulty of gifts to younger
sons, says that this extraordinary rule against being lord and heir
often came into play because such gifts were frequent.[6] In the
rolls the rule is common, and it is yet another thing that may lie
behind more cases than we can see. Although in 1231 justices are
in trouble for directing its application within the general verdict
of an assize of mort d'ancestor,[7] Glanvill thought that the proper

---

[1] For what may be an example of the heir of an elder brother claiming by
escheat on the death of the heir of the younger, *CRR*, VII, *106*, 107 (Windlesores),
218–19, 231; but the case is not straightforward.

[2] (*a*) *CRR*, III, 323–4 (full references above, p. 108, n. 2; notice the demandant
eldest brother's explanation that the middle brother *de eo non tenuit*); (*b*) *Lincs.*,
190.

[3] (*a*) *CRR*, II, 191–2 (argument of sister's son, that brother's son as *filius
feffatoris...non debet esse heres*); (*b*) *PKJ*, IV, 4073; (*c*) presumably *BNB*, 37
(grant to uncle); (*d*) *CRR*, XIV, *555*; *BNB*, 637 (notice argument by eldest son's
son that his own son should be heir).

[4] (*a*) *CRR*, I, *79*; *RCR*, I, 353 (Takele), *354*; *PKJ*, I, *2219*; *RCR*, II, *121*;
and a separate claim by the same plaintiff, *RCR*, I, *193*, 398–9, *405*; *CRR*, II,
302; (*b*) *CRR*, I, *140, 197, 298*, 449 (Richard f. Hamo); *CRR*, II, *18*; (*c*) *Lincs.*,
190; (*d*) *CRR*, IV, 187–8 (full references below, p. 142, n. 1); (*e*) *Gloucs.*, 560.
See too the slightly obscure case in *PRS*, XIV, 32 (Perci).

[5] (*a*) *RCR*, I, *252*, 318–19, *384*; *PKJ*, I, *3522* (and note thereto), *2111, 2776*;
RCR, II, *124*, 254–5; *CRR*, I, *308*; *CRR*, II, *94, 144*, 200; there also survive
entries of litigation between the tenant in this case and the daughter of his elder
brother, especially *CRR*, I, 61; (*b*) *Northants.*, 719; (*c*) *CRR*, II, 191–2; (*d*) *CRR*, III,
24 (Beche; obscure; but demandant clearly meets objection that his elder brother
has a son living by reference to lord-and-heir rule). See also *Glanvill*, VII, 1,
below, p. 141, n. 1.

[6] *Glanvill*, VII, 1: *iuris quidem questiones sepius emergunt.*

[7] *CRR*, XIV, *1331*, 1474; *BNB*, 564 and note following the case; the original
assize has not been found, but the second assize mentioned by the recognitors
is *CRR*, XIII, 1137. Here the question arises as against a stranger. Both this
question, and that between the brothers themselves, are considered by Bracton,
f. 277; and he considers the latter also at ff. 271b–2, in both places citing a case

course;[1] and if it is happening on the earliest rolls, naturally we cannot see it.[2] We cannot even see when the question is withdrawn from the assize because it will be hidden behind a broader exception – namely, that the parties are of the same stock.[3] What is more important is that we do not necessarily see the rule at work even in an action in the right. In 1208 a grand assize declared that a tenant had greater right to hold of a demandant than the demand-ant to hold in demesne. The demandant had counted on the seisin of his grandfather; and if the clerk had recorded in equally common form only the tenant's claim of the grand assize, we should not know even the relationship of the parties. Luckily he noted allegations made by the tenant and confirmed by the knights

from Pateshill's Yorkshire eyre of 1218–19 which is not on the surviving roll; *Yorks.*, pp. xiii f. From other eyres of Pateshill, however, conflicting decisions survive. In 1221 a younger brother is driven to his writ of right when the elder is vouched; *Gloucs.*, 560. And in 1226–7, in a Yorkshire case in the *Note Book*, a sister succeeds against her brother on the basis of the rule; *BNB*, 1857, described by the annotator as *Error*. For earlier cases, see below, n. 2.

[1] *Glanvill*, VII, 1: gift to younger brother who dies childless; donor takes and faces assize by his own two sons; *primogenitus filius uersus patrem et postnatus filius uersus fratrem primogenitum premonstrato modo placitare possunt.* This would probably have been unthinkable later; *CRR*, XI, 645; *BNB*, 949: as against a stranger a son cannot even on a writ of right claim while his father is living, even though the father warrants the claim and would himself be excluded as *dominus*. For the converse case in which the natural heir brings the assize against one entitled by virtue of the rule, Glanvill contemplates enforcement within the assize by way of exception; XIII, 11, below, n. 3.

[2] The rule is rarely mentioned in assizes on the early rolls. It may be raised by a demandant in answer to the objection by a stranger tenant that there is a nearer heir: (*a*) *RCR*, I, 353 and 398–9 (full references above, p. 140, n. 4; both end without a decision); (*b*) *PKJ*, IV, 4073 (ruling that nearer heir should have the assize, but only after tenant's denial of any tenure between the brothers). Or it may be raised by a demandant in answer to a claim by the tenant or his warrantor to be himself the nearer heir: (*a*) *CRR*, II, 191–2 (grantor grants to brother who dies childless; assize by sister's son against grantor's son, who meets argument that *non debet esse heres* by assertion that he has elder brother *qui dominus est*; assize stopped and demandant put to writ of right because parties of one stock); (*b*) *Lincs.*, 190 (one sister died childless; assize by second sister's son against brother's son, who denies that dead sister held of his father; and for this reason demandant put to writ of right).

[3] This exception is very common; see further below, p. 175. It is mentioned in *Glanvill*, XIII, 11, where it is immediately followed by a special exception based upon the rule against being lord and heir. If a father enfeoffed his middle son who died childless, the special exception seems to keep the youngest son in against an assize by the eldest. There is no trace on the rolls, and presumably it would be covered by the exception of one stock, as may have been the converse claim by the youngest son when the eldest has got in; cf. the last two cases in the preceding note.

in a *quia* clause most unusually added to their verdict. The demandant's father was the eldest of three brothers; the tenant is the
youngest; and the grandfather had given this land to the middle
brother for homage, which after the grandfather's death was
renewed to the eldest. There is no mention of lord and heir, but the
rule decided the case; and, whether or not the knights really just
found the facts, its application is represented as their doing and
not that of the justices.[1]

It would be nice to know whether that case would have ended
differently if the homage had not been renewed to the demandant's
father. In the thirteenth century the rule against being lord and
heir may have become a centrifugal force imparted by the original
gift, which held the land as a permanent satellite to the inheritance;
and Maitland even saw this result as a conscious set-off to primo-
geniture.[2] But it is hard to believe that anybody desired the result,
or that the homage so much stressed was just a ceremony attendant
upon each devolution of two self-sufficient ownerships. In the
family context it seems still to be a force which the father of
a younger son can invoke or not. If he does not invoke it, there will
be nothing to keep his heir out. If he does invoke it, the heir will
be kept out even if the younger son dies childless so that the
purpose of the gift has failed. But so long as the results were seen as
flowing from the homage itself, the effect was probably finite.
Glanvill would hardly have written as he did of gifts to younger
sons if the renewal of homage could here be automatically
compelled.[3]

A growing notion that the consequences flowed from tenure
rather than from homage may be reflected in 1219: it is unsuccess-
fully argued that a gift in *maritagium* attracted the lord-and-heir
rule because it was for service.[4] The point of such a gift was to
avoid the consequences of homage. In 1208, on the death of their
aunt without issue, a brother and sister both claim land given on
her marriage by their grandfather. The brother claims it as

---

[1] *CRR*, III, *144?*; *PKJ*, III, *1608, 2384*; *CRR*, IV, 187–8, *290*; *PKJ*, IV, *2632*;
CRR, V, *38–9, 69*, 134–5.

[2] Pollock and Maitland, *History of English Law* (2nd ed.), II, pp. 292 f.

[3] *Glanvill*, VII, 1.

[4] *BNB*, 61; *CRR*, VIII, 73. This may possibly explain why gifts for service
are sometimes called 'free' marriage: (*a*) *RCR*, I, *227, 301*; *RCR*, II, 90 (Ruffus);
(*b*) *CRR*, II, *117*, 228–9. On liability for incidents: (*a*) *CRR*, V, *218–19, 271*, 300
(Valeines); (*b*) *BNB*, 295; *CRR*, XIII, 1143.

maritagium which should revert to the inheritance. The sister says that homage was done, of course by the aunt's husband: her brother is lord and so she is next heir.[1] A gift such as that supposed by the sister can even be called *maritagium* but behaves like a grant to a younger son: homage is done by the husband in the first place, and is repeated at every devolution.[2] The name then reflects only the occasion and the fact that the gift is to the wife rather than the husband. But when Glanvill says that the husband never does homage for *maritagium*,[3] he is referring to the customary arrangement whose special properties will be destroyed when homage is taken. Traditionally that is when the third heir enters, but it may be long before: he is just the first who can insist.[4] In the meantime, the donees under this arrangement are secured by another external force. Like dower, the gift might be made *ad hostium ecclesie*;[5] and Glanvill explains that if the donees have to sue the donor or his heir, they may choose to do so in a church court as on a pledge of faith.[6] But the important difference from the gift to the younger son is its force within the heir's own court. If the gift is proper in amount and otherwise, he is bound by custom to maintain it.[7]

The early rolls suggest that donors and their heirs did concern themselves with maintaining such gifts. If the donee sued in a lay court, it would of course be by writ patent to the heir.[8] But we

---

[1] *CRR*, v, 166–7: nothing tells us who is the tenant, but probably he is the aunt's husband. Cf. the mysterious *CRR*, III, 24 (Beche).

[2] *PRS*, XIV, *29–30*; *RCR*, I, *4, 30*, 39–40: homage to grantor by grantee husband, then by his son, then by son to grantor's son (accompanied by a second relief). The name '*maritagium*' can also be applied to a grant by substitution: (a) *CRR*, IV, 104 (Manneston; full references below, p. 151, n. 8); (b) *CRR*, VI, 201 (Walda; full references above, p. 125, n. 4). Sometimes the tenure by which daughters held may not have been clear: *RCR*, II, *229*; *CRR*, I, 298 (Pilate; for the sisters' relationship to him, see *RCR*, II, 124).   [3] *Glanvill*, IX, 2.

[4] *BNB*, 295; *CRR*, XIII, 1143. Cf. Bracton, ff. 21b–22 and the case to which he refers, *BNB*, 664. Earlier examples of homage taken before the third heir: (a) *CRR*, III, 24 (Beche: by donee husband on succession of donor's heir); (b) *Beds.*, 101 (by donee husband to female donor on death of her husband). For a second heir resisting a claim for homage and relief, see *CRR*, VI, 354–5; *PKJ*, IV, *4487, 4528, 4693*. For a curious reference to the third degree, see *CRR*, IV, 2 (Weston), 76, 118 (king *illam audire vult*), *187*, *219–20, 271*; *CRR*, V, *3*.

[5] *CRR*, VII, *121*, 177 (Warenne). In dower the circumstances of the endowment are most often mentioned when it is supposed to have been *ex assensu patris*: (a) *CRR*, VIII, *137*, 231–2, 351; *BNB*, 91; (b) *Gloucs.*, 1165; (c) *CRR*, I, 323 (Avenell), 361, quoted below, p. 148, n. 5.

[6] *Glanvill*, VII, 18. Contrast Bracton, f. 407b and the case to which he refers; *BNB*, 442; *CRR*, XIV, 575.   [7] *Glanvill*, VII, I, 2.

[8] *PRS*(NS), XXXI, 105, 100–1 (full references above, p. 8, n. 2).

seem also to see donors or their heirs acting of their own motion, at least once even in the king's court, on behalf of the person they thought entitled under the gift.[1] They might also seek to enforce their own rights in their own court.[2] But novel disseisin would prevent this: now they need a writ, and the writ will take the case to the court first of the lord paramount and then of the king. In the king's court we are lucky if we can identify the dispute as between heir and grantee, let alone tell what it was about. Occasionally the heir can be heard to say that too much had been given.[3] But that like all other questions is usually lost behind the grand assize.[4] Nor in the end is it only to the historian that these questions are lost. Like remainders, which seem also to have suffered in the transfer of jurisdiction,[5] such gifts were parts of a system of renewable allocations. In the king's court, the heir's customary obligation to maintain *maritagium* generated an ownership as powerful as that springing from homage, though less ample because until homage is done the land will revert on failure of lineal heirs; and the end of that was to be estates differing only in quantum.

But the difference had been in quality. To take homage was to give independent standing. The *maritagium*, like the allowance, was an arrangement within the inheritance; and for Glanvill the beneficiaries were not independent. He tells us, though it has disappeared by the time of the early rolls, that so long as homage has not been done they cannot claim the land from a stranger without joining the warrantor – that is, the present holder of the inherit-

---

[1] In *CRR*, III, 305 (Sancto Mauro; see Hall, 'The Early History of Entry sur Disseisin', *Tulane Law Review*, XLII (1968), p. 584 at p. 587) it looks as though the heir of a grantor in *maritagium* disseised the donee's second husband in order to instal a son by her first husband. This should be compared with William Butler (above, p. 51), who tried to achieve a like result by action in the king's court.

[2] *RCR*, I, 447–8; cf. ibid. 368. Or, of course, they might seek to enforce their own rights without any judicial process: *CRR*, III, 66 (Truue); *CRR*, IV, *283*. Cf. *CRR*, VI, 140–1, *186*.

[3] See the cases above, pp. 125–6.

[4] *Gloucs.*, 981 (above, p. 126, n. 1). Compare cases in which we can tell that the claim was by the heir of a grantor in *maritagium* against one claiming under the grant, but cannot identify the actual issue (full references to each, above, p. 137, n. 4): (*a*) *CRR*, III, 318 (Waspaill); (*b*) *CRR*, V, 137 (Tresgoz); (*c*) *CRR*, VI, 144 (Ebroicis).

[5] An interesting pair is *CRR*, VI, *135*, 159–60 (claim by 'remainderman' fails); *CRR*, VII, 36 (claim by grantor himself, perhaps on the other's behalf). Cf. *Lincs.-Worcs.*, 256 (lord acting on behalf of remainderman).

ance.[1] The same had probably been true of the gift in alms;[2] and in the early rolls it is still true of dower.[3] In dower it was preserved because the husband could easily make a conflicting grant; and even when the heir becomes unnecessary to the widow's claim as such, he is often vouched by the tenant. But there is more to it than that. As against a third party, the seisin of land held in dower can be attributed to the heir as warrant.[4] We are looking back to a time at which holdings in dower, in *maritagium*, or in alms, for none of which is homage done,[5] were just allocations within the inheritance being carried by the heir.

There remains a practical point about *maritagium*. It was essentially a gift to the daughter, and until a child was born it had no effect beyond providing for her for life. A father might naturally wish to make the provision even though no marriage was in prospect, perhaps for a child who might not marry until after his death. This seems to be the purpose of the gift generally described as *ad se maritandam*.[6] When she married it would behave and be known as her *maritagium*; and there is no telling how many *maritagia* began in that way. Only a difficulty already mentioned brings the *ad se maritandam* stage on to the rolls. A woman may not be able to manage land; and after the death of her husband even a grantee in *maritagium* might incautiously place it and herself in the *custodia* of the heir.[7] For the same reason a father might

---

[1] *Glanvill*, VII, 18: *sine waranto inde placitare non debet, sicut supra de dotibus dictum est.*

[2] Cf. the early cases in which a warrant acts on behalf of his grantee in alms, above, pp. 50–1.

[3] Above, p. 43; *Glanvill*, VI, 8–11. On the writ of right of dower, the question only arises when the case is removed from the warrant's own court. Refusals to answer the doweress without her warrant are common on the early rolls. For a striking example, and one which brings out the difference between this refusal and the power in the tenant himself to vouch, see *CRR*, V, 179 (Lenham); *PKJ*, IV, *3334, 3831,* 4416, *4426*: the doweress says her son is overseas and she does not know whether he is alive or dead.

[4] (*a*) *CRR*, II, 137 (Eddingeton), *302*; (*b*) *PKJ*, III, 997; *CRR*, IV, *19*; (*c*) *PKJ*, III, 2389 (notice unusual indication that writ was patent); *CRR*, V, *24*, 241–2, *308, 314*; (*d*) *BNB*, 345; *CRR*, XIII, 2239.   [5] *Glanvill*, IX, 2.

[6] (*a*) *CRR*, I, 309, 317 (Amundeville; full references above, p. 135, n. 1); (*b*) *CRR*, II, *166*, 268 (Ludesdon); *CRR*, III, *48*; (*c*) *CRR*, VI, 241–2 (full references above, p. 50, n. 1). An alternative phrase is *ad se consulendum*: (*a*) *CRR*, XIII, *2178*; *BNB*, 342; (*b*) *BNB*, 779 (both phrases used). Sometimes a gift described as *maritagium* was evidently of this kind; *Northants.*, 685, *748*. And sometimes *ad maritandum* is used to describe a grant in furtherance of a projected marriage: (*a*) *PKJ*, III, 968; (*b*) *CRR*, VII, *93*, 226 (Alrecumbe); (*c*) *Gloucs.*, 247.   [7] *Lincs.-Worcs.*, 636, *782*.

make such a gift and yet retain actual control; and the examples found all generated law-suits because of uncertainty over the passing of seisin.[1]

The last kind of family gift to be discussed is that to the heir himself, and it brings us back to gifts by substitution. The father can of course make some immediate allowance to his heir apparent; but he must on no account take his homage. The only definitive thing he can do is to step aside and have his heir do homage to the lord. This homage is frequently recited;[2] and the substitution was commonly effected in the lord's court[3] and repeated or proclaimed in the county court.[4] But there had also to be a real handing over of seisin;[5] and this is why, when the father remained in actual

---

[1] Above, p. 134. Donee and land expressly said to have been in *custodia* of donor or heir: (*a*) *CRR*, I, 309, 317 (Amundeville; full references above, p. 135, n. 1); (*b*) *Northants.*, 685, *748*; (*c*) *CRR*, XIII, *2178*; *BNB*, 342. Mort d'ancestor apparently by heir of donor: *CRR*, II, *166*, 268 (Ludesdon); *CRR*, III, *48*. On death of father land taken into wardship, but an inquest does not know whether this was with son and heir or with daughter who claims under such a gift: *CRR*, VI, 220, 241–2 (full references above, p. 50, n. 1).

[2] (*a*) *PRS*, XIV, 25–6 (the father features as tenant in later litigation; *RCR*, I, *352*, 362; *CRR*, I, *125*; *PKJ*, I, *2691*; for other related litigation, see above, p. 99, n. 4); (*b*) *RCR*, II, 134 (William f. John; full references below, p. 148, n. 1); (*c*) *CRR*, II, 213–14; (*d*) *CRR*, III, 240–1 (something apparently wrong), *266*, *328*, *342*; *CRR*, IV, 125; (*e*) *CRR*, VI, *121*, *132*, 211 (Beckele); (*f*) *CRR*, VI, *255*, *259*, 298 (Flammaville; apparently in favour of a stranger with the heir's concurrence); (*g*) *CRR*, VII, 117–18; (*h*) *CRR*, VII, 136–7 (in favour of bastard son); (*i*) *CRR*, VII, *142–3*, 200 (Daneville); (*j*) *CRR*, VII, 316; *Gloucs.*, 257 (in favour of younger son; notice the interval of six years between the two entries); (*k*) *Gloucs.*, 232 (younger son does fealty to lord, elder overseas); (*l*) *Lincs.-Worcs.*, *481*, 519, *262*, 316 (also fealty); (*m*) *BNB*, 95 (full references below, p. 149, n. 5); (*n*) *BNB*, 428; *CRR*, XIV, 457. For early charter examples, both in favour of younger sons, see F. M. Stenton, *The First Century of English Feudalism* (2nd ed.), p. 55 and references there given, and p. 281, Appendix no. 41.

[3] Cases also in preceding note: (*a*) *PRS*, XIV, 25–6; (*b*) *RCR*, II, 134; *CRR*, III, 25; (*c*) *CRR*, VI, 298; (*d*) *CRR*, VII, 136–7; (*e*) *BNB*, 95. Other cases: (*a*) *CRR*, I, 19 (Dacus); (*b*) *CRR*, III, 69 (Carbunell), *243*; (*c*) *CRR*, III, 129 (Ostricer); (*d*) *BNB*, 779.

[4] (*a*) *PRS*, XIV, 25–6 (in both preceding notes; homage *in pleno comitatu et in curia sua*); (*b*) *CRR*, III, 129 (in preceding note; *venit...cum quodam capitali domino...in plenum comitatum et dixit quod ipse deposuerat se de tota terra sua in curia capitalis domini sui*); (*c*) *Northants.*, 846; (*d*) *BNB*, 566; *CRR*, XIV, 1473, *1506*. Cf. *Gloucs.*, 1461 (before justices itinerant).

[5] (*a*) *Lincs.-Worcs.*, *481*, 519, *262*, 316 (*tunc exiuit et absentauit se per aliquot dies*); (*b*) *Gloucs.*, 1461 (question to recognitors); (*c*) *BNB*, 428; *CRR*, XIV, 457 (words of gift *post prandium* and homage to lord, but *pater suus semper fuit in seisina*). In *BNB*, 36, the arrangement between father and son is treated as a *conuencio*, but still apparently given effect against third parties. Cf. *Gloucs.*, 255.

control of some or all of the land, it had to be made clear that he did so as agent or licensee of the son.[1]

The rolls sometimes use '*resignavit*'[2] or '*se deposuit*'[3] for this transaction; but the commonest phrase is '*se demisit*', and that will here be used as though it was a name.[4] Ordinarily it was just an accelerated inheritance having no effect beyond the life of the father.[5] But in one common situation it could permanently alter the devolution of the land. There are two brothers, Geoffrey and John; and the elder dies in their father's lifetime having a son Arthur. When the father dies should it be Arthur who succeeds as heir or John? In the end the decision went for Arthur; but in England it was delayed because a John was king, and this was his own case. For Glanvill, writing when the father of that Geoffrey and that John was still alive and had a yet older son to succeed him, there was a great doubt. He personally favours Arthur but represents the current law as *melior est conditio possidentis*, though subject to an overriding possibility: if Geoffrey had done homage for the inheritance during the father's lifetime, then Arthur is clearly entitled.[6] He does not explain that homage, but it would have followed upon a *se demisit* by the father. A case which first appears in 1199 and is settled in 1205 exactly illustrates his point:

---

[1] Above, p. 134; cf. the charter quoted above, p. 136, end of n. 1.

[2] (*a*) *CRR*, III, 129 (Ostricer); (*b*) *CRR*, IV, *193, 226,* 271 (Hugh f. Robert). The word may also denote a surrender for the benefit of the lord himself, as in Douglas, *Social Structure of Medieval East Anglia*, Oxford Studies in Social and Legal History, vol. IX, Appendix I, no. 34, or in the concord in *RCR*, I, 23–4 (full references above, p. 51, n. 2). In *CRR*, V, 143–4 (full references above, p. 107, n. 1), the beneficiary may or may not be the lord.

[3] (*a*) *CRR*, III, 129 (Ostricer); (*b*) *CRR*, IV, *278*, 303 (Causton); *CRR*, V, *17, 73, 134*; cf. *CRR*, III, *292*, 296–7; (*c*) *CRR*, VII, *142–3*, 200 (Daneville); (*d*) *CRR*, VI, 298 (Flammaville; see above, p. 146, n. 2). The phrase may also be used of a doweress relinquishing her rights to the heir or a grantee: (*a*) *Lincs.*, 451; (*b*) *PKJ*, III, 1017. Cf. *CRR*, XI, *167, 342, 1127*; *BNB*, 947, where *dimisit se* is used in such a case. In *CRR*, VI, 117, a tenant *deposuit se de libero servicio terre sue...et posuit se in servicio vilenagii*.

[4] If the phrase had a technical sense, it was probably just that of a surrender of the tenure; and the association with a surrender in favour of the heir no doubt reflects the rarity of other kinds of substitution. Charter examples: (*a*) Douglas, *Social Structure of Medieval East Anglia*, Oxford Studies in Social and Legal History, vol. IX, Appendix I, no. 6, in favour of heir; (*b*) Madox, *Formulare Anglicanum*, no. c, p. 54, on sale by surrender and admittance. For the latter, *reliquid* may also be found: *Whitby Cartulary*, Surtees Soc., I, nos. cclvi, cclxxxii; *Charters of the Honour of Mowbray*, ed. Greenway, no. 290.

[5] So long as the ancestor lived he might have to be joined; *BNB*, 103; *CRR*, VIII, 287–8.   [6] *Glanvill*, VII, 3. See further on the *casus regis* below, pp. 175–6.

Arthur claims that the father had *se demisit* in favour of Geoffrey, and had held only in *custodia* after Geoffrey died because Arthur was an infant; John denies the *se demisit*, says that the father died seised, *et petit considerationem regni desicut ipse apparens heres fuit in morte patris sui*.[1] In another case it is Arthur himself who has done homage: to secure him against John, his grandmother, whose inheritance it was, asked the lord to take Arthur's homage, and *se demisit* in his favour.[2] In yet another case it is the lord who took the initiative. The Geoffrey of the story

> *accessit ad comitem de Insula et petiit quandam puellam de camera sua ducendam in uxorem; et non placuit eidem comiti, quia in dubio fuit si hereditas ei accideret vel non, quousque pater suus venit in curiam comitis de Insula et se demisit de tota terra sua et petiit comitem ut caperet inde homagium suum; et comes cepit de toto homagium suum.*[3]

This last case is one of many in which the occasion for a *se demisit* is the marriage of the eldest son;[4] and it shows clearly the motives. One concerns dower, and there is evidently an association between the *se demisit* and dower *ex assensu patris*.[5] But more important is the securing of the inheritance for the children. The doubt about representation did not go just to a detail of rare occurrence. It affected every elder son until his father died; and for all we can tell from the records, many thirteenth-century

---

[1] *RCR*, I, *220, 364*; *PKJ*, I, *2248*; *RCR*, II, 134 (William f. John); *CRR*, I, 206; *Northants.*, *555, 636*; *CRR*, II, *152*; *CRR*, III, 25; *CRR*, IV, *59*. The same point may lie behind other cases: (*a*) *RCR*, I, *260, 281, 426*; *CRR*, I, *123*, 125 (Bodham); (*b*) *CRR*, III, 240–1, *266, 328, 342*; *CRR*, IV, 125.

[2] *CRR*, VII, *117–18*.

[3] *CRR*, VII, *142–3*, 200 (Daneville).

[4] (*a*) *CRR*, I, 363 (Burnes); (*b*) *CRR*, III, 52 (Burnard), *233, 319*; *PKJ*, III, *1077, 1483*; (*c*) *CRR*, III, 203 (Hele), *285*; Hunter, *Fines*, II, *64–5*; (*d*) *PKJ*, III, *2259, 2479*; *CRR*, IV, *268, 269*; *CRR*, V, 28–9. Apparently similar cases in which phrase *se demisit* is not used: (*a*) *CRR*, I, 125 (Bodham, full references this page, n. 1); (*b*) *CRR*, II, 213–14; (*c*) *CRR*, II, 273 (Harang), *275*; cf. *CRR*, VII, 297, 316–17; (*d*) *CRR*, III, 6–7; (*e*) *CRR*, III, 129 (Ostricer); (*f*) *CRR*, VI, *121, 132*, 211 (Beckele). Other dispositions on marriage: (*a*) *PKJ*, II, 675; (*b*) *PKJ*, III, 968; (*c*) *Gloucs.*, 247.

[5] The two things seem sometimes to be identified, as in the first four cases in the preceding note. Cf. *CRR*, I, 323 (Avenell), 361; John's widow claims dower *per voluntatem et assensum patris predicti Johannis, qui eo die quo ipsa desponsata fuit filio suo terram illam concessit et dedit ad dotandam ipsam, et inde Johannes saisitus fuit et eam inde dotavit et per quendam cultellum fractum, quem ipsa ostendit, ad hostium ecclesie inde ei saisinam fecit.* But sometimes there is no immediate handing over; *RCR*, I, 365–6; *PKJ*, I, *2039, 2040, 2718, 2727*; *RCR*, II, *95–6, 102, 261*.

actions in the right may have been brought by their descendants against the descendants of younger sons whose succession had at the time seemed proper. Sometimes the father may not even have been looking ahead to the next generation. The whole development shows how inheritance had been seen as depending upon the lord's acceptance; and a father who saw that acceptance as the necessary consummation, even if royal control would compel it, would see the homage as securing the eldest son himself. Sometimes the *se demisit* is not associated with a marriage, and unexplained.[1] Once it is prompted by the forthcoming remarriage of the father: wishing to secure the infant heir by his first wife against a claim to dower by the second, he *demiserat se* and *resignavit* the land with the infant into the lord's hand.[2] Sometimes we can see that the father was old and ill,[3] or was just going away.[4] And in the latter case, or if it was a woman who might not be able to manage the land, it could be disputed whether he or she had truly *se demisit* or had just made the son bailiff or the like.[5] In one such case, the question was to be settled by summoning the lord and his court;[6] and so long as a *se demisit* had the reality so far represented, that was appropriate.

But this reality faded, and the change may prove important. There are two ingredients: the possibility of a *se demisit* without the lord's consent; and the possibility of a *se demisit* in favour of someone other than the heir. At first the lord had to participate,

---

[1] (*a*) *Northants.*, 846; (*b*) *RCR*, II, 134 (William f. John; full references above, p. 148, n. 1); (*c*) *CRR*, III, 240–1, *266*, *328*, *342*; *CRR*, IV, 125; (*d*) *CRR*, IV, 303 (Causton; full references above, p. 147, n. 3); (*e*) *CRR*, VI, 334 (Geoffrey f. Adam; fragmentary); (*f*) *Lincs.-Worcs.*, *481*, 519, *262*, 316; (*g*) *Lincs.-Worcs.*, 742; (*h*) *Gloucs.*, 1461; (*i*) *BNB*, 103; *CRR*, VIII, 287–8; (*j*) *BNB*, 428; *CRR*, XIV, 457.

[2] *CRR*, IV, *193*, 226, 271 (Hugh f. Robert). For a converse arrangement to secure the children of a second marriage, see *Lincs.-Worcs.*, 841.

[3] (*a*) *PRS*, XIV, 25–6 (see above, p. 146, n. 2; the father is an old man); (*b*) *CRR*, VI, *255*, *259*, 298 (Flammaville; *sensit se esse gravatum debilitate*); (*c*) *CRR*, VII, 12 (Luvel; *in infirmitate*); (*d*) *Gloucs.*, 232 (*cecidit in languorem*); (*e*) *Yorks.*, 26 (*debilis fuit et senex et impotens*; see over at n. 2). Cf. *CRR*, I, 437 (Biset): lord, sued in novel disseisin, hands the land to the plaintiff's son with his consent; had the plaintiff been unable to keep up his services?

[4] (*a*) *Lincs.-Worcs.*, *609*, *654*, *750* (*cruce signatus*); (*b*) *Lincs.-Worcs.*, 981 (necessary to say that one who had gone off to pursue his calling and handed his land to his brothers *nunquam demisit se*).

[5] (*a*) Case last cited; (*b*) case in following note; (*c*) *CRR*, VIII, *138*, 228, 238, 290–1; *BNB*, 95; (*d*) *Yorks.*, 26. Cf. (*a*) *PKJ*, II, 490, 534; (*b*) *Northants.*, 474.

[6] *CRR*, III, 69 (Carbunell), *243*.

and presumably he could demand payment for doing so. One lord was given a coat by a father for taking the son's homage.[1] Another was known to dislike the eldest son; and for this reason his mother, who was old and ill, did not dare attempt a *se demisit* but made a sort of bailment instead.[2] So long as there was only the lord's law, there could not be a tenant whom he and his court did not accept. Custom would oblige them to accept the son when his father was dead; but nothing could make them accept him now. But novel disseisin, or rather the consequent shift by which one could be seised although not accepted as the lord's tenant, seems to have deprived this self-evident truth of its effect. What we see in the early rolls is that a dying tenant might send for his heir apparent and make what is called a *se demisit* in his favour, though evidently without the lord's approval or even knowledge. Perhaps he was hoping to save the heir from having to pay a relief;[3] more probably he just wanted to secure him. After his death the heir is disseised, apparently by the lord, and wins the ensuing assize.[4] Of course the death has entitled the heir; and now he can compel the lord to accept him as tenant, which presumably he could not have done while the ancestor was still alive. But if the lord could not put him out, perhaps that acceptance did not much matter. It is a point to which we shall return.

With the natural heir, however, none of this much matters. If it is said that a father *demiserat se* and *inheredaverat* his son, or *heredem constituit*,[5] he made him heir only in the sense of antici- pating nature. But early in this chapter we noticed cases in which *suscepit ut heredem* or *constituit heredem suum* referred to strangers;[6] and a *se demisit* in favour of someone other than the heir would be just a grant by substitution.[7] Other beneficiaries within the family are sometimes found, and we will try briefly to see the matter through the father's eyes. Suppose he has no natural heir, but two bastard sons: he can only anticipate an escheat on his own death by persuading the lord to accept one of the bastards now; and he

[1] *BNB*, 428; *CRR*, xiv, 457. Cf. *CRR*, vii, 117–18 (*tantum inpetravit*).

[2] *Yorks.*, 26. Cf. *CRR*, vi, 340 (Arsic).   [3] Cf. Stat. Marlborough, c. 6.

[4] *CRR*, vii, 12 (Luvel). Similar stories may lie behind: (*a*) *CRR*, vii, 215 (Nuers); (*b*) *CRR*, vi, 334 (Geoffrey f. Adam).

[5] (*a*) *Lincs.-Worcs.*, 609, 654, 750; (*b*) *CRR*, i, 363 (Burnes).

[6] Above, p. 109.

[7] *CRR*, vi, 255, 259, 298 (Flammaville), looks like a dying man making such a grant with the co-operation of his heir. Cf. what looks like a fraudulent trans- action in *CRR*, i, 48 (Wasseburn).

cannot avoid the risk that the one to whom he *se demisit* will die childless, so that the land escheats in his own lifetime.[1] Now suppose he has two legitimate sons, and that he wishes to make reasonable provision for the younger.[2] The obvious danger if the younger son dies childless is not escheat but the rule against being lord and heir.[3] This will keep the elder son out if the gift was by ordinary downward grant, but not if it took the form of a *se demisit*. Two charters dating from before the middle of the twelfth century record just such dispositions,[4] and there are a few examples on the early rolls.[5] In every case the land is said to be the father's purchase, and this requirement seems more natural in the lord's court; but then the whole transaction seems more natural than that which brings homage within the family. Yet Glanvill himself tells us that the lord-and-heir rule often came into play,[6] and the downward grant to the younger son is clearly the common thing; and the likely reason is that suggested early in this chapter. The hereditary claim of the elder son and his issue has made the *se demisit* dangerous not only for the younger son but also for the lord.[7]

Could a *se demisit* be done without the lord? Two law-suits in 1206 resulted from a disposition made by a father who had died at least ten years earlier, leaving a daughter and a much younger son, possibly by a second marriage. In one the son, as heir, claims land from the daughter and her husband; and they plead that it was the father's purchase and that he *se demisit* to them by way of *maritagium*.[8] The other is a *de homagio capiendo* brought by the

---

[1] *CRR*, VII, 136–7. In *Lincs.*, 1335, the father suffered the converse misfortune, failing to make effective livery so that the land escheated on his own death. Both lords made some concession as a matter of grace.

[2] Cases in n. 5, below. In *Gloucs.*, 232, the father fell ill while the elder son was overseas, and handed all over to the younger.   [3] Above, pp. 139 ff.

[4] (a) *Sir Christopher Hatton's Book of Seals*, no. 301, pp. 207–8, discussed in F. M. Stenton, *The First Century of English Feudalism* (2nd ed.), p. 55; (b) Stenton, ibid. Appendix, no. 41, pp. 281–2.

[5] Phrase '*se demisit*' used: (a) *CRR*, I, 78 (Geoffrey f. Warin loses in novel disseisin to his brothers), 359 (brings action in right, they plead *se demisit*); *CRR*, II, *213*; *CRR*, III, *30*; (b) *CRR*, VII, 316; *Gloucs.*, 257. Phrase not used: (a) *RCR*, I, 438 (Bosco; full references above, p. 123, n. 3); (b) *RCR*, II, 88–9 (full references above, p. 107, n. 3); (c) *CRR*, II, 301–2 (grantor *venit in conquestu Anglie*; full references above, p. 123, n. 3). Cf. (a) *BNB*, 183 (to younger brother); (b) *BNB*, 370 (on death of father, lord admits younger son with consent of elder).   [6] *Glanvill*, VII, 1, above, p. 140, n. 6.   [7] Above, p. 111.

[8] *PKJ*, III, 2200; *CRR*, IV, 96, 104 (Manneston), *177*. For another case in which a *se demisit* by way of *maritagium* is alleged, see *BNB*, 779.

daughter's husband against the lord, who refers to the first plea
and declines to take homage until he knows which party is entitled
to the land. Later he takes it; and presumably the jury in the first
plea has found that the father indeed *se demisit*.[1] But the lord had
evidently not taken part, or even known. The *se demisit* had operated
as a private conveyance of the tenement; and because the grantee
had that, he could require the lord to take his homage. The tail is
beginning to wag the dog.

That case concerned a carucate in Suffolk; and perhaps development began in the diluted lordships of East Anglia.[2] What seems
to be developing is the possibility of substitution without the lord's
consent. It was not a central change such as only statute in the end
could make, but almost a trick depending upon the *se demisit*. It
was a surrender without an admittance, but leaving somebody in
whom the lord could not get out. Various threads in this chapter
come together in an assize of novel disseisin brought in 1249 by
a prior against a lord. The lord says that his tenant was proposing
to give the tenement to the house in alms, and all he did was to
send one of his co-defendants to forbid the prior from entering his
fee. We may wonder what effect such a prohibition would have.
But the recognitors find that matters had gone further: the lord's
tenant had actually *se demisit* and put the prior in seisin. Judgment
is adjourned, and no conclusion is recorded.[3] Perhaps the justices
hesitated because this was a religious house; and if they found that
it had become seised as against the lord, there would be no way he
could get them out. Could a lay recipient in such a case go on to
require that the lord should take his homage? 'If a tenant, having
done homage to his lord, *se dimiserit ex toto de hereditate sua* and
enfeoffs another to hold of the chief lord, the original tenant's
homage is extinguished *velit nolit capitalis dominus*, and homage
begins in the person of the feoffee *qui obligatur propter tenementum
quod est feodum domini capitalis.*'[4] What this seems to say is that
the beneficiary of the *se demisit* can be compelled to do homage,

---

[1] *PKJ*, III, *1859, 2364*; *CRR*, IV, 144, 281.

[2] A Norfolk charter recording a *se demisit* to the heir does not mention the lord
as playing any part; Douglas, *Social Structure of Medieval East Anglia*, Oxford
Studies in Social and Legal History, vol. IX, Appendix I, no. 6. But he may be
a witness; cf. no. 7.

[3] *Civil Pleas of the Wiltshire Eyre, 1249*, ed. Clanchy, Wiltshire Record
Society, vol. 26, no. 74. For other cases at this time, see Sutherland, *The Assize
of Novel Disseisin*, pp. 86 ff. For earlier cases, see above, p. 117, n. 1.

[4] Bracton, f. 81; followed in *Fleta*, III, 16. Cf. Bracton, ff. 45b ff.

and it may not follow that the lord can be compelled to take it.[1] But he is evidently compelled to put up with his new tenant; and this is 'Bracton's distinct assertion' without which Maitland would have been unwilling to believe that a new tenant could be forced upon an unwilling lord.[2]

---

[1] For Glanvill, homage would be a condition precedent to demanding services; IX, I, 6. And the receipt of services alone would impose a duty to warrant; III, 7. See above, p. 55, n. I, below, p. 173.

[2] Pollock and Maitland, *History of English Law* (2nd ed.), I, 345.

5

INHERITANCE

Inheritance becomes an automatic succession to what is clearly the ancestor's property. When the ancestor dies, the heir is at once entitled under abstract rules of law and enters without anyone's authority. Just as the lord has no control over alienation or, except for the anomalous power of distraining chattels, over the continuing tenure, so he has no control over inheritance. And the heir's assize of mort d'ancestor is seen as directed against the world at large, against the rival claimant or the mere wrongdoer who has got in first. Like novel disseisin it is a possessory protection, the first line of defence of an abstract property right.

In this long-lived scheme lordship itself is just a property right, a *jus in re aliena*; and its valuable components are the services, a regular income charged upon the tenant's land, and the bonus incidents which accrue when a tenant dies. If there is an adult heir, the lord is entitled to relief, a payment which early becomes fixed in amount. If there is an infant or an unmarried female heir the lord takes wardship, enjoying for his own benefit the lands held of himself; and he, or one of the lords if there is more than one, will be able to sell the marriage for an amount depending upon the total value of the heir's inheritance. And lastly, if the tenant dies without any heir, the land escheats to the lord and is at his free disposal.

These incidents will not be discussed for their own sakes; but they may help to bring out the changing nature of lordship. Their monetary value to the lord depends, like the value of the tenement to the tenant, upon the margin between the amount of the services and the real value of the land. If there was no margin, so that the land was worth no more than the services due from it, getting it back in wardship or by escheat would bring no profit to the lord. To the extent that a tenement was once seen as the pay for services which were desired, therefore, these incidents had no independent value. The pay was just to be at the lord's disposal if the services were not done; and if they were to be done by a new tenant he must be of the lord's choosing.

Increasing concern with the incidents, discussed from another viewpoint in the preceding chapter,[1] reflects a general increase in the margin between value of land and amount of services; and there are two immediate causes. The services are mostly fixed in money and lose their real value, as indeed does the relief. And even at the creation of a new tenure they may be fixed below the annual value of the land: the lord is no longer buying services with land, but selling the land and taking most of his return in a capital payment. To one who has reserved nominal services, for example, a wardship is a windfall as valuable as it is irrational; and the chance of such windfalls is the only thing that makes his lordship itself valuable. But the lordship is a purely economic affair, the correlative of a tenement now just the tenant's property; and we must not read either back.

To say that the general interest of lords shifted from services to incidents is not to say that an individual incident was ever unimportant to the lord concerned. If he was getting the fullest services that the land could support, he had nothing to gain if his tenant died leaving an infant heir: but since on a military tenure the services would cease during the infancy,[2] he would lose unless he could replace them from the profits of the land. From the beginning, therefore, enforcement of incidents mattered as much as enforcement of services; and if the rise of royal remedies seems to be late, it is not because no remedies were needed until the incidents took on the character of independent capital gains. It is because, like the services, they were enforced by lords themselves.

In the course of the thirteenth century a considerable apparatus of royal actions grew up for the protection of wardship, marriage, and escheat. But they are not early. Of the two earliest registers in the Selden Society volume, neither has anything about escheat, and only one has a writ, a *justicies* to the sheriff, by which the lord can recover a wardship to which he is entitled.[3] Nor are royal actions brought by lords common on the earliest rolls. *Custodia* often refers to the control of a husband over the lands of his wife, living

---

[1] Above, pp. 111 ff.
[2] On a socage tenure the fiduciary guardian would arrange for their performance, so that the lord was unaffected by the infancy.
[3] *Registers*, CA54; CA53 is for socage.

or dead, or to those factual arrangements, commonly within the
family, mentioned in the preceding chapter.[1] Feudal wardships
figure as factual ingredients in later disputes over title.[2] But the
lord actually takes the land for himself, perhaps by judgment of his
court; and this may be reflected in an assize brought against him.[3]
If he goes to the king's court, it is in some situation beyond his own
power. There may be a dispute between two lords, especially if the
dead tenant held of both: is it the lord of the older feoffment or the
lord of the greater fee who is entitled to the person of the heir and
the marriage?[4] Or the lord may find that heirs, like villeins, are less
docile than their lands: they go away[5] or have themselves knighted
within age,[6] or have themselves married.[7] In the last case, it is
usually the heiress's husband against whom the lord proceeds,[8]

---

[1] Above, pp. 134 ff., especially the association with *committere*, p. 136, n. 1.

[2] For a good example already considered in another context, see above,
p. 50, n. 1. A disposition by the guardian would usually show itself in a claim
by heir against grantee, e.g., *CRR*, IV, 129 (Sine Averio; full references above,
p. 99, n. 4). But it could turn up in less obvious ways: in *PKJ*, I, *2971*, *2979*;
RCR, II, *98*, 254 (Esturmi), the heir has recovered the land from the grantee and
the grantee has had *escambium* from the lord; but when the grantee dies his
widow claims dower.

[3] (*a*) *CRR*, VII, 81–2 (no mention of judgment); (*b*) *Gloucs.*, 406 (full recital
of judicial process). As against the heir himself the right is not in question, so the
lord could presumably act through his court without writ. Contrast escheat,
below, p. 159, n. 7.

[4] Older feoffment: (*a*) *CRR*, V, 58–60; (*b*) *BNB*, 661. Cf. *Glanvill*, VII, 10.
Greater fee: *CRR*, I, *124*; *PKJ*, I, *2812*, 3114; *RCR*, II, 156. The claimant lord
in this case, or rather Tabari his steward, cuts a questionable figure in other
wardship cases. In one he has removed heiresses from the fee of, presumably,
another lord; *CRR*, II, 26, 70 (though it is not clear who is entitled to their
wardship; *CRR*, II, 172, *259*, *292–3*; *CRR*, III, *3*, *48*, *59*). In another case he
seems to have conspired with the husband of one heiress to secure the whole
inheritance for the couple by making her coheiress a nun. Four actions result,
two brought by an uncle: (*a*) *RCR*, I, *290*, *394*; *PKJ*, I, 2148; *RCR*, II, *124*,
126–7; *CRR*, I, *165*; (*b*) *PKJ*, I, 2506, 3128; *RCR*, II, 160. And two actions are
brought by the victim herself: (*a*) *CRR*, I, 118; (*b*) *PKJ*, I, *2799*. Later litigation
throws more light on the tenurial background, and shows that the girl was
married all right in the end; *CRR*, IV, 80–1, *97*, 102, *124*, 141, *184*, *230*; *CRR*,
V, I, *88*, *196*, *300*.

[5] *CRR*, VI, 237–8, 286. Cf. a remarkable prohibition in *CRR*, I, 175 (Senges),
presumably part of a story hidden behind a series of novel disseisin entries:
PKJ, II, 870; *CRR*, II, *114*, *173*; *CRR*, III, *40*; *CRR*, IV, *198*.

[6] *CRR*, III, 143 (bishop of Lincoln).   [7] *RCR*, I, 10 (Theobald Walter), *114*.

[8] In the case last cited he appears to be bringing a separate action against the
heiress; perhaps the marriage had been annulled. In *CRR*, I, 111 (earl de
Insula); *RCR*, I, 396, the action is once said to be just against the husband, once
against him *et uxorem ejus*. In *CRR*, II, 92 (Carleol), it seems to be against the
husband only.

and one such action is interestingly formulated: *ingressus est in feudum suum et duxit in uxorem filiam...militis sui.*[1] But this is not a claim to the land itself, as was William Butler's with the *maritagium* he had given.[2] It is a trespassory complaint seeking compensation for what should not have happened. Earlier it could not ordinarily have happened: only if the lord consented to the marriage would he take homage, and only then deliver the heiress and the land. And if it did happen, it is likely that the heiress could be disinherited, as could, for Glanvill, the incontinent heiress and even the living tenant having only daughters who presumed to marry them off without the lord's consent.[3] This aspect of the lord's control of his fee has sunk to a monetary exaction needing royal enforcement; but the statute of Merton will still find it appropriate that the lord should compensate himself from the issues of the land, retaining the inheritance as long as necessary.[4]

The enforcement of escheat deserves closer scrutiny. The lord eventually has a special writ, which occurs in its final wording in formularies dating from 1260 or a little after.[5] It seems to have grown from writs formulated with an *ingressum*. But only two examples have been found outside the plea rolls;[6] and, for reasons given earlier, it is hard to tell from the rolls whether any particular *ingressum* is part of the writ or is just alleged in pleading on a writ of right.[7] An example of 1230 goes to the grand assize with special mise; and we cannot be sure that Bracton is right in assuming that it was a writ of entry and attributing the assize solely to the antiquity of the title alleged by the tenant.[8] Another example of

---

[1] *CRR*, VI, 156 (Mauduit), *198, 255*; notice the allegations of damage and shame.

[2] Above, pp. 51–2. Cf. *CRR*, I, 145 (Blac), *212, 246, 452*; *CRR*, II, *15*: mort d'ancestor in right of wife against one apparently claiming under grant from wife's lord; the husband *interrogatus per quem warantum duxit ipsam...in uxorem, dicit quod invenit eam inopem et per se duxit eam.*

[3] *Glanvill*, VII, 12.   [4] Stat. Merton, c. 6.

[5] *Registers*, CC188–91; *Brevia Placitata*, pp. 13, 57, 166–7.

[6] (a) *BNB*, 487, is followed by two precedents: one is a writ 'in the descender' for a claim, like that in the case itself, by the heir in *maritagium* against a second husband (for this situation, see Bracton, ff. 437b–438; and for the case, see also *CRR*, XIV, *395*, 1067); the second precedent has a similarly limited *maritagium* in mind, but is 'in the reverter', the donor claiming as his escheat land into which the second husband has *ingressum* only through the wife under the gift. (b) *Casus Placitorum*, ed. Dunham, Selden Society, vol. 69, p. 30, no. 1: this is also concerned with a donee in *maritagium* dying childless, and also formulated in terms of entry and of escheat.   [7] Above, pp. 97 ff.

[8] *BNB*, 402; *CRR*, XIV, 582. Bracton cites the case at f. 319.

1214 similarly goes to the grand assize: there are two enrolments of the *ingressum* part, and they do not look as though they were written by clerks having the same writ in front of them.[1] It may have been the Charter that encouraged incorporation of the *ingressum* into the writ to show that a *precipe* was not improper.[2] For the present purpose, however, what matters is that lords are driven to use writs at all, whether *precipe* or inappropriate patent. The language of *ingressum* is associated with the downward claim that they would formerly have settled for themselves.[3]

In the early rolls few lords are found seeking the king's help. Escheats turn up as past events recited in proprietary actions more often than as rights being now enforced.[4] The past escheats recited are often *propter delictum*; and these are particularly rare in actions about enforcement, no doubt because the land was in the first instance taken for the king.[5] Actions about the immediate enforcement of an escheat are either claims by the lord to get the land or assizes against him because he has taken it; and claims by him, unless some are hidden behind grand assizes, are rare and late.[6] Assizes of novel disseisin against persons who claim to have

---

[1] *CRR*, VII, *106*, 107 (Windlesores), *218–19*, 231. For another pair, see *BNB*, 462, 597; *CRR*, XIV, 746, 1747; they are close, especially on the rolls themselves, but not conclusively so.   [2] Above, pp. 101–2.

[3] Above, pp. 47 and 92 ff. For a claim to escheat formulated with *quo waranto*, see *PKJ*, IV, *4477*; *CRR*, VI, *342*, 351–2.

[4] Claims by heirs against tenants holding under the escheat: (*a*) *PRS*, XIV, 9 (Piron; escheat alleged to the empress Matilda); *CRR*, I, 173, *184*, 225–6; *PKJ*, I, *3251*; other entries against particular terre-tenants; (*b*) *RCR*, II, *152*, *153*; *CRR*, I, 48 (Jordan f. Avice: in this earliest entry he loses in novel disseisin; the other entries all concern his claim in the right), *129*, 180–1 (showing that Jordan's claim as heir of his mother is resisted on the ground that his father was a felon), *328*; *PKJ*, II, *1067*; *CRR*, II, *138*, *246*; *CRR*, III, 42, 209, *233*; (*c*) *CRR*, II, 110 (Parco); (*d*) *Lincs.-Worcs.*, 942. One who claims under the escheat proves to be not the lord but a grantee, and moreover he has himself at some time been seised; *PKJ*, III, *1817*; *CRR*, IV, *84*, *100*, 111 (Hersin). Notice that lords might allow widows their dower; *PRS*, XIV, 43 (Lobenho); cf. *CRR*, VII, 244 (Dogeman). They might even return the land to heirs; *CRR*, II, 73–4, *81*; *Northants.*, *525*; though this might be carefully restricted to their lives; *CRR*, II, 21 (Broc); cf. *PKJ*, III, 1019 (arising from the same escheat and showing that care was needed).

[5] With the important exception, apparently, of theft; *Glanvill*, VII, 17; cf. I, 2, showing that theft was not a plea of the crown. For a case in which the lord seeks to recover from one claiming under the king's grantee of year and day, see *BNB*, 462, 597; *CRR*, XIV, 746, 1747.

[6] *CRR*, VII, *106*, 107 (Windlesores), *218–19*, 231: *ingressum* by gage from dead tenant, *et pro defectu heredis debet terra illa ei reverti ut escaeta sua* (1214). A little earlier a donor in *maritagium* claims the land from the husband on the

taken escheats are more frequent. Sometimes the plaintiff claims
by gift from the dead man: recognitors find that he had given to
his brother[1] and to his *amica*,[2] but had not made effective livery to
his bastard son.[3] Members of the family just living with him do
not succeed.[4] The surviving husband, whether of donee in
maritagium[5] or of ordinary female tenant,[6] succeeds if children
have been born alive. All these sound like cases of genuine doubt;
and it may be that formerly a lord would have made some *quo
waranto* inquiry in his own court. But now he must not do that,
and the one lord who vouched his court to warrant his taking of an
escheat by judgment brought an amercement upon them as well
as himself: they had acted without writ.[7] No writ will bring the
matter to his own court; so the lord in doubt about a person found
on the land must choose between going to the king's court, perhaps
pointlessly by way of his own lord's, or just entering and risking
the assize. In the early rolls he more often enters; and since he
does not always raise a formal exception against the assize, it may
be more often than we can see.[8]

All this is even clearer in Glanvill.[9] Not only are there no writs
or actions about wardship, marriage, or escheat: there are no

death of the wife *sine herede de se*, and *ingressum* is used but not *escaeta*; *CRR*,
VII, 36 (Autrop f. Hugh; a sequel to *CRR*, VI, *135*, 159–60). But the language of
escheat is commonly used for this situation, as in the two writs above, p. 157,
n. 6, and in *Registers*, CC190. Cf. *CRR*, VI, 140–1, *186*.

[1] *Northants.*, 390, *483*, 601.   [2] *BNB*, 617; *CRR*, XIV, 1896.
[3] *Lincs.*, 1335.
[4] *CRR*, VII, 136–7; father of two bastard sons *se demisit* to one, but all three
continued to occupy together; beneficiary died; lord takes as escheat, wins
when father and brother bring novel disseisin, undertakes to support father but
not brother.   [5] *CRR*, III, 66 (Truue); *CRR*, IV, *283*.
[6] (*a*) *Beds.*, 63; (*b*) *Lincs.-Worcs.*, 357 (husband says lord at time of marriage
consented to his holding for life *siue haberet heredem de ea siue non*); (*c*) *BNB*,
291; *CRR*, XIII, *815*, 1050 (may have been born before the marriage).
[7] *RCR*, I, 447–8; cf. ibid. 368 (escheat on death without heir of son of donee
in *maritagium*). For a lord formulating his claim in the king's court with a
quo waranto, see *PKJ*, IV, *4477*; *CRR*, VI, *342*, 351–2. For what looks like the heir
of a donor persuading the lord to make a *quo waranto* inquiry in his own court,
see *CRR*, III, 161–2. The problem may have been different with a taking in
wardship; above, p. 156, n. 3.
[8] Exceptions: (*a*) *Northants.*, 390, *483*, 601; (*b*) *BNB*, 617; *CRR*, XIV, 1896;
(*c*) *Lincs.-Worcs.*, 357 (but notice the general verdict). Entry ambiguous but
matter evidently raised by defendant: (*a*) *Beds.*, 63; (*b*) *Lincs.*, 1335; (*c*) *CRR*,
III, 66 (Truue); *CRR*, IV, *283*. Pretty clearly no exception, and facts emerge in
special verdict: *CRR*, VII, 136–7.
[9] The principal references in *Glanvill* are these. Wardship: VII, 9–12; IX, 4.
Marriage: VII, 12; IX, 4. Escheat: VII, 17; IX, 1.

problems. The rights are all stated, but nothing is said of their enforcement. Nor does the statement suggest that they are seen as clearly distinct items in some inventory of lordship. They are aspects of the lord's control of his fee. On the death of his tenant, unless there is an undoubted adult male heir, the lord always takes the tenement into his hand; and it is from that posture that questions begin. When and to whom and on what conditions is he going to release it? The distinct incidents grow from the answers: to the infant male when he comes of age, to the husband chosen for the female, and so on. Uniformity must have increased as more questions were subjected to the control of the king's court; but Glanvill's answers are still reflected in the early rolls. They reflect also the routine character of a taking into the lord's hand on a tenant's death. It is said to have been done 'as is the custom',[1] or put forward as evidence that the tenant is dead.[2] There is a general assumption rather than a series of discrete property rights.

Nor is this assumption just proprietary in character. Partly it is governmental. The lord who has taken the tenement into hand may not be protected by novel disseisin: the tenement is not his.[3] He is to ensure that the right thing now happens. If it is not immediately clear what that is, he should hold on until he knows; and this fits uneasily into the scheme of distinct incidents. Glanvill singles out the case in which there is an undoubted heir but it is doubtful whether he is of age: the lord holds until this is settled, and his holding is by way of wardship rather than escheat.[4] But *custodia* probably does not denote for Glanvill the later proprietary entity.

---

[1] *CRR*, II, 213–14 (*sicut mos est*); (b) *CRR*, VII, 168–73 at 170 (*sicut consuetudo est*). Cf. cases in which the routine is assumed: (a) *RCR*, II, 129 (Euersot); (b) *CRR*, II, 110 (Parco); (c) *CRR*, II, 187 (Ginges, possibly a wardship case); (d) *CRR*, I, 28 (Leprosi).

[2] *CRR*, II, 225, 241, 275–6. Cf. the taking of homage as evidence that a tenant was seised. It helps a tenant in mort d'ancestor asserting that a nearer heir became seised after the death: (a) *Lincs.-Worcs.*, 330; (b) *Gloucs.*, 1530 (fealty in lord's court). But it does not enable one claiming as heir to use novel disseisin instead of mort d'ancestor; *Northants.*, 866.

[3] (a) *CRR*, VII, 210 (Lind); (b) *Yorks.*, 28. The same appears to be true of a lord who has taken by judgment for failure of service; *CRR*, I, 320–1.

[4] *Glanvill*, VII, 9: *Si uero dubium fuerit utrum fuerint heredes maiores an minores, tunc...domini tam heredes quam hereditates in custodia habebunt... Glanvill*, VII, 17: *in uno casu* (doubt who is right heir) *intelligitur interim hereditas illa quasi eskaeta ipsius domini, in alio uero casu* (doubtful age of undoubted heir) *non intelligitur esse sua nisi de custodia.*

On the early rolls it means just a holding acknowledged as on behalf of another certain person; and when a tenant died leaving an undoubted adult heir who was at the time in Ireland, the lord took the land *sicut in custodia*.[1] All other cases in which the lord takes because of a doubt are classified by Glanvill as escheat, and the logic appears from the way he puts the matter: lords may and do take the land into hand whenever there is not at the death someone who is without doubt the heir, and may hold it until one comes and proves his right.[2] The proof envisaged is proof against the lord, an 'upward' claim made in his own court;[3] and so long as the land is still in the lord's hand, it does not matter whether there is a rival claimant or not. Ralph may believe that there is no other heir, and be waiting until William proves or fails to prove his right: he is already holding as an escheat, and if William fails this will just continue. Ralph may believe that Thomas is heir if William turns out not to be: but for Glanvill his holding in the meantime seems equally to be an escheat.[4] On the rolls the name has not been found applied to the latter situation; but it is identifiable in too few cases to tell whether Glanvill's usage has changed.[5] But his assumption has not changed: a lord is not infrequently said to have taken the tenement into hand until the right heir comes.[6]

---

[1] *BNB*, 754; *CRR*, xv, 145. For the sense of *custodia* in general, see above, pp. 155–6.

[2] *Glanvill*, vii, 17; ix, 6. Cf. Bracton, f. 252b.

[3] *Glanvill*, vii, 17, quoted above, p. 82.

[4] *Glanvill*, ix, 6 should be read in the light of vii, 17, especially the passage quoted in n. 4, opposite. The lord may of course have committed himself to one of the parties: in *CRR*, iv, 157–8, he has taken in wardship with one daughter in the belief that her half-sister is a bastard; and in *Gloucs.*, 589, he has chosen wrong, taking in wardship with a daughter whose mother admits she was not married to the dead tenant; cf. *Lincs.-Worcs.*, 141.

[5] Doubt in law (half-blood): *BNB*, 44; *CRR*, viii, 50, 221. Doubt over legitimacy of son: *PKJ*, iv, *3781, 3985*; *CRR*, vi, 50 (Nereford), *98, 113* (notice the wrong done in these circumstances in vouching over, and also the further doubt whether this was socage tenure; on the latter see also *Gloucs.*, 406). Doubts as between the heir and one claiming on some other basis: (*a*) *CRR*, i, 205–6, *457*; *CRR*, ii, *77, 81, 169*; *CRR*, iii, *252, 253, 257*, 318; (*b*) *Lincs.-Worcs.*, 256; (*c*) the case discussed above, pp. 151–2, in which the lord is not trying to interfere with the land itself, but is refusing to take homage until a dispute is settled between the heir and a daughter claiming by *se demisit* in *maritagium*. Cases concerning posthumous children: (*a*) *CRR*, iii, 7–8; (*b*) *CRR*, iii, 135–6.

[6] *RCR*, i, 191 (Bigot; *donec rectus heres eum inde requireret*); (*b*) *CRR*, ii, 50 (Roger f. Nicholas; below, p. 169, n. 1; *cum nullus eum requireret de servitio*

For Glanvill, then, no question can arise about enforcing the lord's rights of escheat or wardship, or at least the first marriage of an heiress. The lord has the land; and if anyone has to seek the king's help it will be the heir. Paradoxically, the one incident arising on death for which Glanvill has to mention enforcement is the one that never gave trouble in the king's court. The lord does not take the land into hand if there is an undoubted male heir, and so cannot withhold it until his relief is paid. All he can withhold is warranty, by refusing to take homage; and so long as the relationship seemed to be the important thing, the tenant would often be eager to pay or give security.[1] If this fails, so that the lord does have to take action to get his relief, or indeed his rightful aids, Glanvill prescribes the same remedies as for services: either he proceeds in his own court, as described in the first chapter, or, if he is himself *impotens* to *justiciare* his tenant, he calls in the sheriff with a *justicies* writ of customs and services.[2] Again the rolls bear him out. There are no separate proceedings for relief or aids; and not infrequently it looks as though a demand expressed as for services is in fact for relief.[3] But the primary remedy remained the process of the lord's own court, later to become the disembodied distress of the classical common law.

Before leaving the relief, we may get a larger view by following Glanvill in two digressions. Both concern the king. For baronies and serjeanties, he tells us that the amount is at the king's mercy and pleasure.[4] For the tenants of lesser lords it had long been fixed; and the fixing of the lord's dues was an important part of

suo faciendo vel homagio); (c) Northants., 440; CRR, II, 156–7, 298, 299; CRR, III, 33 (on death of infant heir in wardship, next heir came to lord *et tantum fecit uersus eum quod ipse reddidit ei ut recto heredi*); (d) CRR, III, 135 (Blakemore; *quousque veniret facere ei quod facere deberet*); (e) CRR, VI, 237 (Stokes; similar words), 259, 300; (f) CRR, VII, 210 (Lind; *quousque rectus heres veniret*); (g) Lincs.-Worcs., 150 (heir came to lord *et tantum inpetrauit versus eum quod dominus suus reddidit ei seisinam*); (h) BNB, 219; CRR, XI, 1490, 2227, 2675 (*donec rectus heres ad eos ueniret ad faciendum eis quod inde facere deberet*; and by judgment the lord is to have seisin *saluo herede...cum ad eum ueniret iure suo*); (i) BNB, 291; CRR, XIII, 815, 1050 (*donec rectus heres veniret ad faciendum...quod facere deberet*). For heirs enlisting the aid of the lord, see Yorks., 341.

[1] See Glanvill, IX, 4–6 on *de homagio capiendo*. Cf. VII, 9 and IX, 1.
[2] Glanvill, IX, 8–10.
[3] (a) PRS(NS), XXXI, 96 (Cherebi); CRR, VII, 346; CRR, I, 46; (b) CRR, VII, 333; CRR, I, 36 (Pomerio); (c) CRR, III, 322, 332 (Clopton). Cf. Lincs., 1316, which is expressed to be for relief.
[4] Glanvill, IX, 4. Cf. Dialogus de Scaccario, ed. Johnson, pp. 96, 121.

the process by which a tenant came to 'own' his tenement. After dealing with the church, this was the first of their own grievances to which the barons turned in the Charter of 1215; and the amount of their formal relief too became fixed.[1] But this was partly offset by the long survival of another difference noted by Glanvill. When a baron dies, his barony is taken into the king's hand even if the heir is of full age; and it is not released until a satisfactory arrangement has been made for paying the relief.[2] Centuries later he will still be paying a fine over and above his relief to obtain livery of his lands, and that livery will still resemble a fresh grant: though he may physically have the lands, for many purposes he is not tenant but intruder.[3] Formally he preserves the character of an heir under feudal custom: he cannot be tenant until accepted by his lord, has no superior jurisdiction to which he can turn to compel that acceptance, but still has a customary right to be accepted. Because of this right, the author of the *Dialogus* thinks that reliefs should be recovered as just pecuniary penalties. But he tells us of a harsher view: they are voluntary offerings for something which may be withheld, and if not paid it will be withheld.[4] For him too it is only popular usage that restricts 'escheat' to a failure of heirs. His discussion of relief grows out of his discussion of escheats, and even wardship is a special case of escheat, *escaeta cum herede*.[5] This peculiarity is not explained, but it may link up with another. Glanvill insists that ordinary lords must take the homage of an infant before taking the land into wardship:[6] but the king, perhaps following ancient custom,[7] takes homage only when

---

[1] *Magna Carta* (1215), c. 2; (1225), c. 2; Articles of the Barons, c. 1.

[2] *Glanvill*, IX, 6: *mortuo enim aliquo capitali barone suo, statim baroniam suam in manu sua retinet dominus rex donec heres grantum suum de relleuio fecerit, licet heres ipse plenam habuerit etatem.* Cf. Stat. Marlborough, c. 16.

[3] *Prerogativa Regis*, c. 15. Bell, *The Court of Wards & Liveries*, p. 76.

[4] *Dialogus de Scaccario*, ed. Johnson, p. 121. The harsher view preserves a stronger view of the king's powers over inheritance in general. As late as 1208 a demandant could seek to meet the objection that he had co-heirs by alleging that Henry II had accepted his proffer for the whole (*CRR*, V, 282; Biset; there are many earlier formal entries; see also Sanders, *English Baronies*, p. 1). Contrast *PKJ*, IV, *3733*; *CRR*, VI, *119, 133, 190,* 199–200, 295–6.

[5] *Dialogus de Scaccario*, ed. Johnson, p. 94.

[6] *Glanvill*, IX, 1: *nullam...habere debet custodiam dominus feodi donec ipsius heredis receperit homagium.* Cf. IX, 4: *nullum ius habet dominus feodi in custodia heredis uel hereditatis nisi prius recepto homagio heredis.* Cf. Assize of Northampton, c. 4: *dominus feodi recipiat homagium suum et habeat in custodia illum quamdiu debuerit.* Cf. also Bracton, f. 77b.

[7] Ganshof, *Feudalism*, trans. Grierson, pp. 127–8.

he makes livery.[1] Only then does he formally accept the heir as tenant; and perhaps this is why ancient Exchequer practice did not acknowledge his holding as in *custodia*. The incidents form a pattern of which the main lines all point back to a situation of great conceptual simplicity. The heir does not succeed to his ancestor's property: he has a customary claim against the lord to be accepted as tenant; but only when he is so accepted, when his homage is taken and he is seised, does the tenement become in any sense his.

*   *   *

If anyone dies holding a free tenement, his heir shall remain in such seisin as his father had on the day that he died. . . ; and afterwards he shall seek out his lord and do what he should concerning his relief and other dues. And if the heir is within age, the lord of the fee shall accept his homage and hold in wardship as long as is right. . . And if the lord of the fee denies to the heir the seisin of the dead man which he claims, the king's justices shall inquire by twelve lawful men what seisin the dead man had on the day that he died, and shall restore it to the heir in accordance with what is found. And if anyone disobeys this and is convicted of it, he shall remain in the king's mercy.

This enactment is part of the Assize of Northampton of 1176,[2] and for lords other than the king it broke up the original simplicity of inheritance. The substantive commands are two. The adult heir is not to be made to pay his relief before being let into the tenement, but must be let in at once. And homage is at once to be taken from the infant heir, so acknowledging that the lord's holding is in *custodia* on his behalf.[3] There is no telling how far these were new, and practice may have varied from lordship to lordship. Glanvill's language suggests that the infant heir's homage had become customary;[4] but even if the adult heir in fact often entered on his

---

[1] Hurstfield, *The Queen's Wards*, pp. 168 ff., describes the sixteenth-century procedure.   [2] Assize of Northampton, c. 4.

[3] The text on this point is quoted above, p. 163, n. 6. For the sense of *custodia*, see above, pp. 155–6; and contrast the *escaeta cum herede* of the king, above, p. 163. For the importance of the homage, see above, p. 86, at n. 1, and below, p. 173, end of n. 2.

[4] *Glanvill*, IX, 1, after the statement quoted above, p. 163, n. 6, goes on: *Quia generaliter uerum est quod nullum seruicium, siue releuium siue aliud, potest quis ab herede, siue fuerit maior siue minor, exigere donec ipsius receperit homagium.* But the plea rolls show lords at some levels still taking homage when the ward comes of age: (a) *CRR*, VII, 243–4, 245–6, *308*; (b) *CRR*, VII, 262–3. Cf. *Gloucs.*, 1530 (fealty in respect of urban tenement).

own, it may still have been seen as a matter of convenience and grace. Neither practice, as we have seen, was followed by the king, who did not deny the claim of the heir to be accepted as tenant, but withheld acceptance until his own claims were satisfied.[1] What was certainly new was the regular enforcement of these rules upon lesser lords; and the inquest that the justices were to hold becomes known as the assize of mort d'ancestor.

This identification seems never to have been doubted, and it was accepted by Maitland. He observes, though only in a footnote, that the Assize of Northampton does not expressly give mort d'ancestor against any one but the lord, and that as a matter of fact the lord was a common defendant.[2] And yet he writes: 'The principle...which is the foundation for this assize seems to be this, that whenever a man dies seised...his heir is of all the world the person best entitled to be put into seisin.'[3] He is thinking of an entitlement against the world, and mort d'ancestor is bracketed with novel disseisin as a possessory protection. In one sense of course it was: the relationship between a 'Roman' possessory and a proprietary remedy is curiously mirrored in the relationship between a mort d'ancestor and a writ of right even when both enforce claims polarised against the lord. A tenant *recessit de patria* so that his lord took the tenement into hand: because he did not die seised, his heir must lose in mort d'ancestor; but a grand assize may properly find that he has greater right to hold of the lord than the lord to hold in demesne.[4] It is this analogy in relationship which leaves open some possibility of an ultimate Roman influence in the creation of novel disseisin and mort d'ancestor.

What we must not assume is that at the time lawyers were identifying the substantive concepts involved, *dominium* with the right and *possessio* with seisin. To use Roman language, the Roman pair were *in rem*, the English *in personam*; and this is not just a juridical nicety which the social historian can ignore. Mort

---

[1] Above, pp. 162–4.

[2] Pollock and Maitland, *History of English Law* (2nd ed.), II, p. 57, n. 1; cf. I, p. 148.

[3] Ibid. II, p. 59. The passive mood of the last five words may suggest a doubt.

[4] *CRR*, VI, 142 (Celestria wife of Goldhauec); *CRR*, VII, 93–303; see also *CRR*, VI, 311, and full references above, p. 59, n. 1. Similar stories: (a) *Gloucs.*, 614; (b) *Lincs.-Worcs.*, 981 (in which the absentee is held to have died seised); (c) *CRR*, I, 94; *RCR*, I, 255, 260, 357–8; *PKJ*, I, 2494, 2745; *RCR*, II, 25–6, 197 (tenant gave up freedom of tenement and undertook villein services ten years before death).

d'ancestor was not conceived as an action for the recovery of property which happened at first to be aimed against only one possible class of defendant. It protected one party to a relationship against the other; and as with novel disseisin its initial thrust may have been as much against improper exactions as against simple misappropriation. Maitland's abstract remedy against any stranger came into being, but it is not what the Assize of Northampton meant to create; and this is the only obtrusive incongruity in his picture of the early actions, and therefore of the twelfth-century world.

But the Assize of Northampton is the only obvious evidence of the original orientation of mort d'ancestor; and this ought to be remembered in considering the original orientation of novel disseisin. The legislation creating novel disseisin does not survive, and the only contemporary evidence of its original aim is the wording of the writ itself. If the writ is read without preconception, that evidence is considerable; but there is no other in Glanvill, and what there is in the early rolls does not lie on their surface. If it were not for Northampton, the first aim of mort d'ancestor would be even less clear. The writ contains no revealing phrases. Glanvill mentions the original use in his account of homage,[1] but in his account of the assize itself the only indication is buried in a discussion of infancy of the parties: an infant defendant[2] cannot delay the assize until he is of age if his holding is in wardship.[3] As to the rolls, most entries are as blank as in the case of novel disseisin; and the only facts lying on the surface are that the assize was extremely common and was often brought for small tenements.

As with novel disseisin, it cannot be doubted that the assize came to be used as a remedy in a wider range of situations than that first envisaged. But, if we could hear what was said to and by the recognitors at any period, it seems unlikely that the defendant would often turn out to be a conscious wrongdoer forestalling the heir. There would be a genuine or at least a colourable dispute. But on the early rolls we can rarely make out what it was or how the parties are related. Who is it who says that the demandant is

---

[1] *Glanvill*, IX, 6: *posset quidem assisam uersus dominum suum querere de morte antecessoris sui.*

[2] As in all claims which may be 'upward', the word 'tenant' is confusing.

[3] *Glanvill*, VII, 9; XIII, 15.

a bastard: legitimate heir, lord taking as escheat, grantee from one of those, or casual wrongdoer who has struck lucky?[1] Sometimes we can tell it is the lord: the defendant does not press the point and takes the demandant's homage;[2] or he has taken in wardship with a clearly legitimate child.[3] More often we have only probabilities to go on. Again, who is it who says that the plaintiff is or the dead man was a villein or held in villeinage?[4] Probably it is the lord or one claiming through him; but we shall not be told this expressly. Sometimes the point is not pleaded at all, but just stated by the recognitors.[5] And how often is it the unstated reason for a general verdict? If the ancestor held in villeinage, he was not seised as of fee.[6] As with novel disseisin, it is not impossible that the freedom of a peasant tenement was often the point really in dispute; and if, as may happen, there is a special verdict just setting out the services,[7] we can be reasonably sure that the question had never before been asked in the community concerned.

Villeinage cases may be used to introduce a more comprehensive way in which the seignorial bearing of mort d'ancestor is disguised. It is often not the original defendant who raises the point but his vouchee: the lord has evidently taken the tenement on the death, and granted it away freely[8] or assigned it in dower.[9] But the facts which we can see in such a case may equally lie behind a claim for peasant holdings, a voucher, and a blank general verdict; and the

---

[1] See, e.g., the Hampshire pair at *RCR*, I, 56–7. For a bishop's return, see *RCR*, I, *227*, *302*, 406 (William f. Adam), 413?; *RCR*, II, *42*, *126*.

[2] *Gloucs.*, 1163.

[3] *CRR*, IV, 157–8.

[4] (a) *PRS*, XIV, 133–4; (b) *CRR*, II, 146 (bishop of Winchester); (c) *PKJ*, III, 959; (d) *Lincs.-Worcs.*, 137; (e) ibid. 228. In *Lincs.*, 322, 517, the tenant's vouchee says that one plaintiff is villein, the other bastard. If the lord is not defendant and not vouched, it appears that he cannot intervene; *Gloucs.*, 187: *si voluerit distringat tenementum suum si sit vilenagium suum*, which would no doubt end in an assize of novel disseisin. At least one lord imprisoned a naif who had won in mort d'ancestor; *CRR*, I, 22 (Colleville).

[5] (a) *RCR*, I, 357–8 (full references above, p. 165, n. 4); (b) *Lincs.*, 54; (c) ibid. 155. In *Lincs.-Worcs.*, 279, the assize is expressly conceded, and the recognitors find the ancestor was a villein holding in villeinage. Cf. ibid. 959.

[6] *PKJ*, II, 453; cf. last two cases in preceding note.

[7] *CRR*, I, 120–1, *192*, 216; *RCR*, II, *192*.

[8] (a) *PRS*, XIV, 133–4; (b) *PKJ*, II, 453; (c) *Lincs.*, 322, 517. If the present tenant himself holds in villeinage, he cannot vouch and the demandant must start again against the lord; *Lincs.-Worcs.*, 1287. The same is true if the present tenant holds for years; *RCR*, I, 229, *267*, 355 (Snaring); *RCR*, II, 47.

[9] (a) *Lincs.-Worcs.*, 137; (b) case in n. 7, above.

roll alone will never tell us so.[1] If a vouchee is noted as taking the
demandant's homage,[2] or facing a *de homagio capiendo*,[3] or if
something else tells us that the demandant claims to hold of him,[4]
we know at least who he is though not necessarily why he had
treated the tenement as being at his disposal. And of course there
may be similar indications that the original defendant himself is
lord.[5] But the lord himself may never be a party, either as original
defendant or vouchee. The original defendant must be the person
seised at the time of the writ; and that is why the writ itself contains no seignorial indication. That person may not choose to
vouch, or have the necessary proof. Even if he does vouch, the
assize will not wait if the vouchee does not come when summoned:[6]
it will proceed against the original tenant, who can later pursue an
independent claim for *escambium* if he loses. A lord may face
a *de homagio capiendo* brought by the winner of an assize in which
he played no formal part.[7] Perhaps he had actively put the wrong
person in, and was the main character in a story considered by the
recognitors.[8] Perhaps he had not known or cared.

This is how the assize came to appear as a remedy against the
world at large; and of course the change was not just optical
illusion. The assize greatly reduced the lord's part in inheritance.
But this did not happen all at once. An appeal of felony in 1201
charges the defendant with housebreaking and robbery. It turns
out, as it does in many early appeals, that he is a lord enforcing his
rights: he heard tell that the appellant had recovered in mort

---

[1] *RCR*, I, 333 (abbot of Ramsey), *406*; *RCR*, II, 4, 4–5: note that in the final
enrolment the abbot appears as tenant with nothing to show that he has become
so by warranty.

[2] *RCR*, II, 47 (Snaring; for an abortive assize against the lord's tenant for
years, see p. 167, n. 8, above).

[3] *CRR*, v, *37*, 38 (voucher in assize), 129–30 (assize taken without vouchee),
165, 232 (*de homagio capiendo*, homage taken).

[4] *CRR*, v, 105–6; *PKJ*, IV, *2720*. See also *CRR*, I, 145 (Blac; see above,
p. 157, n. 2).

[5] Express statements: (*a*) *RCR*, II, 191 (Anglicus); *CRR*, III, *279*; (*b*) *CRR*,
II, 15 (Pevensell). Tenant claims to hold in wardship: *CRR*, VI, 130–1. Tenant
has taken homage of another: (*a*) *CRR*, v, 27 (Breusa); (*b*) *PKJ*, II, 111. Tenant
relies on some transaction in own court: (*a*) *RCR*, I, 447 (abbess of Barking);
(*b*) *PKJ*, IV, 4250. Uncertain whether fee or not: *CRR*, I, 430 (Kokefeld).

[6] (*a*) *Staffs.*, 124 (Litelhand), 127; (*b*) *CRR*, VI, 316 (Say).

[7] *RCR*, I, *152*; *PKJ*, I, *2278*; *CRR*, I, 139 (Sandon); *CRR*, II, *11*, *59*; *CRR*,
III, *171*.

[8] Consider the likely part played by the abbot of Angers in *CRR*, I, *226*,
227–8, *249*, 270, 350.

d'ancestor certain land held of his fee; and since nobody came to do homage or perform the service, he occupied the house. The *audivit dici* suggests that the assize had proceeded without any reference to him; but chance preserved the record of its beginning and the tenants had tried to vouch him, only he was overseas.[1]

That appeal was withdrawn. The lord's action within his own fee was certainly not in breach of the king's peace: but it was not necessarily proper, and the appellant might conceivably have won in novel disseisin. In 1214 lurid cross-appeals in Cornwall grew out of a similar incident. A tenant died. The lord *voluit seisire in manum suam, sicut consuetudo est, feudum quod de eo tenuit quousque inde fieret quod fieri deberet*. But the house was barred against his men, allegedly by persons saying there was no king's peace because the king was dead; and hence the uproar and probably the unusual degree of confusion in an unusually detailed record. The truth appears to have been more mundane: the dead tenant's heir *dixit quod ipse intellexit quod ipsi non debuerunt facere nisi simplicem seisinam eo quod etatem habuit, et putavit quod aliter facere voluerunt, et ideo tenuit se in predicta domo*.[2] The phrase 'simple seisin' is only just beginning to appear on the rolls at this time;[3] and in this context it seems to be a short expression of the power described by Glanvill. When a tenant dies leaving an heir of full age, the lord may take into hand *feodum suum cum herede*; but he must do it so *moderate* that he does not disseise the heir.[4] The confrontation between the lord's own law and that imposed on him by the king is reflected in the double language. The heir has not been seised by the lord, but yet has such seisin that he can be disseised; and the lord, who would once have delivered seisin to the heir as the king himself still does, must content himself with a 'simple' seisin *pro recognicione dominii sui*.

Those last words come from the statute of Marlborough, reaffirming the Provisions of Westminster.[5] The Assize of

---

[1] The appeal: *CRR*, II, 50 (Roger f. Nicholas). The assize: *RCR*, I, *378*, 379 (voucher); *PKJ*, I, 2252 (essoin by tenant and also essoin *de seruicio Regis ultra mare* by vouchee); *CRR*, I, 117 (protection), *123*.

[2] *CRR*, VII, 168–73. Cf. *Lincs.-Worcs.*, 256.

[3] The earliest example noted is *CRR*, V, 169 (Mantel): a gagee complains that a sheriff *noluit facere...plenariam seisinam*, but sent his serjeant *qui nichil ei fecit nisi quandam simplicem seisinam de domibus et grangiis, ita quod, cum deberet facere homines ville venire ad faciendum ei fidelitatem, ipse noluit*. See also above, p. 11, n. 1.   [4] *Glanvill*, VII, 9.

[5] Stat. Marlborough, c. 16; Provisions of Westminster, c. 9.

Northampton had provided that the disobedient lord should be made to restore seisin and should be amerced;[1] now he is also to pay damages. The *simplex saisina* of ordinary lords is contrasted with the *libera saisina* taken by the king. And the limitation on lords is carefully restricted, as it was for Glanvill, to the case in which there is one of full age who is clearly heir and recognised as such:[2] if there is doubt, it is assumed that the lord may take the tenement fully into hand. After ninety years, it is still the original function of mort d'ancestor which is modified. And though there are many cases in which the lord is not the tenant named in the writ and is not vouched, it seems unlikely that even then contemporaries could have read them, as we have taught ourselves to do, as though he did not exist.

What were the consequences of this loss of actual control when there was an undoubted adult heir? Perhaps the most important was a change in the look of the thing. In 1201 an assize is brought for three manors of which the demandant's father had died seised. The lord says that the father had held for life only, by grant made after the death of the grandfather, who had on his death-bed forbidden his heirs to claim any right in two but had expressed the belief that the third was his inheritance. Seisin of the third is thereupon adjudged to the demandant. But the recognitors disclose that before the grandfather, the great-grandfather had held the other two; and because of the long tenure they believe the father must have died seised as of fee.[3] This was a fee farm, and the farm for life seems to have been a known entity, whereas a military life estate at this time may not have been; and the factual doubt may therefore not often have arisen. But the case shows how inheritance must have looked when there was only the lord's law and the lord's court. However regular the succession had been in fact, and however powerful the custom binding the lord to make a new grant, it was still only by grant from the lord that each heir entered. Before it was made, the heir could not think of himself as 'owner'. He

---

[1] Amercements for *injusta detentio* on the early rolls appear to be sporadic, but there may turn out to be a principle.

[2] Doubt over who is heir: *Glanvill*, VII, 17; IX, 6. Doubt over age of undoubted heir: *Glanvill*, VII, 9, 17. Compare Stat. Marlborough, c. 16: *si heres aliquis in morte sui antecessoris plene fuerit etatis, & heres ille apparens & pro herede cognitus inventus fuerit in hereditate illa, capitalis dominus ejus eum non eiciat...*

[3] *CRR*, I, 430 (Kokefeld): notice the insertion of *bene sciunt*, no doubt put into the mouths of recognitors who wanted to say only *credunt*. Cf. the similar doubt in *CRR*, III, *340*; *CRR*, IV, 34 (Giffard).

had just his right, a claim *in personam* against the lord to be granted the land. If he died before this was done, for example, the tenement was never his, and his own heir as such had no right to be granted it. The person who now had that right was the next heir of the dead tenant; and only after the *casus regis* was out of the way and representation finally accepted would he normally be the same person.[1]

Traces of all this were long embedded in the law, anomalies attending the mystery of seisin. But it is the equation of seisin with a sort of possession and of right with a sort of ownership that make them appear as anomalies; and that equation partly came about because of mort d'ancestor. The lord was edged out of the ideas which had grown up around him in consequence of being edged out of his actual part. Now the heir does not have to be put in: he goes in by himself, and becomes seised as though the lord had seised him. He begins to look like an owner taking what is already his, rather than just a person having some claim that it should be granted to him. His relief begins to look like an irrational tax, and not the premium for a renewal which could thinkably be withheld. And his homage, once the compact from which flowed the obligations of a relationship, becomes a formality consequent upon the automatic devolution of some abstract title.

But the ideas all had to change together, and it happened slowly. The right did not begin as an abstract title which the king's court could simply declare: the writ patent was an order to the lord, and it was only the lord who could make a tenant. On the ancient pattern of inheritance the lord made him all at once, seising him at the time he accepted his right by taking homage; and to be seised without being accepted by the lord was a contradiction in terms. It is this unity that mort d'ancestor and novel disseisin have destroyed. Now there can be somebody seised who is not accepted by the lord; and so long as the lord's acceptance mattered, this must have been more uncomfortable for those involved than our comfortable possessory language suggests.[2]

Ralph is lord. Thomas has got in, whether by mort d'ancestor or

[1] On the *casus regis*, see below, p. 175, and on its relationship with *se demisit*, see above, p. 147. Notice the simplicity of 'non-representative' inheritance: the son of a tenant who had done homage was entitled before any other relative.

[2] Consider the realities behind an assize of mort d'ancestor followed more than ten years later by a writ of right; *RCR*, II, 276 (Mandeville; the assize); *CRR*, VI, *234*, 243; *CRR*, VII, *56*, 83.

otherwise; but Ralph thinks either that he himself is entitled in demesne or that some third party, William, is entitled to hold of him. If there is a William, he is the only person whose course of action is clear. He brings a writ patent to Ralph: this will decide whether or not he is entitled to be Ralph's tenant of this tenement; and if Thomas vouches, it will decide also whether Thomas has a corresponding right which Ralph must satisfy with *escambium*. William's action, in short, is capable of bringing royal control to bear on both sides of the triangle.[1]

But even if there is a William, he is in no relationship with Thomas; and there is nothing Thomas can do about his claim except wait for it. Thomas can, however, at once seek the king's aid to make Ralph accept him as tenant. If he has a charter, he can perhaps use the writ which comes to be known as *warantia carte*. But his obvious remedy is the writ *de homagio capiendo*, destined to drop out as the seignorial title gave way to an abstract right which the king's court could just declare, but at first a revealing instrument of royal control.[2] Thomas must first make repeated tenders of his homage and relief before witnesses,[3] probably in Ralph's court; and of course he will have been doing this whether or not he has physically got the tenement. If he has not got it, Glanvill prescribes mort d'ancestor;[4] though if he expects Ralph to claim on his own behalf, he may prefer to go straight to the question of right between them with a writ patent. He ought not to use *de homagio capiendo* to claim the tenement itself, perhaps because it is a *precipe* writ. *De homagio capiendo* is appropriate only when Thomas is already in.[5] But it equally goes to the right, and if

---

[1] Above, pp. 41 ff. and 71 ff.

[2] Note that the action is reserved for the king's court; *Glanvill*, I, 3. This seemed puzzling when it lost its importance; *Novae Narrationes*, ed. Shanks and Milsom, Selden Society, vol. 80, p. 100 (B 185). It could also be used upon a change of lord by succession: (a) *PRS*, XIV, 135–6 (full references above, p. 89, n. 4); (b) *RCR*, I, 187, 199 (Bercampo, otherwise Petra Ponte; above, p. 47, n. 2); but apparently not by grant: *CRR*, II, 259–60 (full references above, p. 18, n. 1).

[3] *Glanvill*, IX, 4–6. Cf. the counts in *Novae Narrationes*, ed. Shanks and Milsom, Selden Society, vol. 80, pp. 100 (B 184–5), 274–5 (C 235–8; notice the witnesses to the tender in C 236).

[4] *Glanvill*, IX, 6. For a tenant who seems to bring mort d'ancestor when he has got the tenement, and starts again with *de homagio capiendo*, see *Lincs.*, 161, 436.

[5] (a) *CRR*, I, 86 (Grim; full references above, p. 18, n. 1); (b) *RCR*, II, 29–30, 191; *PKJ*, I, 2511; *CRR*, I, 123, 186; (c) *CRR*, II, 9–10 (full references above, p. 14, n. 5); (d) *CRR*, III, 81, 191–2; (e) *PKJ*, III, 997; *CRR*, IV, 19; cf. *CRR*, IV, 88, 115, 200; *CRR*, V, 2–3, 41. But if the defendant is himself

in answer Ralph claims himself to be entitled in demesne, Thomas can put himself on the grand assize.[1] If the knights declare that Thomas has greater right to hold of Ralph than Ralph to hold in demesne, or if the action otherwise ends in Thomas's favour, Ralph will normally take his homage then and there in court.[2] But this probably cannot be compelled any more than a marriage can be compelled; and if Thomas must have the tenement and Ralph will not accept the relationship, then Ralph must be extruded and Thomas do homage and service to the superior lord.[3] Whether Glanvill envisaged this drastic end is not clear, because at the relevant point he may have left the royal action and reverted to Thomas's private applications to Ralph: the only sanction he states is that so long as the lord does not accept homage he cannot take relief, wardship, or service.[4]

This makes Ralph's own position potentially the most uncomfortable of all. If he thinks that he himself is entitled by escheat, he can claim the tenement, though inappropriately, by writ patent to his own lord, or by way of answer to a *de homagio capiendo* by Thomas. Or he can risk novel disseisin and enter. What he cannot

seised and so chooses, he can allow the right between the parties to be decided in this action; *Gloucs.*, 1495. If a third party is in, the action has no place. In *CRR*, VI, *52*, 80–1, 171, a daughter complains that the lord has taken the homage of the dead tenant's brother, but we do not know why, or who has the tenement.

[1] Examples above, p. 89, n. 4.

[2] (*a*) *PRS*, XIV, 135–6; *RCR*, II, 140 (full references above, p. 89, n. 4); (*b*) *RCR*, I, *187*, 199 (Bercampo); (*c*) *RCR*, II, 200 (Ros); (*d*) *CRR*, I, 95 (Linand); (*e*) *CRR*, I, 451–2 (*warantia carte*); *CRR*, II, 35; (*f*) *Lincs.*, 233; (*g*) *Beds.*, 97; (*h*) *CRR*, II, *37*, 221 (Heirun; for references to related litigation see above, p. 50, n. 1); (*i*) *CRR*, III, 47 (Drope; perhaps a sequel to *Lincs.*, 423, 279; notice the level of tenure); (*j*) *CRR*, III, 313 (Tichesie; *sicut de libero socagio*); (*k*) *CRR*, IV, 176 (Stanham); (*l*) *CRR*, VI, 286 (Scoteny); (*m*) *CRR*, VII, *21*, 38 (Cornhull). It is no doubt because homage would be taken then and there that the plaintiff in this action may not proceed by attorney; *BNB*, 41. The absence of process entries, and in many cases of any sign of contest, may indicate that the object was often to secure warranty by having the homage recorded in the king's court; cf. the homage taken at *Lincs.*, 248, which is made the basis of a claim ten years later; *CRR*, VI, 308, 353–4.

[3] Bracton, ff. 82b, 389. Cf. (*a*) *CRR*, I, 377 (Plaiz; other references above, p. 48, n. 4); (*b*) *RCR*, II, *229*; *CRR*, I, 298 (Pilate). To do homage to the superior lord without cause is of course a wrong to the mesne; *CRR*, V, 77–8 (full references above, p. 117, n. 4; other cases in that note are relevant). For a mesne supposed to have been extruded for a different cause, see *Gloucs.*, 1131.

[4] *Glanvill*, IX, 6: *se in saisina sua teneat et patienter sustineat, donec placeat domino suo homagium suum inde recipere. Quia non prius de relleuio suo tenetur quis domino suo respondere donec ipse homagium suum receperit de feodo unde ei debet homagium.* Cf. *Glanvill*, IX, 1, quoted above, p. 164, n. 4.

do is to proceed by *quo waranto* inquiry in his own court: the mere summons will attribute some tenure to Thomas, and so bring him within the rule requiring a writ and the automatic protection of novel disseisin.[1] For the same reason Ralph must not act on his own authority in his own court if he thinks William is entitled as heir.[2] He can help William to enter extra-judicially, or take the tenement into his own hand on the ground that there is doubt; but novel disseisin has made either course hazardous. Doubt remains a good answer to *de homagio capiendo*,[3] but lords probably take the tenement into hand only when they can get to it before either of the claimants. Since Thomas has got in, the only safe course for Ralph is to wait until William brings his writ patent. But in the meantime he must not accept Thomas's homage, and so cannot take what is due to him from the tenement.

Royal control of the seignorial relationship has largely changed the realities. But the way in which the world is seen has not yet been changed. A lord's acceptance of his tenant is still the ultimate title, the end to which royal action is directed. The fundamental shift in ideas is still to come. Abstract title will reside in the king's court, and warranty will become a contractual addition which the tenant may or may not have. The process involves such piecemeal devices as taking homage with a saving clause,[4] but its important phase is a general stiffening in the requirements to be met by one trying to establish warranty. A largely automatic right to *escambium* is tolerable only so long as the tenant's title truly follows from his acceptance by the lord. If the lord has no control, he must be allowed to acquiesce without thereby providing a guarantee against other claims over which he has equally no control. But generations must die before such new realities can be perceived in terms of new legal ideas, rather than as adjustments to the old order. And the lord's acceptance of the heir was long seen as the essence of inheritance.

Nor should we assume that by the early thirteenth century the

---

[1] *RCR*, I, 447–8; cf. ibid. 368; above, pp. 29 and 159.

[2] *Northants.*, 782 (above, pp. 53–4). Cf. *CRR*, III, 161–2 (above, p. 53).

[3] *Glanvill*, IX, 6. Doubt is expressly pleaded in *CRR*, IV, 144 (abbot of Colchester; discussion and references above, pp. 151–2). If the lord had taken the tenement into hand, of course, *de homagio capiendo* would not lie; above, p. 172, n. 5.

[4] (a) *CRR*, II, 37, 221 (Heirun; above, p. 173, n. 2); (b) *Gloucs.*, 1468. Cf. Bracton, f. 382.

realities had entirely changed and the lord and his court been reduced to a puppet part. At the level of honour courts and military tenures, the customs of inheritance were probably seen as general. But at lower levels the customs resided in each court, and royal control must have been conceived as compelling a proper exercise of power rather than compelling a particular result. This may have been the reason for two limitations on mort d'ancestor. One is not implicit in the writ but appears often in the rolls: the defendant can object that the parties are brothers or otherwise both related to the dead tenant,[1] and then the claim can be made only by writ patent. Perhaps this is because any question between them must turn on the customs of the lord's court.

This was an exception which the defendant could choose to make or not. The other limitation was on the reach of the writ itself. The dead tenant had to be of the claimant's own or the preceding generation, not for example a grandfather. This reduced the occasions on which questions could arise about the canons of inheritance. Consider the king's case, where the dispute is between an Arthur, who is son of a dead elder son, and a younger son John.[2] If Arthur has got in, John can bring the assize, though Arthur can stop it with the exception of kinship. But usually it is John who is in as 'hearth-child'; and Arthur cannot even bring the assize on the death of his grandfather. If it is a yet older brother who has died seised, as indeed in the king's own case, Arthur can of course bring it and sometimes does. Far from excepting, a John in 1201 embarrassingly asks the court to decide which of them is nearer heir: *judicium pendet ex uoluntate domini Regis*.[3] Another John in the preceding year also asks the court to decide which is heir, but he adds an illuminating argument: he has paid his relief and done homage to the lords of the fee. Even so the case was settled, as we learn from a sequel ten years later;[4] and the king's

---

[1] *Glanvill*, XIII, 11. It is common on the rolls.

[2] Above, p. 147. Maitland thought this limitation on the assize showed the novelty of the representative principle; Pollock and Maitland, *History of English Law* (2nd ed.), II, 285, n. 2.   [3] *PKJ*, II, 484, 528.

[4] The assize: *CRR*, I, 187 (Ros). The sequel: *CRR*, VI, 134–5. Another case early in John's reign was given special treatment: *CRR*, I, *153*; *PKJ*, I, *2344, 2457, 3113*; *RCR*, II, *156*, 189 (Vautort): the heir of the elder brother seems to be represented by his guardian (Hubert de Burgh, to be Arthur's jailer); only formal entries survive of the earlier stages, but it seems to be an action in the right; an inquest declares the pedigree and says that the representatives of the elder son *debent esse heredes...ut eis videtur*; the names of the recognitors are

judges took no position on the king's case until after that king was dead, perhaps long after.[1] But this doubt, although prolonged and exacerbated by political chance, had arisen because customs differed;[2] and at humbler levels there must have been many differences.[3] These were largely to be obliterated when the king's court came to decide most cases itself; but that cannot have been intended, and so far as mort d'ancestor is concerned, it looks as though such questions were meant to be left to lords' courts. When this particular limitation on its scope was in effect transcended by the writs of aiel and cosinage, they were objected to as *precipe* writs and within the ban of the Charter.[4] If the objection was not merely formal, it must have been because a question particularly for lords' courts was likely to be taken away from them. It was the question put to them by the writ patent: who is the lord to accept as heir?

*   *   *

We now return to the heart of seignorial jurisdiction, the writ of right patent addressed to the lord. The second chapter concentrated on the part it played between the lord and his accepted tenant. Having taken homage, the lord could not go back on his warranty, whether by denying the tenant's right on his own account or by entertaining the claim of another. Whether he had been right or wrong to accept him, this was his man; and in his own court the bond between them was unbreakable. This was the first sense of the proposition that a tenant could not be made to answer for his tenement without the king's writ; and even the king's writ could often not break the bond without removing the case from the lord's own court to public justice. There the tenant's right to hold this tenement of the lord could be overreached, and the lord made

enrolled (apart from the grand assize, something normally found only when an attaint is contemplated); and then there is a note that the inquest was taken *per preceptum domini Regis non per consideracionem curie vel secundum consuetudinem regni.*

[1] For the position under Henry III, and references to Bracton and to the *Note Book*, see Pollock and Maitland, *History of English Law* (2nd ed.), II, p. 285. See also the case in *Select Cases in the Court of King's Bench*, ed. Sayles, II, Selden Society, vol. 57, pp. clvi f. But a case early in the reign may show the judges considering a new stance: *Yorks.*, 353, 198, 287, 1115 (above, p. 124, n. 4).   [2] Painter, *The Reign of King John*, pp. 1–3.

[3] See the survey in Homans, *English Villagers of the Thirteenth Century*, chapters viii and ix. Differences survived with unfree tenures because the king's courts did not interfere.   [4] Above, p. 84.

to compensate him with another. The mandatory logic of the writ became obscured when novel disseisin protected persons not warranted by the lord; and although always worded as a command, it began to play the part of a required authorisation.[1]

Our present concern is with the demandant rather than the tenant. Who is it who persuades the king to issue so unacceptable an order? That we know from the count, the claim which he invariably makes: he is the heir of an ancestor who was once seised of the land. No other title can be set up by the demandant,[2] and he does not attack or explain that of the tenant. The lord is to accept this demandant just because he is his ancestor's heir, and his ancestor was seised.

What is the ancestor to the lord? Equating 'seised' with 'possessed', we have read back later ideas of abstract title. But to be seised was not an abstract condition: one could only be seised by a lord. The historical fact upon which the claim rests is not a possession but a relationship: the ancestor was tenant of this lord or his predecessor. That is what the demandant's witness undertakes to prove by his body; and if the tenant vouches, he will have to prove it against the lord himself.[3] The nature of the claim is brought out clearly in the case in which the tenant cannot vouch this lord because he claims to hold of another: the demandant must still bring his writ to this lord.[4] His only claim is to hold of him, and its only basis is that his ancestor held of him or his predecessor.

In a sense, though we shall see that it is a special sense, the writ patent is therefore compelling lords to abide by the customs of inheritance. Others have suggested that regular heritability may have been imposed as a consequence of the troubles between Stephen and Matilda, when a disputed succession to the kingdom itself was exacerbated by questionable escheats and dispositions.[5]

---

[1] Above, pp. 58 ff.

[2] For an express statement, unusual with any elementary rule, see *CRR*, II, *150*, 286 (Favarches): the demandant counts on the seisin of his grandfather Robert, who gave him the land; judgment thereon for the tenants, because *non loquitur de seisina sua propria, set tantum de seisina predicti Roberti, qui illam ei dedit...et non dicit quod ei descendere debet jure hereditario ab ipso Roberto.* This may not apply when land is claimed as *pertinens* to some unit not itself in dispute; *CRR*, VI, *11*, *12*, *51*, 75–6; for such claims see above, pp. 75–6.

[3] On proof between lord and man see above, pp. 84–5, where it is suggested that this may have been a factor in the introduction of the grand assize.

[4] Above, pp. 77–80.

[5] Davis, *King Stephen*, pp. 121 ff.; Davis, 'What Happened in Stephen's Reign', *History*, XLIX (1964), 1 ff.

But it is doubtful whether we should think of an essentially legislative act intended to govern the future. Great legal decisions are rare; but great consequences often follow from measures taken to meet immediate problems. And just as the regular civil process of novel disseisin may have grown from criminal inquiries ordered on a particular occasion, so may the great writ of right have grown from a decision equally particular. The peace between Stephen and duke Henry was embodied in a charter which governs only succession to the kingdom itself;[1] but chroniclers tell us of a general provision that those disinherited during the anarchy should be restored to the rights they had under Henry I.[2] The earliest rolls suggest that the writ of right as a regular action grew from this.

So long as the action lasted, counts said not just that the ancestor was seised, but that this was in time of peace and in the reign of a named king. In the earliest rolls, the reign is very often that of Henry I, but even that is not sufficiently specific. The most common form seems to be 'in the time of king Henry the grandfather, namely the day and the year that he died'. The use even under Richard and John of 'the grandfather' suggests that the formula had set hard under Henry II: occasionally it is extended, 'king Henry the grandfather of king Henry the father of the lord king'.[3] Henry I is once or twice identified as father of Matilda;[4] but that unhappy time is usually mentioned only in a statement that the land was taken *tempore guerre*.[5] Another phrase that set hard is 'the day and the year that he died'. Although not infrequently omitted by clerical abbreviation,[6] its omission from the count is a ground of objection. Once this is rationalised:

---

[1] *Regesta Regum Anglo-Normannorum*, III, no. 272.

[2] Davis, *King Stephen*, pp. 122–3.

[3] Probably just a matter of clerical habit. See, e.g., ordinary actions in the right of 1211–12 (only entries of counts noted): (a) *CRR*, VI, 143 (Riebof), 279–80; (b) *CRR*, VI, 259 (Tywe), 335. Found earlier only in exceptional cases, e.g., *RCR*, II, 133–4.

[4] (a) *RCR*, I, 25–6 (note allegation of taking *tempore gwerre*), *125*; (b) *BNB*, 950; *CRR*, XI, *274*, *1484*, *1985*, 2665 (repeated in same form in mise, after oblation *pro habenda mencione de predicto tempore*).

[5] (a) First case in preceding note; (b) *RCR*, I, 93 (Raimes); (c) *RCR*, I, 440–1 (full references above, p. 116, n. 1); (d) *CRR*, VI, 176–7, 287, 296 (after verdict; full references above, p. 25, n. 1). Cf. (a) *PRS*, XIV, 9 (Piron; full references above, p. 158, n. 4; alleged escheat to empress Matilda); (b) *CRR*, I, *390*, 439 (earl Patrick; inquest on seisin *anno et die quibus werra incepit inter Henricum regem patrem regis et H. juniorem...et si occasione illius werre inde fuit disseisitus*); *PKJ*, I, *3400*.

[6] e.g., *CRR*, VII, *38*, 107 Blundus), *121*, 262.

de incerto termino non fit aliqua disrationatio;[1] but when later kings are named, as increasingly they are, there is no closer specification than their reigns. Under Henry III, a court just knows a rule of thumb that you cannot go further back into the reign of king Henry *qui fuit avus avi*.[2] Much earlier, demandants make the mistakes of incomprehension: one speaks of the day his ancestor died in the reign of Henry I,[3] another of his ancestor being seised for a year and a day during the reign.[4] All this lasted until the statute of Merton (itself, as printed in the Statutes of the Realm, making the customary unintelligible abbreviation to *anno et die*) forbade counts to go back so long a time, and fixed the reign of Henry II as the earliest to which a demandant could reach.[5] But what had been fossilised was surely not a period of limitation, and not fixed arbitrarily. It was the last moment of peace and legitimate title;[6] and the entire regular machinery of the writ of right, which ran so long, may have been started to implement the single decision that those put out during the twenty years of anarchy should be put back again.

In a Maitland Memorial lecture delivered many years ago, Professor Thorne ventured a hesitant foot on to the ground this book has so rashly sought to occupy; and he drew much of the fire on heritability.[7] But it is important to be exact about what is and is not now suggested. It is not that kings had never intervened before, but only that the regular machinery of the writ of right started in this way; and this is a relatively unimportant proposition. What is important, and not only in the vexed context

---

[1] *PKJ*, I, *3481* and references in note thereto; *CRR*, II, 12 (Nevill). Cf. other defective counts (other entries not noted): (*a*) *CRR*, II, 265–6 (land specified only by reference to writ, champion not named, and apparently no indication which king Henry); (*b*) *CRR*, III, 34 (Charneles; apparently no reign specified); (*c*) *CRR*, III, 184 (Aurifaber: *nullam sectam produxit nec avunculum suum nominavit nec regem aliquem*).   [2] *BNB*, 280; *CRR*, XIII, 507.

[3] *PRS*(NS), XXXI, *114*; *RCR*, I, *258*, *411*; *CRR*, VII, *349*; *CRR*, I, 69 (Vesci), 277–8, *451*; *CRR*, II, *142*; *CRR*, III, *5*; *Northants.*, *648*.

[4] *CRR*, III, *300*, 343 (Curteis; also fails to produce champion; judgment for tenant).   [5] Stat. Merton, c. 8.

[6] Sometimes the point is made expressly, e.g., *CRR*, I, 158 (Garwinton; full references above, p. 98, n. 5): *tempore pacis scilicet die et anno quo Henricus rex avus obiit*. But of course it could prevent the raising of earlier matters, as is shown by two unusually instructive grand assize verdicts (other entries of the cases not noted) which evidently arise out of gifts to younger sons made before that date: (*a*) *CRR*, IV, 301 (Alexander f. Seman); (*b*) *CRR*, V, 139–40. Cf. the case at pp. 181–2, below.

[7] 'English Feudalism and Estates in Land', [1959] *Cambridge Law Journal*, 193.

of dating, is that the suggestion is not about the heritable principle
as such, but about its enforcement upon lords by the king's court.
In order to bring out the nature of early inheritance as a fresh gift,
Professor Thorne drew a modern analogy: a gardener dies and the
employer takes on his son in his place.[1] But, as analogies often do,
this makes one point at the expense of another; and it necessarily
passes over a background fact without which the matter can be
misunderstood. The employer of the dead gardener makes a choice
governed only by sentiment. The lord of the dead tenant acted
with the advice of his men in his court, and their decision was
governed by custom. They might make a mistake, or might sanction
a rearrangement agreed between the parties. They might even
consciously depart from the usual course – for example because
an elder son was incapable; but they would surely see this as itself
within the customs. What they would hardly ever do is consciously
to defy the customs. Within their own legal framework regular
heritability was well established, and the king's writ of right would
not make much difference to what ordinarily happened. One seeking
to put right the misfortunes of war needed the writ, because
another tenant had in fact been accepted. But normally when a
tenant died, before the writ was in regular use as well as after, the
lord and his court would follow the customs and accept the heir.

So far, then, the suggestion is that a decision taken on a particular
occasion had a limited effect on actual inheritance. The king's writ
of right is working in the same direction as the established customs
of lords' courts, enforcing them in particular cases. But in those
particular cases, in any case in which the writ patent actually
worked, the king's law upset the seignorial result: the lord's
accepted tenant was put out. This was to transform the legal world.
So long as there was only the lord's court, the canons of inheritance,
however clearly settled and however consistently followed, were
criteria for making a choice. They were not rules of law conferring
an abstract right on the heir, but customs about whom the lord's
court should choose; and it was their choice that mattered.
Suppose the heir is passed over: the lord does as Henry I once did
and accepts a younger son because he is the better knight.[2] It is

[1] Ibid. at p. 198.
[2] *Pipe Roll 10 John*, *PRS*(NS), XXIII, p. 113; F. M. Stenton, *The First Century of English Feudalism* (2nd ed.), p. 38; Sanders, *English Baronies*, p. 64 (Marshwood).

done. Isaac should have blessed Esau, but cannot recall his blessing of Jacob. John and not Arthur is the crowned king. The elder son had a claim to be chosen, but he had not and has not a right. The inheritance was never his, and in that seignorial world it now never will be. He is disappointed, has been passed over unjustly: but he cannot by litigation seek the ouster of the one preferred.

That this was the original nature of the canons of inheritance may be important for our understanding of twelfth-century society. To the present writer it is important also for a reason unconnected with the theme of this book. He has suggested that most substantive law came into being as rational modes of trial compelled legal consideration of the facts underlying disputes.[1] This was a slow process; and some have seen a difficulty in the early existence of so considerable a body of substantive rules as the canons of inheritance. But the canons did not emerge *ex post facto* in law-suits. Whether the right or the wrong man had been admitted in the past was not a question which could arise, except in recrimination or war. The question which lords' courts had to answer arose every time a tenant died: whose homage should be taken now? The canons grew from what they customarily did. But what they actually did was conclusive in the particular case.

This conclusiveness was the important thing that the writ of right was to destroy. The lord has in fact accepted somebody other than the heir, and taken his homage. The question is no longer closed. It is still closed in the lord's own court, and hence the king's writ with its provision for removal. In the county or the king's court the heir makes his claim, essentially against the lord, as though the question was still open and the tenement still vacant. That it is not vacant is the lord's business: by taking homage he has conferred warranty on the present tenant. But this warranty now carries only a right to compensation if the heir wins: it is no longer the conclusive title to this tenement.

Nor is it only a recent decision of the lord and his court that may in this sense be reopened. One Bernard had lived and perhaps died in the time of Henry I. Three reigns later, in 1199, the grandson of his elder son claims land from the son of his younger son. What had actually happened is clear enough: the elder son had been incapable, and on Bernard's death the lord had accepted the younger son. At the time this was no doubt seen as proper, and as

[1] 'Law and Fact in Legal Development', *Toronto Law Journal*, XVII (1967), 1.

affecting nobody but the two sons: the elder son was rightly passed over in favour of the younger, and when the younger died a new decision would have to be made. But by 1199 the matter can no longer be seen like that: there is now a sort of heritable ownership over which the lord, having made his original grant, has no further control. The son of the younger son therefore omits all mention of Bernard: he just says that the lord had granted the land to his father. The grandson of the elder son, thinking in the same terms, rests his claim on Bernard; and he explains the transfer to the younger son as a sort of wardship.[1]

But we have not yet plumbed the depths of the change. At least in that case the parties thought they knew what the dispute was about; and by good fortune we for once know it too. Each side had a story, and the stories met at a particular past event. Although the question had to be cast in anachronistic terms, it was definite: what had happened when Bernard died some sixty years before? But in many cases under Richard or John based on a seisin under Henry I, it is likely that nobody knew what had happened. Perhaps it was a taking during the anarchy, perhaps a mistake or malice by some predecessor of the lord. The parties may not have known any more than we do; and it did not matter. Perhaps the lord warrants this tenant as he warranted his father and grandfather before him; perhaps neither has ever heard of the demandant. Bad luck: if the demandant's ancestor was seised and if the demandant is his heir, then the tenant must go and the lord must find him *escambium*.

The canons of inheritance are unchanged. They can be stated in the same words at the end of this development as they could have been at the beginning. But their operation has been transformed. In prescribing who is the heir, they used to be criteria for making a selection; but this was on the practical basis that the selection itself was final. Right or wrong, there was no going back. Now there is. They are rules of law, harbouring an abstract title in some sky; and it can come down to undo what happened long ago.

*   *   *

[1] *RCR*, I, *253*, 360 (Walter f. Hamo): notice also the tenant's assertion that his father was seised on the day Henry I died; cf. above, p. 179, n. 6.

If the beginning of the writ of right as a regular action has been rightly seen, no general change was intended: lands lost during the anarchy were just to be restored. Even if a general enforcement of the hereditary principle was intended, the change would have seemed small. Lords did in fact follow the customs; and it would not make much difference to require it at the instance of heirs passed over. And yet the writ of right was the first and perhaps the decisive step in bringing down the seignorial world. In England and in modern times the essence of that world was most clearly seen by Sir Frank Stenton. Describing arrangements made in lords' courts around the middle of the twelfth century, he observed that the lord was the 'supreme authority'. He was writing of great lords, of a 'feudal state in miniature';[1] but the juristic consequences follow at all levels of lordship. They are most fully preserved for us to see in the later records of courts dealing with unfree tenures. These were not subjected to royal control, and the lord and his court remained the supreme authority.

In such a world, it is in the lord's court that rights are created, exist, and can be ended; and a decision of that court, whether in admitting an heir or sanctioning a grant or settling a dispute, will be final. There were reasons for the decision: the customs, the consent of the grantor, the outcome of the proof. But what matters is the decision itself, the court's acceptance of the result, the lord's acceptance of the new tenant. When once a tenant is accepted – for example, as heir on the death of his ancestor – there can until his own death or surrender hardly be a question about the right to the tenement. The lord may seek to take it back for some breach of duty, or there may be a trespassory invasion or a dispute about appurtenances. But a proprietary dispute about the tenement as such can hardly arise: this is the lord's tenant, and that is all there is to it.

The writ of right alone would have broken this up. For the tenant, his unique seignorial title is no longer final, but subject to unpredictable hereditary claims. For the lord, his warranty may be overridden as the title to this tenement, but still binds him to compensate his tenant. Consider the possible effects on a grant.

---

[1] *The First Century of English Feudalism* (2nd ed.), pp. 47 ff., esp. at p. 51 on the earl of Lincoln and at p. 54 on earl Ferrers. Note too the observation on p. 55 that a transaction in the court of Henry de Port 'curiously anticipates the surrender and admittance of the copyhold tenements of a later age'.

So long as they were the supreme authority, the lord and his court would agree or not to accept a new tenant in place of the old: yes or no, there was an end of it. But now their decision is not the end of it. What is to happen if some heir of the grantor, ignorant of the facts or otherwise, makes his hereditary claim? It will be removed to the king's court, and the lord may have to find *escambium* for the grantee. Would it not therefore be better if the grant itself were now sanctioned in the king's court instead of the lord's? But then may not the king's court sanction a grant to which the lord would not have agreed? There is no end to it; or rather the end must always be in the king's court, in this case indeed a fine. What had moved up was the power of final decision, and everything was bound to follow.

It is even possible that the writ of right had begun to change the idea of seisin. When the lord's court was the supreme authority, it was there that homage was taken and the tenant was seised or invested with the tenement. The lord's part in the idea was obvious from his part in the transaction; and the effect of that transaction endured at most for the life of this tenant. But when a demandant may go back to the time of Henry I, some sixty years before the earliest rolls, some forty years before the grand assize, some twenty years even before Henry II became king, he goes back beyond the memory of his lord's court, which has anyway witnessed a later transaction and committed itself to the present tenant. It is to knights of the county that the grand assize puts the question, not peers of the fee; and the question they can answer is not whether the demandant's ancestor was accepted by the lord's court, but whether he enjoyed the tenement.[1] The lord and his court are left out of the question, and in the end will be left out of the idea. Language may show us this happening. It seems to be under Henry II that the noun comes into common use. 'Seisin' concentrates on the tenant and the tenement, and the lord's assent is an implication which will fall away. 'In seisin' comes to mean something like 'in possession'; and we have accustomed ourselves to reading 'seised' as a synonym. But it could not be so when 'to seise' was a verb having one person as its object and another as its subject.

The abstract noun, denoting a relationship between person and

[1] Cf. Thorne, 'Livery of Seisin', *Law Quarterly Review*, LII (1936), 345, esp. at 355 ff.

land which can exist without the lord's concurrence, and even against his will, is mainly a product of novel disseisin. Seisin is what the assize protects, and is enlarged as the assize comes to be used against other defendants than the tenant's lord and by other plaintiffs than the lord's accepted tenant. Mort d'ancestor contributes to the same process, as the heir becomes seised without the lord playing any part. But the larger effect of this was that seen by Professor Thorne.[1] Inheritance begins to appear as just a succession to property and not as a grant to the heir, not even a grant that the lord is obliged to make by the king's writ as well as by custom. Except for warranty, all the ideas have become abstract. And the lord and his court, once the supreme authority inherent in all of them, can dissolve and yet leave a coherent system.

All this may have been inevitable from the first interference of the writ patent. Controlling jurisdictions have a habit of taking over the functions they control. How much of it could be seen to be happening is the hardest kind of question to answer. Conceptual changes are never visible as they proceed; and linguistic symptoms such as 'simple seisin' show awareness only of some practical adjustment.[2] As to the practical changes, the realistic question is whether anybody could ever see what was happening clearly enough to resist it, and this turns upon how fast it happened. Leaving aside for the moment the first introduction of the actions, the one change which must have been rapid is the extension of novel disseisin from its original use. But the only aspect of that which really diminished lords' powers was the prohibition of proceedings without writ against persons whom they did not accept as their tenants;[3] and that may not have happened quickly, and never protected wrongdoers so blatant that no judicial proceeding was necessary. That the ultimate result of the changes was not intended cannot need saying. Probably there was no intention to change the framework at all, not even to take jurisdiction. Indeed we may be doubly wrong to think of a transfer of jurisdiction. The great mass of land litigation in the thirteenth century may largely have been generated by these changes. It is not that disputes which would have arisen anyway are brought gratefully to a preferred jurisdiction. They are the miserable products of uncertainty, of

---

[1] 'English Feudalism and Estates in Land', [1959] *Cambridge Law Journal*, 193 at 201–2. [2] Above, p. 11, n. 1, and p. 169.
[3] As in the case of the countess Amice, above, pp. 45–6.

the ending of that conclusive seignorial title. But of course that was itself something that nobody could see. All that could be seen were many points at which old institutions were suddenly causing friction. The piecemeal result was the legislation of the thirteenth century, so long unmatched in nature and volume. It was the product not of great vision, but of changes too large to be perceived. The vision can only be piecemeal.

What vision was it that first produced the actions themselves? Historians have pitted native inspiration against Roman books, have used the word 'genius':[1] but that would still be a grudging word for an achievement on the scale supposed. Great things happened; but the only intention behind writ of right, mort d'ancestor, and novel disseisin was to make the seignorial structure work according to its own assumptions. If the ideas in this book have seemed difficult, one reason is that they do not follow the assumptions behind modern work in this field. In departing from Maitland's great framework, they cut laboriously across the grain of our thinking. But they do not see Henry II and his advisers as cutting across the grain, as meaning to depart from the framework of their world.

[1] e.g., D. M. Stenton, *English Justice between the Norman Conquest and the Great Charter*, pp. 22 ff., esp. at p. 26.

INDEX

Persons involved in law-suits are entered, with further identification in brackets, only if they are named in the text: they are not indexed from footnotes, where a name is given only when needed for ready identification of the reference (see p. ix). The entries of *modern scholars* do not include references to editorial work. *Legislative acts* are listed in a chronological table under 'statutes and documents'.